Sacred Sites and the Colonial Encounter

Sacred Sites and the Colonial Encounter

A History of Meaning and Memory in Ghana

Sandra E. Greene

INDIANA
University Press

Bloomington & Indianapolis

This book is a publication of

Indiana University Press
601 North Morton Street
Bloomington, IN 47404-3797 USA

http://iupress.indiana.edu

Telephone orders   800-842-6796
Fax orders   812-855-7931
Orders by e-mail   iuporder@indiana.edu

The paper used in this publication meets the minimum
requirements of American National Standard for Information
Sciences—Permanence of Paper for Printed Library Materials,
ANSI Z39.48-1984.

Manufactured in the United States of America

Library of Congress Cataloging-in-Publication Data

Greene, Sandra E., date
  Sacred sites and the colonial encounter : a history of meaning and
memory in Ghana / Sandra E. Greene.
     p.   cm.
Includes bibliographical references and index.
  ISBN 0-253-34073-X (cloth : alk. paper) — ISBN 0-253-21517-X
(pbk. : alk. paper)
  1. Anlo (African people)—Religion. 2. Anlo (African people)—
Cultural assimilation. 3. Sacred space—Ghana. 4. Body, Human—
Social aspects—Ghana. 5. Ghana—Colonial influence. I. Title.
  DT510.43.A58 G75 2002
  966.7′004963374—dc21

                                                    2001004947

1 2 3 4 5   07 06 05 04 03 02

To Kafui and Kwaku

Contents

Maps and Figures

MAPS

FIGURES

Preface and Acknowledgments

RESEARCH FOR THIS study was conducted in 1996, but its foundation was laid some twenty-two years earlier, in 1974. In that year I attended the funeral of a University of Ghana student who was from Anlo and a fellow resident of Mensah-Sarbah Hall. Like many of the other students who boarded buses for the 2-hour bus trip to the deceased student's home town, I had never been to the Anlo area. So I went as much out of curiosity as from a desire to support the efforts of my fellow students to see one of their own given a proper farewell. For me, however, it was also a cross-cultural experience. I found it odd that the grave dug for the burial was not located in a cemetery but rather was relegated to a rather isolated area, far from the town, from which the Keta Lagoon had only recently receded. Yet there *were* cemeteries around. Why was the burial in that location rather than elsewhere? At the time, I did not it give much more thought than that. There was so much else to take in: the wailing and shouting that accompanied the lowering of the casket into the grave, the attempts by the deceased's girlfriend to jump into the grave after the casket, and the noisy exertions of the deceased's male friends to keep the girl from hurting herself. In time, I simply consigned my questions about the grave's location to that mental file of interesting but seemingly not-so-important puzzles. More experiences, more questions were to follow, however.

When I returned to Anlo in 1977 as a graduate student researcher, for example, I was strongly advised by a number of Anlo friends to establish my local research base in Keta, not in Anloga as I had originally planned. They had concerns about my welfare. Again, this meant nothing to me, and since my friends didn't push the issue, I opted to ignore their advice. Everything I had read about Anloga suggested that though it was a traditional political center, it was a small town in Ghana like so many others. Why such concern? But when I did indeed establish myself in Anloga, I found it curious that so many of those I interviewed considered it important to discuss with me, even without my prompting, the location of certain sites in the area: this pond, that shrine, the fact that where certain groves once stood, there now existed a church, a police station, a school building. The town of Notsie was mentioned repeatedly as well, perhaps a bit too often and too consistently. I heard the same stories told again and again by both young or old. I recorded all, but much of what I heard and experienced about the meanings of place and space remained for me isolated fragments, information that raised questions but ones that I did not bring together into a clearly formulated set of queries.

Only in 1987 did all this begin to come together. In that year, violence erupted in Anloga between a group of traditional religious believers and a number of evangelical Christians. The clash was the talk of the town. Everyone seemed to have their own explanation about the causes of the clash and the motives of those involved. But what especially caught my attention was the fact that virtually no one disputed the fact that the violence took place at a site that was of tremendous cultural and historic significance. Some thirty years earlier, the same site had been the location of an important confrontation between traditional believers and the colonial government. And more than 100 years before this, the identical site was used by the political and religious leaders in Anlo to counter a threat to its religious authority. Remembered by the Anlo as a place of historic political importance, it was also a site of sacred significance. If this location—one I had passed by many times—was associated by the Anlo with such complex meanings and memories, perhaps so too were those locations (the 1974 burial site of my student colleague, the town Notsie, and Anloga itself) that had earlier struck me as curious because of the way my Anlo acquaintances had subtly signaled their significance. But what meanings were these, defined and remembered at what pivotal point in time and by whom? In what ways did these meanings and memories inscribe or reinforce, challenge and become challenged by which previous understandings?

This text offers answer to these questions, but first I would like to acknowledge the fact that in the process of seeking these answers, I enjoyed the support and assistance of many people over so many years. This book is not the result of one or two research trips; it is the result of the many bits and pieces of information I gathered and was given over the more than twenty-five years I have been visiting Anlo and working on the history of this area. Central to this study (and to my own understanding of Anlo history and culture) are the many interviews I conducted and conversations I have had with Anlo residents. Their knowledge and insights, which they freely shared with me, gave me a sense of how many Anlo viewed, and in some instances still do view, their environment. Comparing these contemporary views with the observations published by late-nineteenth- and early-twentieth-century German missionaries and British colonial officers allowed me to understand what the residents of Anlo had both remembered and forgotten about the meanings associated with specific places, with specific spaces, and with the body. This comparison also helped me interpret the Bremen and British accounts. The oral information I was given allowed me to determine what the Europeans resident in Anlo saw and didn't see, what they understood and misunderstood because of their own subject positions and beliefs. Most of the oral interviews were conducted with the help of the many research assistants I have had the pleasure of working with over the years, but most helpful for this project was Elvis Adika. His assistance was invaluable and greatly appreciated.

The documentary sources I used—the Bremen Mission published accounts, the British colonial documents about their efforts to introduce Western health systems and regulatory measures into Anlo, the many undergraduate long essays and honors theses that provided time-sensitive understandings of Anlo rituals and their meanings—were located in a number of libraries and archives. These included the individual department libraries at the University of Ghana, Legon, and the university's Balme Library; the libraries at the University College of Winneba (Ghana), Cambridge University, the London School of Hygiene and Tropical Medicine, the Wellcome Institute, and the University of London's School of Oriental and Asian Studies; and Olin Library at Cornell University. I also used archival holdings at the Bremen Mission in Germany, the Ghana National Archives in Accra, the British Library, the Public Record's Office at Kew, and Oxford University's Rhodes House Library. In all cases, the librarians at these institutions were most helpful in locating materials, providing space for me to work, and making arrangements for photocopying and obtaining copies of photographs. For all this I am most grateful, for this study would have been impossible without their assistance.

Equally important for the successful completion of this study was the financial, institutional, and logistical support I received from the Fulbright Program, the United States Information Service in Accra, Cornell University's Department of History, the College of Arts and Sciences and the Society of the Humanities at Cornell, the Department of History at the University of Ghana, Legon, and G. K. Nukunya, colleague, friend, and then pro vice-chancellor at Legon. To all I convey my heartfelt thanks.

I also benefited tremendously from exchanges about this study with colleagues, friends, and relatives: Emmanual Akyeampong, Kodjopa Attoh, Sena Attoh, Innocent Guilty Aka, Margaret Ahiadeke, Tamara Loos, Maria Cristina Garcia, Susanne Pohl, Zillah Eisenstein, Leslie Adelson, Solace Nyadroh, Mary Roldan, John Hanson, Rachel Weil, Michael Kammen, Larry Yarak, and the members of the Comparative History Colloquium at Cornell University. Many listened patiently as I struggled at times to articulate what I was trying to do. All gave me invaluable advice, even though for some my research interests were far from their own. Others read a chapter or two; some the entire manuscript. For all their assistance, advice, and willingness to take the time to push me to think more deeply about this project, I am especially thankful.

The maps that appear in this text were produced in a most timely and professional manner by David Wyatt and Teresa Howley. I thank them and the

Bremen Mission, which allowed me to reproduce the late-nineteenth- and early-twentieth-century photographs that appear in this text. I also wish to thank the very many students, graduate and undergraduate, German and American, who assisted me with the translation of the Bremen Mission materials into English. Without their assistance and that of so many already listed above, especially the residents of Anlo, this book would not have been possible. *Akpe akpe.*

A Note on Ewe Orthography

THE EWE LANGUAGE was committed to writing by missionaries associated with the North German Missionary Society (Norddeutche Missionsgesellschaft) in the mid-nineteenth century. They chose to use a mix of Roman and phonetic symbols that to this day constitute the Anlo alphabet. But in more recent times, authors who have written about the Ewe have tended to use the Ewe alphabet rather selectively. It is common, for example, to find most spellings of the word "Ewe" written as indicated even though the correct spelling according to the Ewe alphabet would be "Eυe." Similarly, it is rather unusual to find any author using the Ewe alphabet to spell the word Aŋlɔ (Anlo). Individuals sometimes use the letters "or" to replace the Anlo letter ɔ, or "p" to replace the bilabial fricative *f*. Such usage is quite inconsistent, however.

In this study, I have used the English spelling that is most common for proper names. When listing a specific Ewe term for an English word, however, I use the following equivalents for the Ewe letters.

o̲ = the open sound found in the English word "fought," written as ɔ, in Ewe
w̲ = the voiced bilabial fricative, written as υ, in Ewe
f̲ = the voiceless bilabial fricative, written as *f*, in Ewe.
e̲ = pronounced like the English long "a" sound, written as ɛ, in Ewe
d̲ = a voiced retroflex stop, written as ɖ, in Ewe
x = a voiceless dorsal-velar fricative, like the "ch" in the German word *hoch* (high)

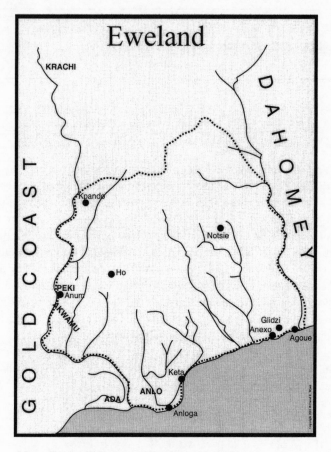

Map 1. Eweland (Ghana and Togo), Showing Major
Towns.
Based on D. E. K. Amenumey, *The Ewe Unification
Movement* (Accra: Ghana Press, 1989), p. 3. Modified to
highlight the noted features by David K. Wyatt.

A History Outlined

As a study that focuses on the individual histories of particular sacred sites, this text does not attempt to document chapter after chapter an unfolding story of linear change. Yet such a chronological approach can reveal much about the factors that have shaped Anlo understandings of their landscape. To facilitate this understanding, to provide a sense of the ongoing dialogues that have occurred within Anlo and between Anlo citizens and the missionaries and British colonial officers who operated in the area, I include below a select listing of dates, names, places and events. Together, these citations illustrate in chronological order Anlo efforts, from pre-colonial and colonial to post-colonial times, to make their landscape ever meaningful.

c. 1450   Notsie, home of the deity Mawu, is well established by this date as a regional religious center.

c. 1650   The Anlo Nyaxoenu lineage (later part of the Adzovia clan) obtains the politico-religious symbol of authority from Notsie, upon which the Adzovia and Bate clans base their right to provide the Anlo *awǫamefia.*

c. 1750   Notsie's position in Anlo as the home of the most powerful god in the region is challenged by the arrival of another deity, Se.

           By this date, the ocean is associated by the Anlo with a number of spiritual forces, some of which are also worshipped on the coast to the east of the Anlo area.

c. 1769   The Adzovia and Bate clans' exclusive right to rule is challenged by the Dzevi clan on the basis of the military prowess of the Dzevi god Nyigbla.

c. 1840   The Portuguese-speaking stranger Baeta settles in the town of Atoko and introduces the use of barrels for constructing wells, be-

ginning the process of declining belief in the deity-controlled availability of potable water.

1853   The Bremen Mission opens its first station in Keta.

1875   Great Britain extends the boundaries to incorporate Anlo into the
        Gold Coast Colony.

1877   The Bremen Mission publishes its version of Anlo's historic connec-
        tion to Notsie.

1878   By this date, the Anlo annual pilgrimage has become much less
        regular.

1878   The Gold Coast Colonial Government passes its first ordinance re-
        quiring the establishment of public cemeteries.

1881   Violent confrontation between the Yewe religious order and the
        Christian convert Stephano Kwadzo Afelevo occurs in Woe.

1890   The Roman Catholic Church is established in Keta.

1899   The African Methodist Episcopal Zion Church begins services in
        Keta.

1900   The first effort to bring Christianity to Anloga fails.

        By this date, the Keta hospital is established, drawing more than
        2,000 patients a year from the Anlo area.

1905   Mission schools in Anlo introduce into the curriculum lessons on
        sanitation and health science.

1906   Awoamefia Amedo Kpegla, remembered as a staunch opponent of
        European influence in Anlo, dies.

        Priests associated with two of the most influential deities in Anlo
        ban the use of sails on the lagoon.

1907   Cornelius Kofi Kwawukume, a mission-educated businessman, be-
        comes the Anlo *awǫamefia* and begins his reign by refusing to abide
        by many of the religious rituals and regulations that have governed
        the position since the seventeenth century.

1908   The Bremen Mission baptizes its first Christian converts from Anloga.

1911   The British colonial government passes an ordinance stipulating
that chiefs lead the way by developing local cemeteries.

The town of Anloga is destroyed by fire and rebuilt in accordance
with a "modern" grid system.

Chiefs in Anlo appeal to local traditional priests to help alleviate a
drought.

1914   Sri II defies the ban prohibiting sails on the lagoon by ordering his
sub-chiefs to allow canoes with sails to operate on the Keta Lagoon.

1915–37 The British colonial government engages in several efforts to ban
the Yewe religious order, which is closely associated with the belief
in a deity-controlled ocean.

1920   Physical education that emphasizes the body as machine is added to
the school curriculum.

Chiefs in Anlo appeal to the colonial government rather than to the
local priests for assistance in filling the dry Keta Lagoon with water.

c. 1930 Worship of a new god associated with the ocean, Mami Wata, is introduced into Anlo.

1934   Anlo State School at Keta is established by disgruntled Anlo teachers to encourage students through a revised curriculum to appreci-
ate both Anlo culture and the worth of Western scientific values.

1945   A ritual murder in Cape Coast is traced to an Anlo belief system
about the spiritual aspects of the body.

1950   By this date, most Anlo citizens have stopped the practice of house
burials and have established public cemeteries.

Urban growth in Anloga undermines the sacred character of the
pond Blolui.

The religious order Brekete abandons its emphasis on witch-catching
and witch-accusations that rely on a belief in the ability of the spiritual aspects of the body to cause harm to self and others.

1953   Anloga explodes in riot after a religious ban on the discussion of taxation is ignored.

1954   Reconciliation efforts begin to cool animosities left in the wake of the Anloga riot.

1955   United Nations plebiscite vote results in the Ewe-speaking peoples of the British Togoland opting to join the Gold Coast/Ghana.

1956   Agbobo Festival held in Notsie. All versions of the Notsie story are brought into line with the one created and published by the Bremen Mission in 1877.

1957   Ghana (including Anlo) gains its independence from Great Britain. Ewe nationalist fervor begins to decline.

1959   Togbui Adeladza II succeeds Togbui Sri II as *awǫamefia.*

1960   Togo gains its independence from France.

Early   Togbui Adeladza sanctions the sacrifice of a cow to the Anlo tradi-
1960s   tional deities on behalf of all Anlo to help control the sea erosion at Keta.

1962   Anlo develops the Hogbetsotso Festival based on the Bremen Mission understanding of Notsie's historic significance, a significance put to use to foster greater pride in Anlo culture and (in subsequent years) support for local economic development.

1968   A delegation from Anlo goes to Notsie for spiritual assistance in alleviating a drought.

1984   T. S. A. Togobo, businessman and advisor to the *awǫamefiawo* Sri II and Adeladaza II, dies.

1985   The Church of Pentecost violates a ban on drumming during the days leading up to the Hogbetsotso Festival, but unlike in past years, their drums are seized by the Traditional Council in Anloga.

1986   The Asogli Traditional Area (which includes the city of Ho) establishes the Gligbaza to promote local development and local cultural pride through the use of the Notsie story.

1987   Conflict erupts between Christians and traditional believers and their supporters in Anloga.

Anlo Christians protest the sending of a delegation to Notsie.

1996   The Notsie narrative is performed at the Hogbetsotso Festival as a slapstick comedy.

Conflict erupts between Christians and traditional believers and their supporters in Anloga.

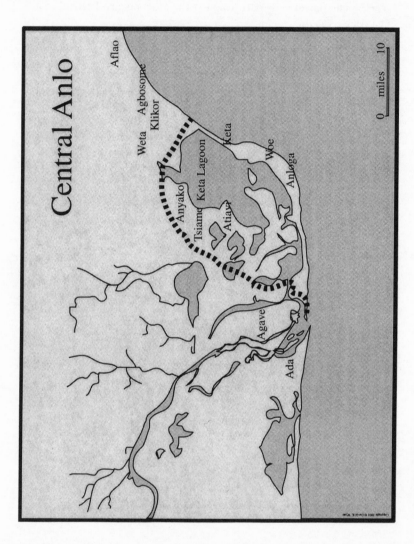

Map 2. Central Anlo.
Based on Sandra E. Greene, *Gender Ethnicity and Social Change on the Upper Slave Coast* (Portsmouth, N.H.: Heinemann, 1996), p. 84.

Sacred Sites and the Colonial Encounter

Introduction
Managing the Modern

THE PERIOD BETWEEN THE 1850s and the 1950s marked a profoundly important period for the polity of Anlo (located in what is now the southeastern corner of Ghana in West Africa). During those roughly 100 years, the Ewe-speaking peoples of Anlo encountered the evangelical zeal of German Pietist missionaries determined to spread their religion. They also had to cope with the political, economic, and cultural consequences of their incorporation into the British Empire. Both encounters, separately and together, had a tremendous influence on Anlo culture and identity. European colonialism did more than accelerate changes in the Anlo political and economic institutions, which were already altered by centuries of contact with other African communities and the West. And it did more than generate changes more rapid than had ever been seen before in social relations and religious beliefs. European colonialism destabilized the very terms by which the Anlo had come to understand themselves and certain elements within their physical environment.

We know, for example, that prior to the late nineteenth century, the Anlo had defined certain physical realities—the human body, the ocean, burial sites, and specific towns in the region—as entities consisting of more than their material properties. The human body, for example, was more than blood and bone, muscle and flesh. Certain towns were more than an assemblage of houses and streets, markets and farms, individuals and families organized into a defined political community. These sites and others were also associated with the sacred. They were locations defined as much by their physical properties as by the spiritual forces that the Anlo believed occupied and operated from these locations. The ocean was understood to be a seemingly endless body of water over which one could travel to reach a desired destination. But it was also associated with a number of deities that had the power both to generate bumper harvests of fish and to consume through drowning the lives of those who depended on the ocean for their sustenance. The human body was understood to be a material entity that could experience pain and sickness, health and death from natural causes. But it too was intimately associated with separate spiritual forces that had the power to induce both sickness and health, life and death in the physical self and in others. These sites were sacred, locations where the separate and intimately related worlds of the material and the spiritual came together. They were the sites from which spiritual forces operated to influence human life. But they were also interactive sites, places where humans could influence the sacred as well through the performance, or the lack thereof, of particular rituals.

Anlo understandings about sacred sites also deeply influenced the dynamic character of their political, religious, and social culture. We know, for example, that prior to the nineteenth century, Anlo's political leadership based their authority, in part, on both the material and spiritual association they maintained with the town of Notsie. As a physical site, it was claimed as the ancestral home of their ancestors and a number of their non-Ewe political allies. Yet it was also a sacred site, the home of Mawu, the most powerful deity known to the Anlo, the place from which the Anlo leadership derived their symbol of office, a stool, that had both material and spiritual properties and that underpinned the claimed right to rule. The Anlo leadership's connection to such a spiritually powerful site, a material reality to which they made periodic pilgrimages to renew their physical and spiritual relations, constituted the very basis of their power. Yet it was also this belief in the sacredness of particular sites that generated dynamism within pre-colonial Anlo culture. Those who could claim a relationship with an equally or more powerful alternative site, one imbued with the power to influence even more positively than Notsie the lives of the Anlo people, could use that relationship to challenge the preeminence of the Notsie connection. And this is precisely what happened in the late eighteenth century. But this is getting ahead of our story. More important is the fact that any site defined as sacred by the Anlo could become the means through which an individual or a group could attain influence within the community. Thus, this notion (that there existed physical entities through which one could interact with the spiritual and that could also be harnessed to achieve particular ends) constituted the very basis for Anlo understandings of their human and physical environment (a totality I will call the landscape).

It was this understanding that was so profoundly affected by European colonial rule. Those who came to Anlo as colonial officers and missionaries understood the world in very different terms. Shaped by the European Enlightenment that defined the material and the spiritual as not only distinct but completely separate domains of existence, and convinced of the superiority of their own beliefs, they attempted to impose their understandings on Anlo. They used their schools, churches, and hospitals as well as colonial policy and individual exhortations to challenge the ways in which the Anlo viewed themselves and their environment. In the hands of German missionary efforts, for example, Notsie was stripped of its religious significance and remade into the exclusive home of all Ewe-speaking peoples rather than, as the Anlo had understood it, a place of both material and spiritual significance that gave sacred significance to their political organization and defined them as related not only to other Ewe-speaking peoples but also to some of the Akan-speaking communities in the region. Under the influence of Western technology and science education, various water bodies lost their sacred aura and were thus rendered spiritually irrelevant to the quotidian rhythms of daily life. Anlo burial grounds—once considered both mundane material locations and sites made sacred because of their association with the spiritual power of the dead —were redefined by the colonizers as purely material entities, to be understood according to "modern scientific principles" and/or European Romantic notions about their contemplative value. At the same time, the beliefs of the Anlo were disdained as primitive and unscientific. According to dominant thinking in nineteenth-century Europe, the material world was quite separate from the spiritual world. It was a world to be understood according to physical and biological principles, not religious belief. It was a world that could be controlled by human action alone, where prayer and devotional exercises operated in a separate realm, for spiritual rather than direct material benefit.

The meeting of such disparate worldviews through colonization has been the subject of many studies on both the colonizer and the colonized. And most make it clear that colonial efforts to define, control, and position the colonized according to terms dictated by and of principal benefit to the colonizer impacted the very bases upon which all involved with colonialism understood themselves and organized their societies. Colonizers were forced to rethink the terms they had once used to define racial, class, national, sexual, and gendered identities for themselves and others. Some began to question increasingly the validity of dominant medical practices, others were compelled to reevaluate their own religious beliefs.[1] The colonized, in turn, were forced to adjust when their political leadership structures were altered, when their legal systems became ossified under colonial tutelage, when older production and distribution networks were incorporated into the new and made to operate largely for the benefit of the colonizer. As new political and economic conditions challenged pre-existing social relations and religious beliefs, the colonized modified the very terms by which they organized and defined themselves as individuals, as members of social, political, and religious communities. But in what ways did colonialism affect not only institutions and individuals, economic and political life, intra- and inter-group relations and identities but also the very terms by which the colonized, in particular, understood and interacted with their landscape, that physical and human environment where certain material sites were also considered to have spiritual meaning?

This book addresses this question by exploring the history of colonialism among the Anlo-Ewe. It focuses specifically on the changes in meaning that the Anlo effected with regard to a number of sites that they had once associated with great spiritual significance. It reconstructs the interactive and dynamic character of early-nineteenth-century, pre-colonial Anlo understandings of their human and physical environment and links this understanding to the ways the Anlo actually used these sites to define themselves and the relationship between the material and the spiritual. It examines the challenges that the Anlo faced as these understandings were ridiculed, ignored, and/ or selectively appropriated by German Pietist missionaries and British colonizers in their efforts to impose on the Anlo their own notions about the relationship between the spiritual and particular material sites through their schools and churches and through colonial regulatory measures. And it explores Anlo responses to this challenge, responses that involved both resistance and acceptance and every form of accommodation that could possibly exist between these seeming polar opposites.

This book also explores the question of why the Anlo reconfigured their understandings of and interactions with their landscape in such diverse ways. Why did certain sites retain their sacred character despite the acceptance by many Anlo of European scientific approaches to and religious beliefs about the world? Why did others lose that sacred quality? Why were the meanings associated with still other sites displaced to new locations? What was the cultural logic, the underlying principles, that influenced how the Anlo constructed new understandings of their landscape, understandings that retained traces of the old despite the press of "modernity" yet also embraced selected aspects of the new?

I argue that after their encounter with colonialism, the Anlo attributed more varied and sometimes contradictory meanings to sites in the region in which they lived because the Anlo themselves varied in the ways they constructed new understandings about themselves and their environment. Some retained many of their beliefs about the interactive relationship between the material and spiritual world. And this, in turn, set the terms by which Western beliefs and practices were incorporated into one form of an Anlo modernity. But others more fully embraced European beliefs and practices, and this, as well, had profound consequences for how they constructed their own understandings about the spiritual and material significance of place, space, and the body. Of course, no single approach ever completely dominated Anlo understandings of themselves and their physical environment prior to the arrival of German missionaries and British colonizers. But colonialism certainly complicated tremendously Anlo efforts to operate collectively according to a common set of beliefs. Not only did differences within earlier understandings about self and the physical world continue to operate in colonial and postcolonial Anlo, colonialism also introduced new beliefs and practices. These the Anlo selectively adopted and adapted to local concerns, but they did so in ways that generated another set of notions about the appropriate handling of place, space, and the body and new contestations about the meanings associated with these sites.

MEANINGS, MODERNITY, AND MEMORY

The complexity characteristic of such colonial cultural encounters is not easily captured in words. During the 1970s and 1980s, the terms "bricolage," "synthesis," "accommodation," "adaptation," and "syncretism" became popular means to describe the mixture that resulted when individuals and groups brought together diverse cultural elements to form that which was neither a replica of the old nor a replica of the new. But these terms failed to account for the range of cultural responses that emerged as a result of these encounters, a range that included minimalist appropriations of surface characteristics and more profound responses that involved the abandonment of whole ways of thinking about self and the world. Often overlooked as well was the extent to which unequal power relations also influenced cultural encounters. In colonial situations, for example, colonized peoples "struggled, in diverse ways and with differing degrees of success, to deploy, deform and defuse" the cultural values and forms imposed on them by European missionaries and colonizers.[2] But it was also the case that the ability of the colonized to choose what to accept and what to reject was circumscribed by the power dynamics embedded in the colonial enterprise.

By the 1990s, scholars had begun to recognize some of these oversights and thus began to include in their studies an analysis of the role power played in colonial cultural encounters. Some redefined their terms to take this new emphasis on power into account. Others opted to employ new expressions. Among the more popular were those that made reference to "the modern," a phrase associated with historical trends in Western Europe: "the growth of scientific consciousness, the development of a secular outlook, the doctrine of progress, . . . individualistic understandings of the self . . . and so on."[3] Instead of simply appropriating the term for their use, however, those interested in studying colonial cultural encounters reconfigured "the modern." They made it plural ("modernities") and then attached to this plural form a number of prefatory expressions ("cultural," "alter(native)") to critique the assumptions that had informed the most common ways in which the term "modern" had been used. These assumptions stated that "the modern" was qualitatively better, that progress for non-Western, colonized peoples was associated with their acceptance of "the modern," a process that was inevitable once these "traditional" cultures had encountered the West because of the obvious superiority of the latter. Critiques took a number of forms. Some documented the fact that the West itself has been by no means of one mind on the value of "modernity." Emphasized in these studies is the notion that "modernity" has its own history. Its acceptance was neither inevitable nor complete. Others interested primarily in colonialism noted as well that the colonizers themselves often fell short, deliberately, of the "modern" ideal and that the "modernity" they did bring not only reflected contestations in Europe but also, once transplanted to colonial territories, were frequently modified or rejected by the colonized according to their own concerns and interests.[4] The colonized not only managed the colonizer but also "[made] themselves . . . as opposed to being 'made' . . . modern."[5] The term "modernities," then, was coined to emphasize the multiple ways in which "the modern" was selectively adapted and made into "alter(native) modernities," especially by the colonized, according to their own priorities and concerns. This new orientation in colonial cultural studies in particular made power dynamics central to the study of cultural encounters. It also continued the decades-long effort to contest the notion that in their encounter with "the modern," the colonized lost all control over their definitions of how best to manage the present and the future.

Yet I would argue that the more recent approaches to the study of colonial cultural encounters (while correct in debunking the notion that the modernity of the West is an unquestioned good that will inevitably spread to the rest of the world) obscure yet another reality. Colonialism certainly generated "alter(native) modernities," but it also had more profound consequences. I document, for example, the reality of unequal power relations in colonial Anlo, and I discuss the fact that the Anlo managed this power as best they could, taking advantage of the cracks and fissures, the contradictions that existed within the beliefs imposed on them, to generate a range of creative adaptations. But I also argue that colonialism generated more than simply a myriad set of "alter(native) modernities." It also—in some instances— transformed the very terms by which many of the colonized understood themselves and their physical environment. Most in Anlo today, for example, simply no longer associate the existence of naturally occurring potable bodies of water with the actions of particular deities. Technological innovations and a school curriculum that emphasized the greater value of using scientific methods have altered the very terms by which the Anlo understand their physical environment. Similarly, most Anlo no longer view the human body as a material entity whose spiritual power is both part of and separate from one's physical self, a power that can protect as well as wreak havoc on the self. Again, the very terms by which the Anlo understand and manage their selves have undergone profound change.

Such terms as "bricolage" and "syncretism," and even the expressions "cultural modernities" and "alter(native) modernities" fail to capture both the more superficial and the more deeply transformative ways in which the colonized reconfigured their notions about the spiritual and material characteristics of their human and physical environment. Studies on the cultural legacy of colonialism, for example, often focus on only one particular form of African modernity. Scholars study syncretic churches but rarely include as well an analysis of mainline missionary-founded religious establishments. Art historians tend to focus on "traditional" artists or on those who use the formal techniques of the West (painting, for example), but not both. This specialization, of course, has its benefits. Such studies provide more in-depth information about a particular institution or practice. But they do so at the cost of producing a fractured image of African responses to the legacy of cultural colonialism, images that then too easily reinforce notions of an "authentic," "traditional" Africa juxtaposed against an "inauthentic," "Westernized" Africa.

Individual African societies need to be studied comprehensively in all their diversity in order to illustrate the range of cultural forms that can exist within a single society, forms that most often coexist peacefully but which can at times clash, producing eruptions of violence. Only then can we move beyond simply celebrating the ingenuity, the agency, the creativity of the colonized, of Africans, to understand as well what particular historical circumstances have fostered the development of tolerance for diverse cultural forms and even different epistemologies operating within the same society and why tensions that have arisen from this diversity have sometimes led to intra-communal conflict. This book addresses this concern by examining the many different "alter(native) modernities" and the more profound epistemological differences that arose among the Anlo-Ewe as a result of their encounter with European colonialism. It also explores the circumstances that led to the development of new consensual meanings about place, space, and the body; but in instances where no new consensus could be devised, it explains why one finds to this day the continued existence of deep tensions and periodic outbursts of intra-communal violence.

Modernity and meaning are themes central to this study, but so too is the topic of memory. Colonialism not only challenged older ways of thinking about self and the world by offering alternative meanings, it also encouraged the development of different memories about the past. Bogumil Jewsiewicki and Johannes Fabian emphasize this point in their discussions about Zairean painter Tsibumba Matulu. Both note, for example, that Matulu's paintings of the Zairean past exhibit both local ways of remembering the past and colonial historical epistemologies.[6] But to what extent can these paintings tell us about the colonial impact on memory in Zaire more generally, given the fact that the paintings studied were produced not by society at large or for a particular group but rather arose from the imaginative rememberings of an individual artist?[7] How do we move from a focus on the individual to the truly collective? What do we even mean when we speak of a collective memory? Perhaps the most useful answer to these questions is provided by Maurice Halbwachs and elaborated upon by Paul Connerton. According to both, remembering is an individual activity and should be understood as such. But the framework for these individual memories is provided by the society of which one is a member. That is, individuals "situate what [they] recollect within the mental spaces provided by the group." These mental spaces are composed of ideas (how one thinks about past experiences), language (how one speaks of what one remembers), and places (the material sites that support our mental images). Accordingly, to speak of a collective memory is to refer to those sets of assumptions and experiences—whether conveyed through the written word, socialization, commemorative ceremonies, rituals, or bodily practices—that encourage thinking about and remembering the past in common ways.[8] I draw upon the work of Halbwachs and Connerton by defining the framework used by early-nineteenth-century Anlos as one that included beliefs about the physical and spiritual characteristics of certain material sites. The town of Notsie, for example, was understood to be the physical place from which the Anlo migrated before they settled in their present homeland. But it was also the home of the deity believed to be the most powerful god in the region. Periodic pilgrimages organized by the leading families in Anlo and the recitation of oral traditions and explanations about the cause of disasters that affected the entire society all reinforced, for most, the importance of remembering and remaining connected to Notsie. Similar notions structured the way most Anlos remembered past experiences with the bodies of water in the area, the dead, and the living.

In focusing on the framework that structured Anlo memories, however, I move beyond Halbwach's and Connerton's emphasis on delineating the fact that memory is socially constructed (and influenced by the hierarchies of power within that society) in ways that facilitate "social persistence." I analyze as well the phenomenon of change. I document, for example, how certain memories about the Anlo past (for example, those that emphasized the population's connection to Notsie and the Anlo capital, Anloga) informed how most Anlo came to understand and remember the significance of certain sites. I note how these prevailing collective memories were reinforced through oral traditions and ritual enactments—bodily practices that reinforced existing power relations—but they also became the basis for challenges to the political authorities in pre-colonial Anlo. I then document European colonial and (later) Ewe nationalist appropriations of these collective memories. I describe how these appropriations transformed the memories associated with particular sites. And I argue that as the Anlo embraced (selectively and with much contestation) the new meanings that the colonial encounter had begun to encourage them to accept about sites of historical significance, these new meanings gradually gave rise to new collective memories and the bodily practices that supported them. I demonstrate as well the fact that the history of collective memory is more than the history of the production of group remembrances.[9] It concerns the study of historic mentalities, where memory is indeed understood to be influenced by the social and the political and riddled with contestations, but where it also exists as part of a "shared *symbolic* universe."[10] Colonialism disrupted this universe by introducing different symbols, beliefs, and practices. It "upset long-consecrated patterns of socialization."[11] The result was the demise of certain collective memories and the bodily performances that reinforced their significance, but these memories the colonized and, in this study, the Anlo replaced with new memories and structures (actions, beliefs, and symbols) because they reinforced new (though still contested) ways of thinking about self and the world.

ON LANDSCAPE AND HISTORY

Individuals and societies locate meanings in and associate collective memories with a variety of places and practices: speech, bodily gestures, the written word. This book, however, focuses specifically on the landscape, defined here as those places and spaces as well as the human body that are visible to the eye and that have also been the focus of collective ritual activity. Geographers have been perhaps the most attentive to the way particular landscapes have been the focus of meaning and memory, whether sacred or secular.[12] But they have not been alone. Anthropologists have long explored this topic, expanding it by redefining the notion of landscape (as I have) to include places and spaces as well as the human body.[13] They, along with many geographers, have also taken particular interest in emphasizing the extent to which the meanings attached to a particular landscape can both reinforce and disrupt our individual and social identities and cultural values while also generating tensions and contestations about meaning, often among unequally empowered groups and individuals.[14] Frequently treated only cursorily in all these studies, however, is the issue of change, how meanings of place and space have shifted over time.[15] For a more focused discussion on this topic, one must turn to history. Here, a number of studies, including several that focus specifically on Africa—by Thomas McCaskie, J. Matthew Schoffeleers, and Patrick Harries, for example—have discussed how Africans and/or Europeans in Africa during pre-colonial times understood particular natural environments—the landscape in general or particular hills, caves, pools, and forests—in what is now Ghana, Malawi, and Southeast Africa, respectively. These same authors have also examined how these understandings influenced the ways that different African and/or European communities interacted with their physical environments and with each other.[16] More recently, in *Voices from the Rocks*, Terence Ranger has focused on the extent to which European colonialism generated new and different meanings about the Matopos Hills in Zimbabwe. Once associated with the graves of revered Ndebele ancestors and the god Mwali, the Matopos later came to be known among Africans and Europeans alike as the last resting place of Cecil Rhodes, as a site of African rebellion and resistance, as a venue for devilish un-Christian practices, and/or as a landscape that should be unsullied by human habitation.[17] Religious practices are given a prominent place in all these studies about the history of certain sites, but religious change is rarely linked to larger epistemological shifts. To what extent did changes in the religious meanings attributed to place and space (and the body as well) not only mark a shift in how the landscape was understood but also indicate a more profound shift in how Africans in particular understood themselves and their environment as both material and spiritual?

This book seeks to answer this question by embracing insights from anthropology, religious studies, and geography about the importance of understanding place and space through the meanings that communities attribute to them. It reinforces the importance historians attach to understanding meanings in the context of changing religious beliefs, practices, and concerns. But it also does more. It emphasizes the notion that changing meanings associated with landscape, especially in the context of colonial cultural encounters, can also reflect both limited and more profound epistemological shifts in how people came to understand themselves and their environment. It emphasizes this point by focusing on those material sites once considered by the Anlo to be intimately associated with spiritual forces.

The sites examined include such "natural" features as the ocean, permanent potable water bodies, and forests. But they also include other features of the Anlo landscape: burial grounds and sacred religious centers as well as the gendered human body. In focusing on the history of these sites, this text does not claim to offer a comprehensive analysis of Anlo understandings of their entire landscape—the sites, sounds, smells, images, peoples, places, and spaces that the Anlo have imbued with meanings and memory. It is not a narrative history structured to document, chapter by chapter, a successive set of societal changes. Rather, each chapter addresses the question of how a particular site was conceptualized by the Anlo prior to colonial rule as both material and spiritual. Each chapter also explores, where sources allow, the ways a particular site was harnessed for personal or political gain, under what circumstances this conceptualization was challenged first by some in Anlo and later by German Pietists and/or British colonial officers during the colonial period. All the chapters discuss how the Anlo in part and together responded to this challenge and why tensions within Anlo created by this clash of understandings about how to understand the Anlo landscape were resolved or have continued to simmer and sometimes boil to the surface. Yet each chapter is also different from the other. Every site examined is associated with a different set of meanings; each site faced challenges to its pre-existing meaning that came in a different form. And the ways in which the Anlo handled these challenges also varied from site to site. In exploring these very different sites in a single study, I de-emphasize the differences that distinguish one from another, man-made as opposed to "natural," human as opposed to inanimate (as defined by contemporary Western thought).[18] Instead, I emphasize the similarities, the extent to which according to Anlo thought all these sites had spiritual significance because of their association with the sacred. Such spiritual forces may have been defined as either "nature" spirits (occupying certain natural formations in the Anlo landscape) or ancestral ones to which man-made shrines were built, but all had the power to occupy material entities (whether human or inanimate). And all were subject to the vicissitudes of time and space, occupying certain sites for a period of time but vacating those same sites if offended or ignored and thus rendered irrelevant for the day-to-day lives of the Anlo. Focusing on the history of several sacred sites rather than that of a single location within the Anlo landscape allows one to identity the very terms by which nineteenth-century Anlos understood and defined their material and spiritual landscape, a landscape within which they also constructed identities of themselves and others and developed their social, political, and religious institutions. It allows one to document the unevenness and varieties of change—the fact that certain sites retained their previously sacred meanings while the meanings associated with other sites were displaced to new locations or were lost altogether to contemporary Anlo residents.

In Chapters 1 and 5, for example, I examine the sacred character of the towns of Notsie and Anloga and the ways in which these communities during the pre-colonial period constituted (not without challenge) two of the pillars upon which nineteenth-century Anlo constructed its identity as a religious and political community. But the meanings and memories associated with these two towns took quite different turns. During the colonial period and under the influence of post-colonial developments, Notsie saw itself appropriated by German Pietist missionaries and French colonial officers in ways that encouraged the Anlo to associate the town (whose physical and spiritual distance from daily life in Anlo had already dimmed its religious significance) with solely secular meanings. Ewe nationalists and those interested in local development later reshaped these new understandings for their own purposes. The result: Notsie lost for the vast majority in Anlo its meaning as the home of a "traditional" religious god and became instead the center around which to celebrate—through festivals and ritual reenactments—an Anlo (and Ewe) ethnic identity. The town of Anloga was also associated by the Anlo during the pre-colonial period with religious meaning. And like Notsie, it too found its image as a sacred site under attack by European colonizers and missionaries. Unlike their response to the attacks on Notsie's meaning, however, the citizens of Anlo rallied to Anloga's defense. This led to a confrontation around meaning and memory that has only served to reinforce its religious significance. The result: Anloga—unlike Notsie—stands for the Anlo as a site of continual tension and conflict as different groups struggle to maintain or contest those meanings and memories with which it was once and is still associated. The histories of these two sites illustrate the extent to which meanings and memories associated with sites of spiritual significance have shifted in diverse ways under the influence of colonialism and post-colonial developments as different ways of understanding have become incorporated into Anlo ways of understanding self and the world.

Chapter 2 examines the meanings and memories associated with the numerous water bodies that dot the Anlo landscape. Here we also see the uneven impact of European colonial ways of knowing on Anlo understandings of the material and spiritual aspects of their landscape. Where Western technology embraced by the Anlo rendered the permanent potable water bodies in the area spiritually meaningless to contemporary Anlos, the ocean has not suffered the same fate. It continues to evoke a sense of awe as the failures of Western technology to control coastal erosion, the continued belief in disembodied spiritual forces, and the sense of identity an untamed ocean provides for male fishermen keeps alive the sacred character of the sea.

Chapter 3 examines the early-nineteenth-century Anlo belief in the spiritual power of the dead as demonstrated in the use of particular burial practices. It documents the impact that the entrance of Western public health concerns and German Pietist notions about the relationship between the living and the dead had on the placing and spacing of the dead. And it explores the ways in which the Anlo displaced those beliefs that had previously informed the spatial handling of deceased family members by attaching them instead to the notion of a ghost uninfluenced by ritual actions on place and space.

Chapter 4 expands the discussion of Anlo conceptions about the spiritual power of the body by shifting the focus from the dead to the living. It documents early-nineteenth-century notions about the power of the spiritual aspect of the human body to influence the health of the self and others. And it examines the entrance of Western medical knowledge systems. It then discusses the struggles that ensued between both colonizer and colonized and within Anlo society as individuals and groups therein sought to reconcile old beliefs with the new by creating new understandings about the body and the causes of illness in light of the changes wrought by colonial and post-colonial developments in the health and educational institutions of the Anlo. These chapters can be read successively as they move from a focus on a regional site of significance (Notsie) to sites of increasingly local importance. They can be read randomly. One can also read them in sets. As noted, Chapters 1 and 5 focus on towns of religious significance and the successes and difficulties in reaching some community consensus on how to interact with these sites despite epistemological differences. Chapters 3 and 4 focus on the body, giving comparative attention to the changing meanings associated with the dead and the living. However one reads them, together the chapters document both the creative adaptations and the failures of certain local understandings about the African landscape to survive the onslaught of European epistemologies. They illustrate the ways in which this encounter, which was deeply influenced by the unequal power relations embedded in the colonial encounter, produced both myriad "modernities" and more profound epistemological shifts. They demonstrate the ways in which these changes became the basis for a new consensus about how one should understand and interact with certain sites within the Anlo landscape. And they illustrate how these same developments continue to produce tensions and conflicts that periodically erupt into violence.

1

Notsie Narratives

THE TOWN OF NOTSIE (located in south-central Togo) evokes quite specific memories among the Anlo and other Ewe-speaking peoples of southern Ghana and Togo. To most, the town is remembered as the common home of their Ewe ancestors, a place where a king ruled with tyrannical power, a location where this tyranny led to the great dispersal of Ewe-speakers throughout what is now southeastern Ghana and southern Togo. Ewe and non-Ewe alike draw upon these memories for a range of purposes. Historians study them as one of the few indigenous sources of early local history.[1] Others have explored the importance of this exodus narrative as a charter for delineating what is deemed to be socially and politically acceptable behavior.[2] Some argue that these memories explain why Ewe-speaking peoples have historically eschewed centralized political power,[3] while still others deploy them to demonstrate the notion that the Ewe once were and could again be a power to be reckoned with. In the nineteenth century, however, Notsie meant something quite different. To the German missionaries who had begun working in the region after 1847, Notsie was a convenient way to conceptualize as simply as possible the historical origins of a very diverse collection of communities. To those Ewe and non-Ewe in the region who had to deal with these German conceptions, however, this understanding of Notsie was only vaguely familiar, for they had their own understandings of their individual histories, languages, cultures, and origins. Most recognized that the town had been important historically, especially as a religious center, but it was only one of many such centers. Equally significant is the fact that these local nineteenth-century notions obscured, in their own way, an earlier history that identified Notsie as a major economic center within the region not only for local residents but also for European traders operating on the coast in the mid-sixteenth century.

Of particular interest in this chapter is the fact that despite these shifts in meanings and memories, Notsie has defied the erosion of time.[4] Its decline in political, economic, and religious significance by the eighteenth century; its colonization by Germany and then France in the early twentieth century; its post-colonial economic and geographical marginalization as a poor upcountry town in the impoverished nation-state of Togo[5] have done nothing to displace the cultural significance of Notsie in the minds of many in the region. This chapter explores the extent to which Notsie has served as a geographical site through which many Anlo and many others in southeastern Ghana and southern Togo define themselves. It examines the way memories and meanings associated with Notsie have been shaped by political, religious, and economic agendas. But perhaps more significant, it seeks to explain why this site has proven so powerful to so many for so long. I argue that Notsie existed in early-nineteenth-century Ewe memories as a ritual trace, a site of religious significance, but one of limited importance in the lives and imaginations of those in the region. It was this quality that made the site attractive for continuous redefinition as a place of memory and meaning.

PRE-COLONIAL NOTSIE NARRATIVES: FROM THE
FIFTEENTH TO THE EIGHTEENTH CENTURIES

Archaeological studies and the few documentary sources that mention the town indicate that Notsie was of major regional significance from at least the mid-fifteenth century. During this period, the political leadership of Notsie began the construction of a wall that ultimately measured, even though it was never finished, 14,450 kilometers at its perimeter and enclosed 14 square kilometers. It was not built for defensive purposes but rather was designed to symbolize the town's status as a major economic power and ritual center within the region.[6] Serving as a center of pottery production from the sixteenth to the mid-eighteenth centuries, Notsie operated as a regional site for economic exchange.[7] More important, Notsie was also where the shrine for the regional god Mawu existed and where its priest served simultaneously as political and religious head of the community. From the sources currently available, we cannot know how the people of Notsie conceptualized Mawu—as male, female, androgynous, as a lesser deity or the Supreme God. We do know, however, that others in the region believed Mawu to have great power. European traveler accounts from the seventeenth century indicate, for example, that in the town of Whydah (known locally as Glehue and located on the coast east of the Ewe-speaking region where the population spoke Peda, a language closely related to Ewe) Mawu was known and viewed as the Supreme Being. In Dahomey (located north and east of Whydah, where Fon, another language closely related to Ewe, was spoken), oral traditions state that the god Mawu is said to have brought order into the world.[8] In the Ewe-speaking polity of Anlo (located immediately east of the Volta River estuary), it was to Notsie that one of the most prominent immigrant groups, the Nyaxoenu lineage, resorted in the early- to mid-seventeenth century when it became entangled in a dispute with another immigrant family about which lineage had the religious authority to share leadership of the town with the indigenous inhabitants. It was from Notsie that the Nyaxoenu family obtained its *tsikpe* (rain stone), an object of great spiritual power that allowed them to assert their right to provide (in alternation with the Bate clan) the Anlo spiritual and political leader, the *awǫamefia.*

Most contemporary analyses of the religious beliefs of the Ewe (and of those beliefs in the Whydah and Dahomey) often argue that Mawu (with its base in Notsie) was historically conceptualized as the Supreme Deity in the entire region. This ignores a more complex reality, however. Indigenous notions of a supreme god were far from static. A deity perceived at one point in time as the most powerful was defined as supreme, but it could lose that designation if its power appeared to diminish in relation to other gods. Thus I noted that Mawu was worshipped as a supreme deity in the seventeenth century in the coastal town of Whydah.[9] By the eighteenth century, however, the worship of Mawu is said to have taken on more of the attributes of a lesser god.[10] In the coastal polity of Anlo, Mawu continued to be worshipped as the Supreme Deity, but by the eighteenth century it had to share this designation with another god, Se, which was associated with the Yoruba Ifa divination system.[11] By the nineteenth century, Ewe-speaking peoples of Agu no longer defined Mawu as the supreme deity. Rather, Kpaya held that distinction, and Mawu was conceived of as a lesser god in the town.[12] Similarly, among the Ewe-speaking people of Peki, there existed no concept at all of Mawu as a supreme deity; the Peki assigned that designation to their god Dzingbe.[13]

These accounts indicate that Mawu's preeminent stature in the sixteenth century among the Ewe-speaking peoples of Peki, Agu, and Anlo and among the Peda of Whydah had declined significantly by the nineteenth century. No longer considered the single most powerful deity, in Anlo Mawu had to share the designation of Supreme Deity with another god; in Agu it was demoted to the status of a lesser deity; in Peki it was simply replaced by a god thought to be more powerful.

Numerous events appear to have precipitated this turn of affairs, but all were linked to the rise in demand by Europeans for enslaved African labor. Beginning in the late seventeenth century, the Akan polity of Akwamu launched a series of successful imperial wars against the numerous Ewe-speaking communities that lay to its east in an effort to control the trade routes that funneled goods along the coast and between the coast and the interior. Akwamu's control waxed and waned during the next two centuries, but the consequences of their political and economic influence generated significant changes in the region.[14] Notsie lost significance as a religious and economic center, while deities located on the coast, where the European demand for slaves had begun to bring enormous wealth, gained in stature with the rise of new centers of economic exchange on the Atlantic littoral. For example, the incorporation of the coastal Ewe-speaking polity of Anlo into an Akwamu sphere of influence opened new trade ties with communities along the coast and in the northern hinterland for the Anlo. It also propelled the Anlo into the many political and military conflicts that came to characterize the region as different states sought to dominate the increasingly lucrative business of exchanging slaves for European manufactured goods.

This development, in turn, precipitated a crisis in leadership in Anlo. In 1769, an ethnic outsider group known as the Dzevi successfully challenged the right of the Adzovia and Bate clans to serve exclusively as the political and religious leaders of Anlo. They were able to do so in part because the Anlo had suffered a series of terrible military defeats between 1702 and 1750. These losses eroded the Anlo population's belief in the ability of the Adzovia and Bate gods to spiritually support them in battle. Both of the deities had gained prominence in the seventeenth century because of their ability to produce rain when droughts were both severe and frequent.[15] By the eighteenth century, however, a deity's prowess in war was of far greater importance than its ability to produce rain. This loss of authority, especially on the part of the Adzovia, appears to have had a significant impact on relations with Notsie, for the Adzovia claimed to have obtained their deity, a *tsikpe* (rain stone), from this town. Annual pilgrimages to Notsie became less frequent,[16] and much more attention was given to the Dzevi's local war god, Nyigbla. In addition, during this same period, political, economic, and religious contacts with communities to the east brought to Anlo a new divination system, Afa, that introduced the god Se. This god not only coexisted with Mawu as a separate conception of the Supreme Being;[17] for many it also superceded Mawu in importance. Se became the Supreme Deity to which prayers for daily guidance were directed, and the coastal towns to the east where the god Se was said to have originated became the more common destination for religious pilgrimages. This in turn resulted in a redefinition of Mawu and the significance of its home in Notsie. Both came to be defined as physically and spiritually distant from the day-to-day concerns of the Anlo; many conflated in their own minds Notsie's geographical distance from the coast with its limited religious significance.

This is not to say, however, that Mawu and the town of Notsie lost all significance for the Anlo or others in the region, however. In 1812, British traveler G. A. Robertson observed that "the town of Oache [i.e., Notsie] is a privileged place" and that "many of the inhabitants of the adjacent country resort thither to participate in the benefits of his prayers and protection."[18] But by this time, Notsie no longer commanded the kind of respect or undivided attention of those polities in the region that it had in the past. Thus, by the late nineteenth century, British colonial officer A. B. Ellis noted that in Anlo and elsewhere on the coast:

> Mawu . . . [with its principal shrine at Notsie] is regarded as the most power-ful of the gods but he is not a supreme being or a creator. Although he is chief, he is but one of many independent gods. I am aware that this is not the view commonly held by the German missionaries, who are the only class of Europeans who ever seem to try to discover what the religious beliefs of the natives really are. They are of opinion [sic] that Mawu is held to be the lord of the terrestrial gods, who are subordinated to his control and some even go so far as to say that he created them; but though one may occasion-ally obtain from natives who inhabit the seacoast towns, and who, having all their lives been in contact with Europeans, have become familiar with the European notion of a creator and supreme god, statements that go to cor-roborate this, yet it is evident that this is a modification of the more original conception of Mawu and is due to European influence; for natives who had not been subjected to that influence distinctly hold the view that Mawu, though most powerful, is simply one of many gods. . . . Sacrifice is never di-rectly offered to him, and prayer rarely. The natives explain this by saying that he is too distant to trouble about man and his affairs, and they believe that he remains in a beatific condition of perpetual repose and drowsiness.[19]

The situation in the coastal towns described by Ellis in 1878 was also true for the interior communities. In the vast majority of these other Ewe-speaking communities, Mawu had no priest. No local interests existed to manage and control the definition of this god. Notsie, the home of Mawu, existed for the majority in the region as a site to which only occasional pilgrimages were made (and then only in dire circumstances) and/or it stood as a site used to give religious authority to existing political alliances. For example, to re-inforce their mid-eighteenth- to late-nineteenth-century political and eco-nomic relations, the Anlo defined Notsie not only as a spiritual center but also the physical home of both their own ancestors and those of their allies, the Akan-speaking Akwamu. Thus, by the eighteenth century, Notsie (as a site that had commanded the religious interest of a region populated by Ewe- and non-Ewe-speaking peoples alike) had declined substantially since the mid-fifteenth century in significance and meaning. Changing times had encour-aged the population to adjust their religious beliefs and practices in concert with the developments that were affecting their daily lives. By the beginning of the nineteenth century, Notsie had become a center that was largely empty of everyday meaning, an emptiness that made it available to be comman-deered and filled with alternate meanings and memories by anyone with the will and capacity to do so.

COLONIAL NOTSIE: MISSIONARY AND NATIONALIST NARRATIVES FROM THE NINETEENTH TO THE MID-TWENTIETH CENTURIES

European missionary activity in what is now southeastern Ghana and southern Togo began in 1847 with the arrival of the Bremen-based Norddeutsche Missionsgesellschaft (NMG). In that year, Lorenz Wolf established a mission station in the Ewe-speaking polity of Peki. Six years later, in 1853, however, the mission was forced to abandon its first station because of local political disputes. It then shifted its headquarters to the coast and from there expanded over the years back into the interior and eastward.[20] By the outbreak of World War I (which marked the beginning of the end of direct German missionary activity in the area), 53 Europeans and 215 local assistants attended to 8,274 Christians in 8 mission centers and 160 outstations throughout the region.[21] During this period of missionary activity, the Europeans associated with the NMG (also known as the Bremen Mission) were guided by a common set of beliefs that influenced how they pursued their goals. These beliefs included the notion that

> originally all people on earth had been united by one language and the worship of one God. Yet, when human beings had tried to contest God's power by building a tower that would reach heaven, God . . . punished them by dispersing them and making them speak different languages. . . . This dispersal had led to religious and linguistic degeneration; the rise of polytheism and the loss of linguistic unity went hand in hand.
>
> It was the task of the mission to lead all these scattered peoples back to the Christian God whom they had worshipped in a very distant past. But rather than reuniting all people in one language, God [showed] at the occasion of Pentecost that he accepted the existence of different languages and rather wanted the Gospel to be preached to the "heathens" in their own mother tongue.[22]

In emphasizing the power of language to reconnect the Ewe to their monotheistic past, the missionaries took it upon themselves to define the various Ewe-speaking peoples in the region as a linguistic community. They did so, in part, by ignoring Anlo notions that not only Ewes but also the Akan polity of Akwamu had its origins at Notsie. They also promoted language standardization. Using the coastal Anlo dialect as their guide, they created a written language deemed to be a "worthy container for the accommodation of the Gospel"[23] which all Ewe who attended the schools and churches established by the mission were forced to learn. This, in turn, encouraged the development of an Ewe identity where none had existed before.[24]

According to Birgit Meyer, the Bremen missionaries' desire to foster a common identity had its roots in German notions about how all peoples should see themselves. The missionaries, for example, saw themselves as members of a *volk,* a people that shared a history, a culture, and, most important, a language, features that distinguished them from others. It was this concept which they also applied in their mission work; they encouraged the Ewe to see themselves as a separate group which, if developed to its full capacity within Christianity, would allow its members to realize their potential as human beings created by God. Critical to this concept of *volk* was the question of origins. According to this view, by recapturing one's shared history as found in one's origins, a people could reinvigorate their *volksgeist,* their shared ethnic national spirit.[25] As part of their effort to foster a sense of oneness among the Ewe-speaking peoples of the region (a oneness that the mission could then use to delimit the linguistic and territorial limits of their operations), the missionaries selected Notsie as the site from which all Ewes would be encouraged to believe they originated. They did this in spite of the fact that the towns of Ketu and Tado (now in the Republics of Benin and Nigeria, respectively) were also cited as places of origin among some Ewe communities. They did this even though they knew that not every Ewe-speaking group within the region claimed an origin in Notsie.[26] To manage this rather messy situation, they simply ignored the divergences in the origin traditions found among the various Ewe-speaking communities and published this refurbished history in their quarterly mission magazine in 1877. Eventually the same basic account appeared in the Ewe readers (Ewegbalexexle) first published in 1901 and 1906,[27] which they then used to encourage the students in their schools to see themselves as Ewes. This refurbished history emphasized a common identity and origin grounded in shared oppression and a successful escape from Notsie.

> All the people from Ewe . . . come from a common homeland in the northwest. . . . This old homeland they call Nodschie which is about 8–10 days travel from the coast where the Anlos now live. . . . They lived there under a king who had great power and prestige and who was also the most influential priest. All of his subjects had to live for his sake and thus they were no more than slaves, but the king also had to care for his people through the elders and his representatives. He made sure that if they worked for him and his household and the elders, they could also plant and work and work for themselves. The king did well; the land was prosperous.
>
> In time however, the king grew old and died. After him . . . a young king came to the throne. This young king had all the elders killed because he feared their influence on the people. They might encourage the people to rebel against his often childish and incomprehensible behavior. Without the king knowing it, however, his subjects failed to carry out completely his command, and rather allowed several elders to live.

Figure 1. Bremen Mission missionaries, wives, and deaconesses, Keta, late nineteenth to early twentieth centuries.
From *So Sahen Wir Africa* (Bremen: Staatsarchiv Bremen, 1984), p. 28.

One day, when a group of young men was working for the king, the sovereign commanded that all should report to work without exception. When they appeared he told them they must build him a great house worthy of a king. The suggestion pleased the people and they were willing to do so. Thus he separated the people into groups ... and they prepared a great pile of earth for building. When the earth was thus prepared, the king had water poured on it so that it could be trampled down by foot. Then he commanded them to gather cacti and thorns and spread them over the earth so that they would be kneaded together with the earth. When they stopped their work because of the wounds they received on their legs and feet, the king became enraged and ordered them to do whatever he told them.

The next day, before dawn, the people went to these elders who were still alive to explain their desperate situation. The elders comforted them and advised them to go back to the work that the king had delegated to them. The king then demanded that they turn into rope the earth they had mixed with the thorns and cacti so that they could use this to bind the king's house. Their attempts failed, and as a result their hands were full of thorns. They then went again to one of the elders to express their desperate need for advice. The elders told them they should ask for a piece of old cord to use as a model. Perhaps his ancestors had made such a rope and they could examine it carefully and use it as a model to make another. Such words did not please the king and he declared that this idea could not have come from them. "There must still be one or more elders who told you to say this." The king then urged the people to tell him were they got this idea so that he could kill those in question.

Filled with indignation, they all went home and when night fell, they gathered and decided unanimously to leave the king by [breaking through the
wall that surrounded the town and] moving away. . . .

The last ones to leave . . . kept their [old] homeland in sight . . . by walking
backwards. . . . When dawn came and the people did not arrive at work, the
king heard about the mass emigration and promptly sent out his people in
all directions. But the footprints of those who were fleeing pointed in the
direction of the homeland which astonished and confused those who were
searching.[28]

In addition to using this narrative to emphasize a common origin and
a shared history, the Bremen Mission also worked in tandem with the German colonial government that controlled the Togo territory (and therefore
the town of Notsie) to secularize the town, both in the imaginations of their
Ewe students and in reality. Accounts of Notsie and the exodus in the Ewegbalexexle texts omitted all mention of the fact that Notsie was the home of the
regional god Mawu. Emphasis instead was placed on describing Notsie as a
secular town. The German colonial government reinforced this conception by
altering the reality of traditional rule in Notsie. When the governing council
of Notsie was forced to interact with the colonial government, they appointed
during the early years of German rule an elder to communicate with the colonial officials on behalf of their leader, who by tradition remained secluded
from public view. The German colonizers not only accepted this individual as
a spokesperson but later recognized him as the official chief of Notsie. This
effectively separated (as had never been the case before) the connections that
had existed between the religious and the political in both the functions of
the Notsie chief and the imagery of the town.[29] Notsie was no longer to be
viewed as the home of a priest-king who was associated with Mawu. And
Mawu was no longer to be viewed as a powerful but distant god, one of many,
who was uninvolved in the daily affairs of mankind unless specifically requested. Rather the god—like Ewe history, Notsie's political structures, and
Notsie town itself—was stripped of its previous content. Mawu was instead
designated the Supreme God of the Christians and assigned all the attributes
of the Christian god: omniscience, omnipotence, and omnipresence.[30] Notsie
town was redefined as simply a town from which all Ewes emigrated because
of the tyrannical rule of Agokoli. Of even greater significance is the fact that
this redefinition of local identities and the memory of Notsie subsequently
became more than the way in which many Ewe-speaking peoples began to
view themselves and their history; it also provided the foundation for the later
development of an Ewe nationalist movement.

As early as 1914, local Ewe-speaking elites embraced the concept that the
Ewe were a single people unified by language, culture, and history and encouraged others to embrace it as well. In that year, mission-educated Anlo

paramount chief Togbui Sri II offered 10,000 men to the British government to help defeat the Germans who had exercised colonial control over Togo since the 1890s. He did so—while refusing to allow Anlo citizens to partici-pate in the war in East Africa—because of his specific desire to eliminate the hardships that those with whom (in his words) the Anlo were so closely affili-ated suffered because of the particularly harsh character of German colonial rule. After World War I ended and the Ewe-speaking polities in the former German colony found themselves occupied by both French and British forces, several chiefs and mission-educated local elites sponsored a delegation in 1918 to meet with Lieutenant Colonel Rowe, the officer in charge of the Brit-ish forces. Their goal was to encourage the British to support the inclusion of all Ewe-speaking peoples into the British colony of the Gold Coast in or-der to mitigate the social and economic difficulties that resulted from the sev-ering of family, village, and economic relations through incorporation into the colonies of two different European powers. Their efforts failed, however, and the League of Nations formally recognized French and British control over the former German colony of Togo. In the 1930s and 1940s, Ewe nation-alist organizations continued their efforts but adopted sometimes quite dif-ferent goals. Some sought Togoland unification, which would have excluded those Ewe-speaking polities that had already been incorporated into the Gold Coast during the nineteenth century. Others advocated Ewe unification but with the option of being independent of both France and Britain.[31] Despite these differences, all accepted and asserted the notion that Ewe-speaking peoples constituted a single people whose origins were located in Notsie; an idea that had been defined in their mission-authored school texts. This em-brace of a mission-authored construct of Notsie's significance for an imagined Ewe *volk* reinforced the secularization of the town and extended its appeal to those who had not experienced directly the ethnic nationalizing influence of missionary education.

By the 1950s, the power of this combination of a mission-based and nationalist-reinforced Ewe identity formation reached its apogee.[32] In 1956, the United Nations held a plebiscite in British Togoland. The purpose was to allow the residents of that section of the former German colony of Togo that had been separated from Togo after World War I by the League of Nations and given to Britain to administer to determine whether they wished to join formally the Gold Coast, which was in the last stages of becoming an inde-pendent Ghana, or to continue under British trusteeship. Ultimately, those in British Togoland opted to join Ghana, but supporters of an independent state decided to register their protest by organizing a festival—the Agbogboza—in September of 1956. This event brought together in Notsie for the first time since their reported dispersal "all the important personalities in Ewe country (kings, chiefs, leaders of political parties accompanied by important delega-

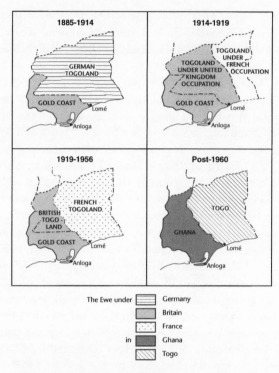

Map 3. The Partitioning of the Ewe.
From Sandra E. Greene, *Gender Ethnicity and Social Change on the Upper Slave Coast* (Portsmouth, N.H.: Heinemann, 1996), p. 146.

tions) from all the communities that claimed to have their origins in the exodus from Notsie."[33] Traditions that had not experienced the standardizing influence of the Bremen Mission were brought into line. More important, the memory of Notsie as a secular town from which the once-unified Ewe had originated assumed an authority of its own. This nationalist-inspired memory was steeped in a political agenda shaped less by missionary ideology and more by ethnic concerns that will be discussed below. But it was this memory that came to dominate not only Ewe conceptions of their historic identity but even the self-image of the non-Ewes who lived in the region. Paul Nugent describes the situation in the Central Togo language community of Likpe.

[Several] factors ... help to explain why people from Likpe ... have ... claim[ed] a Notsie ancestor.

During both the German and British rule, the Ewe Presbyterian and Catholic Churches relied upon the Ewe language as the medium of religious proselytization and of tuition in the schools. Those Bakpele who first attended schools were therefore assimilated into a cultural milieu in which proficiency in Ewe—and the Anlo dialect at that—was considered essential. Significantly when a future headchief of Likpe, himself a mission product, wrote a short history of his stool in 1909, it was in the Ewe language. Moreover, the surviving schoolbooks of another future Paramount Chief, Nana Soglo Allo III, demonstrate that the Notsie tradition was being actively disseminated in the classrooms during the 1930's. It might have seemed preferable to such a young man to imbibe Ewe history rather than face the implications of having no history of his own to recount. As his exercise history book reminded him: "A nation who has no history of its own has lost one of the precious things in the world."

The articulation of Ewe unificationist demands after the Second World War attached even greater importance to the putative relationship between historical connections and ethnic goals. . . . Amongst the minorities, a willingness to support the Togoland Congress [the most active Ewe nationalist group in the region] rested partly on the perception of a shared heritage with their northern Ewe neighbors. The Congress enjoyed a great deal of support within Likpe, right up to the moment of [Ghana's] independence, from a mixture of people. . . . The level of support for the Togoland Congress demonstrated the resilience of the Notsie paradigm.[34]

The development, consolidation, and embrace of nationalist readings of Notsie was not the last transformation in meaning and memory that was to occur, however. Post-colonial times have generated yet another set of associations that have kept Notsie in the forefront of people's imaginations despite its decreasing stature as a sacred site.

POST-COLONIAL NOTSIE

After the UN plebiscite which saw British Togoland opt to become part of the Gold Coast, the people of Togo voted in 1958 for a 1960 date for independence from France. This development and the years which followed entrenched the divisions that had begun to develop among the different Ewe-speaking populations who had been split administratively between France and Britain since the end of World War I. Ewes in both newly independent countries focused not on furthering Ewe unity but rather on taking advantage of the services available to them in their respective countries.[35] Job opportunities, years of education in either the Ghana English-language or Togo French-language schools, constant exposure to national integration efforts by the Ghanaian and Togolese governments, and the cultural differences that developed as a result saw Ewes identify more with the nations of which they were a part and with the local districts from which they came rather than as Ewes who should come together in one nation-state.[36] This, in turn, impacted the meanings and memories associated with Notsie.

As early as the 1960s, various Ewe communities began to define Notsie not so much as a basis for defining an Ewe identity and not so much as a place of religious significance but rather as a convenient focal point around which to rally a sense of *local* cultural pride. This development is perhaps most evident in the Ewe-speaking coastal polity of Anlo. In 1962, Anlo developed what became an annual festival commemorating the exodus from Notsie. Named Hogbetsotsoza (from the Ewe words *hogbe* [homeland], understood to be Notsie; *tsotso* [exodus therefrom]; and *za* [festival]), the organizers used this particular title because Notsie (or Hogbe) was known to every Anlo who had either been taught or had heard about the history of the Ewes in school or from local traditions. In the first year of its organization and in all those festivals held since, however, emphasis was placed not on a larger Ewe cultural identity but rather on identifying and taking pride in Anlo culture. For example, in 1996 in the first official brochure for the festival, considerable attention was given to descriptions of the traditional political organization of the Anlo state, historic places in the capital of Anloga, the importance of reconciliation *within* Anlo, and the cultural value of Dodede, the traditional approach to sanitation. In subsequent years, musical groups from other parts of the Ewe-speaking areas in Ghana and Togo were invited to perform, but local culture and history was still emphasized.

In addition to a focus on the local, the festival also attempted to encourage those who had left the area for greater economic opportunities elsewhere in Ghana to return psychologically, physically, and financially so they could contribute to the development needs of the district. In 1966, for example, a special subscription dinner was organized as part of the Hogbetsotsoza to support the *awoamefia*'s palace-building fund as there was no official residence that could serve as a symbol of the power and respect that should be accorded the paramount chief of the Anlo district.[37] In subsequent years, the organizing committee made even more explicit their concern that the festival be used to rally support, not only to reinforce a sense of oneness and cultural identification with Anlo and Anlo culture but also to garner support for development projects. In 1973, the foreword to the Hogbetsotsoza brochure penned by Togbui Adeladza II, the *awoamefia* of Anlo, stated that

> The theme for this year's festival is "Charity Begins at Home." . . . The central Government, of course, has certain definite responsibilities to each community in the country, but it is now abundantly clear that the initiative for real development must come from the local community itself. This is as it should be because it is the local people who know their own problems most intimately.

> Such major works as building the sea defense at Keta or the road from Srogboe to Dabala are obviously beyond the resources of any local community. But whatever we can do for ourselves we should never neglect to do. In

Figure 2. Re-enacting the Notsie exodus through dress at the Hogbetsotsoza, 1996.
Photo by author.

the past, our people built their own schools, dug their own wells, and constructed their own feeder roads. We still continue to undertake such self-
help projects, but the rate does not appear to match our requirements. By
the force of circumstances, most of us stay far away from home doing our
jobs to earn a living. But you must always remember that Charity Begins at
Home. Everybody must make provision in his monthly budget not only to
build a house at home but also to make some contribution to development
projects undertaken in the community.[38]

This emphasis on the local has had a significant impact on the meanings and
memories associated with Notsie. Increasingly for many, the town's significance is an ever-more-distant memory, unconnected to any specific political,
religious, or everyday concern.[39] The town comes to mind only during those
rare discussions of Anlo or Ewe history, once a year when a delegation is sent
to Notsie seeking blessings for the festivities immediately before the Hogbetsotsoza, or when a new *awǫamefia* is installed. The remoteness of this connection is again best illustrated by examining the festivities of the Anlo, who are
probably connected to Notsie in more ways than most among other Ewe-
speaking peoples in the region. Since its inception, the organizers have included at each Hogbetsotsoza a dramatic reenactment of the Notsie narrative.
By the late 1970s and early 1980s, however, interest in this aspect of the festival had begun to falter. In 1978, for example, when I first attended Hogbetsot-

soza, a clan elder who was widely respected for his knowledge of the oral history of the area presented a most dignified and movingly eloquent account of Notsie's history and the exodus that mesmerized those who attended. The audience was sparse, however, and over the years it attracted even fewer interested observers. By 1989, the audience had dwindled to an embarrassingly small number. Refusing to abandon the very heart of the festival, the organizers had opted by 1996 to pursue another approach. That year, they invited a drama troupe from Accra to perform the exodus reenactment. The response was overwhelming. In years past, the Traditional Council office's courtyard (where the drama is staged) was largely empty. In 1996, however, it was difficult to find even standing room within the walls of the quite large compound. Significantly, to attract such a crowd, the troupe took considerable artistic license in dramatizing the events leading up to the exodus. Agokoli was portrayed not as the insensitive tyrant of the well-known Notsie narrative, but in slapstick form as a drunken, lecherous, bumbling ruler who was presented as more an object of amusement than abhorrence. The fact that only a more light-hearted account that deliberately played fast and loose with the traditional narratives about the town and the exodus could draw such an engaged crowd illustrates the extent to which older meanings and memories have undergone yet another set of transformations. Under the pressure of rural-to-urban migration, Notsie has been harnessed to ever-more-local agendas through the use of a popular transnational artistic form in response to agendas dictated not, as in the past, by religious or ethnic nationalist sentiments but rather by the demands of a post-colonial, global capitalist world in which poor communities are increasingly urged to fend for themselves using what few resources they may have to rally support for their development.

Even more significant is the fact that while pre-colonial, colonial, and post-colonial meanings have come one after another with increasing intensity, the meanings and memories associated with these different periods co-exist (if uneasily at times). This has helped sustain the importance of the town in the individual and collective imaginations of the Ewe-speaking peoples in the region. In 1969, for example, the Anlo State participated in the ethnic nationalist-oriented Notsie festival, Agbogboza, despite the emphasis in its own Hogbetsotso festival on local culture, history, and development concerns. In 1986, the Ewe-speaking Asogli Traditional State with its capital in the city of Ho commemorated the significance of Notsie for their own history by organizing a festival they entitled the Gligbaza (wall-breaking festival: *gli* [wall]; *gba* [break]; *za* [festival]) Designed to commemorate the exodus of the ancestors of the Asogli state from Notsie, its focus was very much on the particulars of Ho culture and history, but it too celebrated unabashedly and with enthusiasm an Ewe identity and culture in which Notsie was given pride of place.[40] Likewise, Notsie's historic religious significance is regularly acknowledged. As mentioned above, the polity of Anlo periodically sends delegations to Notsie to receive religious blessings. This occurs on the ascension of a new *awǫamefia,* immediately before the annual Hogbetsotsoaza, and when particular environmental circumstances demand spiritual intervention. In 1968, under the leadership of the paramount chief, Togbui Adeladza II, a delegation traveled to Notsie seeking assistance in alleviating severe drought conditions in the polity. When subsequently in that same year so much rain fell that floods devastated the area, many farmers attributed this turn of events to the petition that had been sent to the sacred grove in Notsie.[41] In 1987, when the usual delegation was to be sent to Notsie before the annual festival, dissension developed within the Lafe clan (*hlǫ*) (one of the five that was officially designated to represent Anlo) because of rumors that secret rituals had been performed late in the night for unknown purposes just before the delegation was about to depart. The secret ritual is said to have included a request that the gods accept the soul of one of the delegates as a sacrifice in exchange for the blessings to be received.[42] The content of this story appears to have been based on local traditions about the events that transpired in Anlo after those who left in the original exodus from Notsie arrived in their present area. According to these traditions, the first leader of the Anlos, Sri I, discovered that he had forgotten his stool of office in Notsie only after having arrived in Anlo. When a delegation returned to Notsie to retrieve the stool, they were told that they could have it only in exchange for the severed head of Sri. After consulting with one another, the delegation decided to kill a servant attached to the delegation and to present not his head (which would have been recognized as not belonging to Sri) but his arm, which had been scarred by yaws, the same disease that had similarly marked Sri. The ruse is said to have worked. Agokoli released the stool and the delegation returned with it to Anlo. Those who heard about secret rituals being performed in 1987 before a delegation was to depart for Notsie apparently thought that a sacrifice like the original one would be necessary again, for the leader of the Lafe clan absolutely refused to allow anyone from this *hlǫ* to participate in the delegation, and his views influenced others who also declined to send a member from their clan with the delegation. Even in their refusal, however, it was the memory and meaning of Notsie that so influenced their actions.

Thus, all of these instances—the development of the Hogbetsotso and Gligba festivals, the continued holding of the Notsie Agbogboza, the sending of the 1968 delegation concerned with drought conditions, and the dispute in 1987 over the delegation sent to Notsie prior to the Hogbetsotsoza—indicate the extent to which Notsie continues to evoke a range of memories and meanings despite the massive transformations in the religious, political, and economic cultures of the region and in the individual Ewe-speaking communities and towns in southeastern Ghana and southern Togo.

THE NOTSIE PHENOMENON EXPLAINED

Given the discussion of Notsie's place in the historical and cultural imaginations of the Ewe, certain developments emerge as clearly contributing to the longstanding status of the town as cultural icon in the region. In the precolonial period (from the sixteenth to the early nineteenth century) Notsie was not only an economic center but, more important, a religious center to which many in the region resorted. It was the home of Mawu, a very powerful god from which the political authorities in a number of communities such as Anlo derived their spiritual authority to rule. By the middle of the nineteenth century, however, its status as the single most important religious center in the region had been undermined by political and economic events in the region. This decline was exacerbated by the Bremen Mission's embrace of the town as the site they sought to define as the historic home of an Ewe *volk*. In selecting Notsie, the missionaries effectively stripped much of the religious power of Notsie from the minds of many who embraced Christianity and Western education. At the same time, however, this refurbished memory of Notsie reinvigorated its status as a regional center (albeit for ethnic nationalist rather than indigenous religious purposes). The growth of an ethnic nationalist movement among Ewe elites and their efforts to deepen a sense of Ewe-ness among the communities in the region further reinforced the regional significance of Notsie. Even with the decline of nationalist sentiments and the growth of more local concerns based on the nation-state, Notsie continued to serve a variety of interests. Those who sought to encourage local development by harnessing the resources of migrant Ewes used Notsie to rekindle a spirit of cultural oneness with their respective communities. Those who maintained their belief in the indigenous religious system and those who continued to value the age-old cultural practices of their ancestors made sure ritual pilgrimages to Notsie continued, even if only periodically. And those who defined themselves in opposition to these beliefs also found themselves having to take into consideration a Notsie that has continued to play a role in the affairs of their communities.

Thus, the "staying power" of Notsie can be attributed, in part, to the fact that so many over such a long period of time found in Notsie something around which to shape an identity. For Ewe-speaking peoples in the precolonial period, Notsie was a regional religious center, a center that stood at the heart of their political and spiritual institutions. For those schooled by the Bremen missionaries, a refurbished Notsie defined the historic home of an Ewe *volk*. For Ewe nationalists, it was the symbol of their hope for a reunited Ewe nation. And for those Ewe communities that have more recently established festivals to commemorate the history of the town, Notsie served to reconnect members living abroad with their home communities so that their collective resources might be harnessed for the good of their communities of origin. This explanation does not explain, however, why individual Ewe-speaking people responded so positively, especially to missionary and nationalist initiatives to change, and yet also kept alive the memory of Notsie. Why did identity politics resonate so well with the Ewes of Ghana and Togo? The answer, I believe, lies in understanding the dynamics of the colonial and post-colonial encounter as the Ewe-speaking peoples of southeastern Ghana and southern Togo interacted with their British, German, and French colonizers and their non-Ewe neighbors in independent Ghana and Togo.

Studies on Africa in the nineteenth and early twentieth centuries have documented with great precision the extent to which British, German, and French colonial rule brought massive challenges to those who were colonized. Indigenous political systems were severely disrupted or destroyed altogether. Local and regional economies were reorganized for the primary benefit of the colonizer. Ideological notions that accompanied colonial rule devalued the cultures of those whom the Europeans conquered and greatly influenced the milieu in which the colonized were forced to operate. "Natives" were defined in the most negative terms according to nineteenth- and early-twentieth-century European notions of proper dress, sexual behavior, gender relations, technological achievements, education, linguistic development, mental capacity, and so forth. Africans were exhorted to adopt European culture and religion if they ever hoped to become "civilized." They were encouraged to abandon those customs and beliefs that held them in a primitive state. Adoption of European practices, however, rarely guaranteed acceptance, and this fueled further frustration among the colonized. Resistance took a variety of forms, from open rebellion to passive resistance to selective adoption of European culture and beliefs. The impact of colonialism on the Ewes of southeastern Ghana and southern Togo and the various ways in which they sought to resist these developments were no different from that described above.

Of particular interest here, however, is the fact that Ewe communities used local narratives, and the Notsie narrative in particular, as a means to cope with the assault on their culture. One such assault involved the undermining of the traditional political culture. In the early years of British and German rule, individuals who had no legitimate right to represent their communities were often elevated to such positions by the colonizers despite the objections of the legitimate political rulers and/or the councils of elders, the governing bodies that operated in most Ewe-speaking communities. Even after efforts were later taken by the colonizers to work with only those leaders who were recognized by both the local communities and themselves, the very nature of the colonial system allowed and sometimes encouraged these local leaders to abuse their authority. This contributed to a decline in respect for the authority of the elders. This decline was then exacerbated by the fact that new economic opportunities generated by the colonial economy allowed many young men and women to establish more control over their lives than had been the case in the past, when they were much more dependent on their elders to generate the resources they needed for marriage and the accumulation of material goods. Resistance to this change in the culture of authority in the area took a number of forms, but perhaps the most interesting was the popularity of narratives that reinforced elderly authority. One such narrative from Anlo (quite popular from at least the 1930s)[43] was the story of Tsali and Akplomeda.

> One day in a fit of anger, Tsali . . . challenged his father to a public display of supernatural powers (*amlimatsitsi*). In response to this challenge, the father [Akplomeda], removed his own intestines, washed them in a herbal preparation and dried them to give more years of life to himself. Tsali turned into a hawk and carried his father's intestines away into space. Tsali searched in vain for the tallest tree on which to settle and swallow the intestines of his father. But Akplomeda [had] commanded all the trees in the vicinity to be dwarfed. [He then] turned himself into the tallest tree upon which Tsali came to settle. Before Tsali could swallow his father's intestines, Akplomeda reached out his hands and Tsali dropped the intestines right into his father's unseen palms.
>
> Akplomeda [then] ridiculed his son with the words: You know how to turn into a hawk as I had taught you, but you don't know how to turn into a silk-cotton tree.[44]

The story clearly admonishes the young to remember their place—that the father is more knowledgeable than the son and the son should therefore show due respect. The Notsie narratives, despite the many different versions that have come into being, emphasize this same point. A young, foolish Agokoli seeks to rid himself of the confining advice of his elders by ordering all to be executed. His Ewe subjects, however, are successful in saving a few from death by hiding them. When Agokoli then orders his subjects to construct a palace using swish (adobe) mixed with thorns and to construct a rope out of mud, it is the elders who advise the young people on how to respond to the demand. And it is the elders who successfully lead them out of Notsie when they make their escape.

The Notsie narrative's popularity was further enhanced during the colonial period among the ordinary and the average in the region as a result of local efforts to make sense of their own traditions in light of the Biblical narratives introduced by the Bremen Mission. Instead of embracing the notion that they were the children of Ham who had diverted from the path of God and who needed the guiding hand of the missionaries to lead them back onto the road of righteousness, many among the Ewe associated their exodus from

Notsie with the Jews' escape from Egypt. The Ewes were not heathens but instead had been one with the Israelites. I encountered this interpretation in
1978, held with great conviction by an old woman who passed her formative
years during the height of colonial rule.[45] It is also present in a number of recent popular local histories published for an Ewe audience.[46]

Thus, while it is certainly the case that missionary efforts elevated the
status of Notsie during the colonial period by widely propagating the narrative in schools and mission publications in order to create an Ewe identity, it
is also the case that Notsie loomed large in the imagination of the Ewes because many Ewes themselves found the Notsie narrative useful as a means of
reinterpreting and resisting the efforts of the colonizers and the missionaries
to denigrate and destroy their cultures. For some, that reinterpretation was
cast in a Biblical idiom; for others, it meant reasserting the traditional religious significance of Notsie. Both approaches, however, placed Notsie at the
center of the discourse.

Many among the ordinary and the average of the Ewe also embraced a
nationalist-defined Notsie during the colonial period, and many continue to
do so in post-colonial times, as we have seen with the celebrations of the Agbogboza in Notsie and the Gligbaza in Ho. For these individuals, Notsie served
during the colonial period and continues to serve in independent Ghana as a
cultural anchor in their relations with non-Ewes. During the colonial period
when many Ewes migrated to work in the Fante- and Twi-speaking areas of
the Gold Coast, they not only found themselves to be a distinct linguistic mi-
nority but also encountered persistent stereotypes in which they were defined
by others as thieves, kidnappers, sorcerers, and ritual murderers.[47] This imagery has persisted in post-colonial Ghana and has expanded to include notions that the Ewe are also secretive, inward-looking, and tribalistic and that
they practice nepotism. Ewe and non-Ewe peoples in Ghana also often interpret the competition for political power and the distribution of economic
development projects in ethnic terms. For an Ewe who accepts this interpretation, the lack of development in the region where most Ewes live can be explained, at least in part, by their ethnicity.[48] In resisting what they see as the
consequences of such negative stereotyping, many celebrate the very ethnic
identity that others have used against them. They do so, in part, by acknowl-
edging a common link to Notsie for all Ewe. Such a response by many Ewes
in Ghana is evident in the numerous local histories that have been published
by Ewe scholars. Virtually all of these histories emphasize the existence of a
single Ewe people connected to one another through language, culture, and a
common connection to Notsie.[49]

Ethnic concerns in Togo have followed a rather different historical trajec-
tory, but they too have reinforced the central place of Notsie in the Ewe imagination. In Togo during the colonial and the immediate post-colonial period,

Ewe-speakers held some of the highest positions in government because of their long history of missionary education. This situation changed, however, in 1967 when Gnassingbe Eyadema, a military officer from the northern Kabye ethnic group, launched a coup and overthrew the government. To compensate for the lack of development and educational opportunities in northern Togo, the government under Eyadema inaugurated an affirmative action campaign to encourage those in the north to obtain the skills needed to contribute more fully to the country's development. This in turn generated considerable disquiet among many Ewes in Togo, who felt that the subsequent expansion in opportunities for northerners would work to their disadvantage. According to Vernay Mitchell, resistance among the Ewe has taken a number of forms, including "manipulating history [and] symbols" in which the place of Notsie is emphasized as absolutely central to Ewe identity. According to Mitchell, widespread sentiment exists, especially in Notsie, that the town should not become just another administrative center dominated by civil servants from the north. It is central to Ewe identity and should be recognized first and foremost as such.[50]

These examples of popular interest in Notsie from the colonial and post-colonial periods in Gold Coast/Ghana and Togo (in conjunction with the earlier discussion) indicate that while Notsie's identity as a sacred site has declined significantly (beginning even before the advent of colonialism), the town's central place in the imagination of the Ewe-speaking peoples of Ghana and Togo has remained. This is the result of a multitude of factors that have not only converged but have reinforced one another over the decades. Mission-generated notions of a secular Notsie engendered among some in the region a refusal to forget the historical and religious connections that tied many communities to Notsie. They also generated a nationalist embrace of Notsie as the center of an imagined Ewe nation. This in turn facilitated, with the advent of the post-colonial period, the use of Notsie to encourage local cultural pride and economic self-help. Perhaps most fascinating, however, is the fact that all this was made possible because trace memories of Notsie as a sacred site from the early nineteenth century were substantial enough yet largely devoid of everyday meaning to allow Ewe and non-Ewe alike to create new memories and meanings around which to build an identity for a changing world, an identity that came to be firmly centered at Notsie.

2

Of Water and Spirits

To ENTER THE central district of Anlo is to journey into a land of water, where lagoon and sea, pond and creek are ever present, where even the location of farms and fields exist as reminders of where waters once stood. All that separates the littoral residents from the Atlantic Ocean and the inland Keta Lagoon is a narrow sandbar (not more than a mile wide), on which the Anlo villages are clustered "like beads on a string." Water is at the center of Anlo culture. As a liquid, it is seen as necessary for life itself, yet it is also believed to be capable of bringing great hardship. Death from drowning and the destruction caused by the waves of an ever-encroaching Atlantic Ocean have been an all-too-common reality of life since at least the nineteenth century.[1] Periodically, the Keta Lagoon also overflows its banks, bringing destruction to fields and crops. This has profoundly shaped land-tenure patterns and residential development.[2] Yet water is also part of everyday life. From the normative offer of water to visiting guests to the use of this substance in the many rituals surrounding birth, death, and religious worship, water is believed to have the power to cool the hearts of men and gods, mediate relations between humans and the spiritual world, and purify the physical both literally and ritually. In its natural state, it has evoked in the imaginations of the Anlo awe and respect, but at the same time it can be so ubiquitous as to be taken for granted.[3]

This chapter will examine the many memories and meanings associated with a number of water bodies that exist in Anlo. In so doing, I give little attention to the ritual use of water—its symbolic role in ceremonies marking birth and death, in the enstoolment of chiefs, in the purification of ritual objects, and in prayers to the divine. Rather, I focus primarily on places, specific water bodies whose histories, spiritual significance, and meanings have been transformed by environmental change, technological innovation, colonial rule, and missionary influence.

Of particular interest is the question of why certain water bodies have lost their former meanings while others have withstood the weathering (and in some instances destructive) influence of time. We know, for example, that in nineteenth-century Anlo, many of the ponds that first provided the Anlo with their drinking water when they first migrated to their present home on the Atlantic littoral were associated with particular deities. It was these spiritual forces that all believed had the power to provide continuously the fresh drinking water needed by residents who lived in an area where salt water was far more abundant. Taboos and prohibitions governed the ways in which men and women were to utilize these sources of fresh water. Various life forms—real and imagined—served as the physical embodiment of the gods, punishing those who failed to demonstrate respect and rewarding the pious with the very substance necessary for life. Today, however, more than 100 years later, many of the ponds stand neglected, remembered only by the very elderly. The same can be said of the Keta Lagoon. Once the principal source of salt and fish for the Anlo, a major transportation route, and the home of a respected deity, this water body, too, no longer commands the respect, the veneration, the attention of those residents who live near it. Some elderly male residents explain this turn of events by decrying the actions of the young, who, in no longer believing in the power of the gods, have driven them away. "Young girls on their menses approach sacred groves and shrines, abort babies here and there. . . . With all this moral morass prevailing today, how can Anlo deities demonstrate their once-indispensable power?" Despite the obvious despair and resignation that resounds in such sentiments, not all water bodies in Anlo have lost their former meanings. The ocean retains its power for many in Anlo. Deities that the majority at the turn of the twentieth century associated with the ocean (Wumetro,[4] Mami Wata,[5] and Agbui or Awleketi[6]) still maintain their hold over the lives of many in Anlo. Given this, we must ask what factors, what historical events have allowed the ocean to maintain its identity as a sacred place among the Anlo, and why have the ponds of Anloga and the Keta Lagoon lost that aura of spirituality? How did technological change and new religious belief systems introduced by colonial rule, missionary influence, and post-colonial developments affect the memories and meanings associated with these sites? In the previous chapter, we saw that the emergence of identity politics in the colonial and post-colonial periods have contributed tremendously to the maintenance of memories of Notsie even as the meanings of this town have shifted and changed with time. Yet no such memories exist for the vast majority in Anlo when they think of the lagoon and the ponds. Why? How have the Anlo been able to maintain a sense of the sacred when interacting with the ocean when the spiritual aspects of Notsie are now of limited interest to most and when the spiritual aspects of the first ponds and the lagoon are barely remembered at all?

In this chapter, I address these questions by examining the history, memories, and meanings of the ponds of Anloga, the Keta Lagoon, and the ocean as these memories and meanings have shifted and changed under the influence of new technologies, missionary influence, colonial rule, and post-colonial development policies. I demonstrate that all these factors influenced both a series of forgettings and a continued vitality in certain memories and meanings. But of particular importance have been Anlo understandings of the spiritual, understandings that have continued to mediate Anlo interactions with their natural environment.

TAGBAMU AND THE POTABLE WATER PONDS OF ANLOGA

The existence of freshwater ponds in an area otherwise saturated with salt water has been a phenomenon of some interest to both Western-trained scientists and the Anlo who live in the area. Both have their own explanations of how such ponds could exist in the midst of an overwhelmingly salt-water environment. Scientists, for example, state that the sandy soil of the spit on which the Anlo live is actually a former sandbar. After centuries of geologic activity, this sandbar enclosed the body of salt water that later became known as the Keta Lagoon. In the lengthening and widening process, the bar developed different elevations: some places rose higher above the saltwater table formed by the ocean and the lagoon, other places were lower. All, however, had a thick layer of sand, which allowed rainwater to percolate down to the saltwater table. Because fresh water has a lower specific gravity than salt water, it does not mix with the latter but instead "floats as a layer on top, rather as oil does on water."[7] In those areas where the elevation was low, fresh water existed as a standing body, easily accessed without even digging below the sand's surface. Such is the scientific explanation, one concerned with relative specific gravities, soil types, and geological change.

Anlo oral tradition, of course, offers a very different explanation. It is one that reveals very little about hydrological processes but illustrates instead how the Anlo interacted with, understood, and remember their environment. According to these traditions, the very existence of fresh water, easily obtained and seemingly permanently available, was critical to the decision by the Anlo's ancestors to settle on the coast. In the areas where the Anlo's ancestors had lived for some time, for example in Fiahor northwest of the sand spit, supplies of fresh water were a problem, especially during the periodic droughts that affected the region. Thus, the existence of fresh water that was both easily accessible and permanently available was most attractive. Perhaps in recognition of the critical nature of these water bodies, and hoping to ensure their continued existence, the Anlo imbued these sites with spiritual significance. All were associated with a set of deities known as the *dzokpleanyiwo* that are said to have been the first inhabitants of the area. It was these gods who are said to have created the ponds that later became known as Welifome, Klalavime, and Atsiwume.[8] Welifome, for example, is said to have been the property of Gbaaku, the same deity that was invoked during the Nyiko custom and whose name became associated with the grove (Gbaakute) that existed near the Welifome pond. Klalavime and Atsiwume are associated with the deities Duto Konyi and Agodzo, respectively.[9]

More significant, the spiritual meanings associated with these three ponds —so critical as sources of drinking water for the residents of Anloga—seem to have been forgotten except by the most elderly residents of the town. Although all are cited in the Hogbetsotso Festival brochures as historic sites, only one, Atsivu, has been permanently preserved as a means of protecting it from being destroyed by residential development. The others have been largely ignored. Even in the festival brochure, the particular ponds cited are remembered exclusively for their utilitarian function:

> [Klalavime, Welifome and Atsivume] . . . were the first sources of potable water for men and beasts on the settlement of the area. The importance of these ponds must be assessed from the fact that they made the founding of the town possible, for without water there could be no development of the area.[10]

Similarly, the memories of even the most elderly residents of Anloga[11] more often recall the ponds as part of the quotidian rhythms of the community: as places where one regularly collected drinking water and children could fish; as sites where young women—teasingly aware of their budding sexuality— gathered under the admiring, playful eyes of the young men in the community; as locations where heavy rains would swell the ponds to the point that they would flood the surrounding areas; as water bodies that were indeed created by certain deities but where this now has little meaning for the daily lives of the men and women, even the elderly of Anlo today.[12] That sacred quality that so influenced how the Anlo understood, interacted with, and remembered these early sources of drinking water no longer exists. Instead, the ponds of Anlo have been rendered spiritually meaningless, rarely remembered even in the quotidian rhythms of daily life.

The same can be said of the memories and meanings associated with the Keta Lagoon. Known locally as Tagbamu, this body of water is well remembered in Anlo oral traditions as the first major water body that the Anlo encountered on their arrival in the area in the early to mid-seventeenth century. According to these traditions, the ancestors of the Anlo were struck by the sheer expansiveness of the lagoon and thus called it Tagbamu (wide river). It quickly became one of the principal sources of protein for the Anlo, available to all no matter what their economic, social, or religious standing in the community, yielding rich harvests of "exquisite fish and crabs, . . . oysters [which were] so common . . . and prawns . . . particularly large and well-flavored, some of them being upwards of six inches in length."[13] And after the introduction of more stable types of boats and salt-making techniques from the more established saltwater communities to the west in the late seven-

Figures 3 and 4. The pond Welifome (overgrown with weeds) and the pond Atsivume (cemented for preservation).
Photos by author.

Figure 5. Keta Lagoon in the late nineteenth to early twentieth centuries.
From the postcard "In der Keta Lagoon," Staatsarchiv Bremen, 7, 1025/105.

teenth and early eighteenth centuries, Tagbamu connected Anlo to communities to the east and the north. After periods of heavy rainfall, for example, the Keta Lagoon expanded so greatly that it became connected to a series of inland lagoons that stretched from the Volta River to Lagos.[14] Boats would then be poled and paddled up and down the coast within this inland lagoon system, providing easy and quick communication between the many communities that existed along what was known as the Slave Coast (that section of the Atlantic coastline east of the Volta River but west of the Bight of Benin that included Anlo, Anexo, and Lagos, among others). Exchanges between the Anlo littoral and inland communities were likewise facilitated by Tagbamu, as this water body became the principal resource used for transporting locally produced goods to the roads that connected the communities on the Keta Lagoon to the interior, where the slaves and ivory demanded by the Europeans and the "red earth" used by the Anlo in their ritual activities were exchanged for Anlo's salt and fish and the manufactures purchased from the Europeans operating on the Atlantic littoral.[15]

Despite this central presence in the everyday activities of the Anlo, Tagbamu was more than a waterway for communication and a rich source of fish and salt.[16] Its expansiveness, its periodic flooding and drying, its seeming unpredictability as a source of both abundance and destruction prompted the Anlo to associate it with several deities, one of whom is remembered today as Tovuntsikpo. It is said to have once been a very powerful god, for "no matter how heavy the rainfall . . . its shrine [in Anloga] near the lagoon . . . would never be submerged. Tovuntsikpo stopped the floodwaters from occupying the town. It also generated more fish in the lagoon."[17] Associated with the Lafe clan, Tovuntiskpo protected the entire town, just as it offered its harvest of fish and salt (collected to the east and north of Keta) to any male who wished to tap its resources. Women—whether on their menses or not—were barred from entering the lagoon. Individuals who had recently eaten leftover food were advised to stay clear of Tagbamu if they wished to avoid weakening Tovuntsipko's ability to provide abundant harvests of fish.[18] No one was allowed to travel on the lagoon at night.[19] These beliefs and practices—like those associated with the ponds of Anloga—held sway in Anlo, governing everyday practices through much of the colonial period.[20] Yet over the remainder of this last century they too have come to occupy a meaningful place only in the memories of the very elderly. Why this is the case has much to do with the influence of missionary education and the technological efforts on the part of the British colonial government to "domesticate" and "modernize" the meanings and memories associated with Anlo's watery landscape.

MISSIONARY TEACHINGS AND WESTERN TECHNOLOGY

The majority of the missionaries who operated in Anlo during the late nineteenth and the early twentieth century were associated with the Norddeutsche Missionsgesellschaft, North German Missionary Society (NMG), also known as the Bremen Mission. Most came from working-class (farming and artisan) backgrounds in southern Germany and were deeply influenced by the Awakened Pietist tradition that was embraced by the Bremen Mission. This tradition defined itself in strict opposition to those forms of popular religion that were still quite common in rural Germany: belief in the power of certain spiritual forces to influence one's life and consultation with those who are said to have the ability to bring wealth, health, or harm. Pietists opposed these beliefs and practices but, significantly, they did not deny their power. Instead, they argued that these forces were either the "agents of Satan" or Satan himself, evils that prevented one from knowing the true God. This approach defined the work of the missionaries who operated in Anlo.[21] They saw themselves as freeing the Anlo from the clutches of the Devil by opening their eyes to the satanic character of the Anlo religion and encouraging them to fight the Devil by embracing Christianity.

The struggles of the Bremen missionaries to convert the Anlo to Christianity are well documented in their many reports published in the mission's publications. Of interest here is the way in which this conversion effort impacted Anlo views of their own physical environment, for one of the principal goals of the missionaries was to convince the Anlo that the spiritual forces that they believed occupied material substances were either manifestations of the Devil or simply did not exist. In 1909, for example, Bremen missionary Forster participated in what he and other Christians in Anlo considered to be a massive achievement: the baptism of the first converts from Anloga, the political and religious capital of Anlo, a town considered to be both a "bastion of heathendom"[22] and a major impediment to the spread of Christianity. In describing the baptism, Forster noted that an especially important aspect of the ceremony was the public disavowal of any ritual objects that the converts once believed had efficacy. Each baptismal candidate was thus asked to hand over to the missionaries their "fetishes and magic things" before a crowd of more than 1,000 "heathens." The purpose: "to show all the people that [these objects] were harmless,"[23] that they had no power to predict the future, protect one from harm, or cause harm to others. In performing the baptism itself, minimal significance was ascribed to the water used in the ceremony. Less than a single sentence was used to describe the actual ritual. Instead, emphasis was placed on the converts demonstrating their knowledge of the Bible and making a public profession to illustrate their seriousness, their inner conviction to embrace Christianity. The water—while symbolic—could not wash away their sins, separate them from their former lives, or cleanse their consciences. The baptismal water had no such power. Rather, it was the individual and the control they exercised over their own conscience that gave the converts the ability to communicate with and know God. This same approach— one that emphasized the feebleness of relying on a material-based spiritual force to influence one's life—was still being used almost twenty years later in 1927. In that year, Bremen missionary Carl Spiess reported with jubilation the success he and his fellow missionaries were having in encouraging schoolchildren to abandon the belief that spiritual forces could occupy physical objects. No mention is made of Satan or devilish practices, but the emphasis on refuting the existence of spirits occupying the material remains.

> There it lay, the great Tree of God, uprooted by the storm, the huge Tree of God on the ground directly over the often-traveled bush path. . . . The powerful crashing noise that shook the surrounding forest called [the heathens] out of their huts.

> They stared at it. Oh if you could truly see the frightened heathens! I see them in front of me now. I can read the inner doubts in their faces: "Where is our god, who for decades, for centuries lived in this huge tree? Where has he gone; to what place has he returned? We don't know, the other gods don't know. Ask the priests." "No, our village and our tree's godliness has not

left this place. The old trunk is still holy." The priest says it, so the others mumble to one another.

Weeks passed. . . . The "giant of the forest" lay where it had fallen, unmoved, still there. Women carrying water in large clay pots, men returning from the fields, children accompanying their parents—they all obediently went around the holy place on a newly trampled bush path on the side; none of them would dare set a foot on the trunk, quietly stand over the tree or disturb something in its path. Bad luck would meet them and the spirit that lived in the tree, injured by their footsteps[,] knew enough ways to seek revenge on such perpetrators.

More weeks passed. . . . I heard songs, school students' songs. . . . School students! I saw them coming . . . 20, 30, 40 in number. One, two, three—they all set foot on the "Giant of the Forest." . . .

"Are you not afraid?" "No, we are not afraid of the gods because there aren't any. There is only one God who lives in heaven and loves us."

Is that not something of a victory for the Gospel![24]

The accounts of Forster and Speiss—separated by almost twenty years—speak to the missionaries' persistent attacks on the Anlo's belief that spiritual forces could occupy material substances and in so doing be close to, in communication with, human beings and influence their lives.

Rarely, if ever, however, were these attacks directed specifically at Anlo notions about the Keta Lagoon or the water bodies from which the Anlo collected their drinking water. Instead, they were diffuse, directed more broadly to counter the notion that any external spiritual force existed, could be the source of anything good and holy, or had material reality. A more focused attack had to await the development of an Anlo Christian community that had the power to enforce more broadly throughout Anlo (and not just among the community of converts) a different understanding of the natural environment. This occurred in 1907. In July of that year, the elders of the Adzovia clan installed Bremen Mission–educated Cornelius Kofi Kwawukume under the name of Fia Sri II as the *awǫamefia,* or political and religious leader of Anlo.[25] They were guided by the conviction that only with the ascension of a mission-educated king would the Anlo be able to direct what they felt was the necessary "modernization" of Anlo. Miafiaga Nyaxo Tamaklo and Togbui Joachim Acolatse I were two of the elders who strongly supported the election of Sri.[26] Both had already reaped tremendous financial rewards by simultaneously supporting British colonial rule and using their connections with the British to gain the information they needed to exploit loopholes in the British colonial administrative structures designed to end smuggling operations over the British Gold Coast/German Togoland border.[27] As a popular oral account indicates, Tamaklo equated the Europeans with the loofa sponge: "*Yevu kutsa de wodia nutsi*" (The Europeans are like the sponge; they make your skin smooth).[28] That is, they can be used to make the place nice. Both Tamaklo and Acolatse also strongly supported the various Christian missions that had expressed interest in operating in the area. Although he remained a patron and member of the Yewe religious order until the very last years of his life, Tamaklo donated land in Keta and in his home town of Whuti for the building of schools by the Catholic Church and the Bremen Mission, respectively.[29] Acolatse also donated land in Keta for the building of the African Methodist Episcopal Zion Church.[30] Both took advantage of the opportunities provided by the various missions operating in Anlo to educate their own children because they saw the advantages such education brought for strengthening their ability to conduct business throughout the Gold Coast and German Togoland.[31] Thus, Acolatse and Tamaklo deemed anyone who did not understand the usefulness of the Europeans as "ignorant"[32] and they threw their considerable support behind the election of Kwawukume as the new *awǫamefia*.

On his ascension to office, Sri II immediately embarked on a campaign to challenge the power of the Anlo priests and their gods to dictate how the Anlo were to understand the material and spiritual world. He refused to participate for the full six months that had customarily been used to spiritually fortify any new *awǫamefia* before they officially assumed office. And thereafter he also refused to remain in seclusion, as had also been the tradition for the Anlo *awǫamefia* since at least the late seventeenth century. Instead, he traveled freely and openly throughout Anlo, riding a bicycle from one end of the littoral to the other. He supported the opening of Anloga to Christian churches and schools. He defied the ban on sewn clothing that had been imposed in the early nineteenth century by the Nyigbla religious order by allowing anyone who wished to to wear European-style clothing in Anloga.[33] Most significant for the discussion in this chapter, he challenged traditional religious control over the water bodies that existed in Anlo. In 1906, for example, priests associated with two of the most well-known and influential deities in Anlo (Mama Bate and Togbui Nyigbla) declared a ban on the use of sails on the canoes that traveled on the Keta Lagoon. According to the priests, "When the winds blew, they normally drained away the lagoon waters [and then the lagoon] became shallow. Since sailing boats could not function without the wind, to permit their use on the water was an indirect way of encouraging the winds to blow and so drain away the lagoon waters."[34] In 1914, eight years after the ban and seven years after his installation (having already instituted many of the reforms already noted), Sri ordered his sub-chiefs to allow canoes with sails to be once again used on the lagoon. He noted that since the ban, the lagoon had dried repeatedly even though all had obeyed the priests. Thus, it was obvious that the use of sails had little to do with the water level in the lagoon.[35] Sri launched a second challenge shortly thereafter when sand

Figure 6. Fia Sri II in the early twentieth century.
From the author's collection.

accumulated in the channel that connected the Keta Lagoon to the Volta River, blocking what was at that time a vital means of communication between Anlo and the rest of the Gold Coast. According to the priest of the Anlo god, Gbotonya, the barrier had been erected by this god and therefore was not to be disturbed. Sri defied this religious pronouncement by summoning workers and then personally supervising the removal of the barrier.[36]

In pursuing these actions, Sri directly and deliberately challenged the authority of the priests who had been so influential in shaping the political and religious culture of Anlo. He did so, however, not because he believed, as the missionaries did, that by following their traditional beliefs, the Anlo were engaged, often unwittingly, in doing the work of Satan. Rather, his primary motivation had to do with his desire to take advantage of those innovations that he thought would further the "modern" development of Anlo. In taking this approach, however, his actions only reinforced the challenge first presented by the Bremen missionaries to the Anlo's religiously inspired understanding of their natural environment. The result was a gradual secularization of the Keta

Lagoon and Anlo's potable water bodies, a secularization that was further facilitated by yet another set of developments: the introduction of a number of
technological innovations beginning in the mid-nineteenth century.

In 1840, a man by the name of Baeta—identified by the British as Portu-
guese—settled in the town of Atoko, several miles to the west of Anloga.[37] At
that time, the Anlo littoral had become a convenient site for the clandestine
sale of slaves, because such commerce in the Accra area to the west had been
made extremely difficult by British efforts to stamp out the sale of human beings. Taking advantage of Anlo's proximity to the Accra area and the lack of
British anti–slave trade patrols in that area, Baeta—with the blessing of the
local political leaders in Atoko—established residence in the town and immediately embarked on the business of supplying the American, Brazilian, and
Cuban vessels that operated off the coast with human cargo. As part of his
operations, he erected a building (sections of which still existed in 1996) as a
holding cell for the slaves he intended to sell overseas. He also built a well in
order to supply his human cargo with drinking water from a readily accessible
source until the arrival of the ships that would transport this cargo to the
Americas.[38] Built out of barrels that were sunk into the ground, this well,
known locally as Batewudo, Baeta's sunken well, created quite a sensation in
the area. This was the Anlo's first introduction to the notion that one could
make a continuously available potable water source anywhere that was convenient.[39] Prior to this, the Anlo had access to only two sources of drinking
water. They could make shallow diggings in the sand, which yielded a supply
of fresh water for only a very limited time, or they could rely on those pools
that they believed never dried because the residents were diligent in maintaining good relations with the deities that created them. The introduction and
widespread acceptance of the technology that made Baeta's well possible gave
the Anlo much greater control over this vital natural resource. But it also was
the beginning of a demystification of the waters of Anlo that only accelerated
under the influence of the Bremen Mission and Togbui Sri II.

The impact of new technologies on Anlo notions about the spiritual character of certain water bodies in the area is perhaps most evident in the ways
this population attempted to control the water levels in the Keta Lagoon. We
know, for example, that in 1906, when the priests of the deities Mama Bate and
Togbui Nyigbla issued their order prohibiting the use of sails on the Keta Lagoon, the majority in Anlo complied. They believed in the ability of the gods
to fill and empty the lagoon of the water that was so vital to their lagoon-
based fishing industry. They abided by the ban. In 1911, four years after Fia
Sri II's installation and his first attacks on such beliefs, the vast majority of
Anlos still responded positively to support religious interventions to stem yet
another phase of drying in the Keta Lagoon. As the British district commissioner in Keta at the time, Harry Newlands, noted, there was overwhelming

support for the priests' efforts and little that Fia Sri II or his fellow Christians could do.

> Fetishism has a very great hold on the people in this district and I have known many instances where professing Christians here have abandoned their new faith and gone back to that of their forefathers in times of stress.

> For instance, in the year 1911, a public subscription was opened to collect funds for the fetish priests who had made the annual intercession for rain to fill the lagoon. A very large sum was collected—well over £100 I understand —and presented to them as a mark of gratitude for the unprecedented success which had attended their efforts in 1910 and to spur them on to similar efforts as the lagoon was rapidly drying. This subscription was remarkable for the large amounts given by native Christians not, probably, so much because they had any great faith in the efficacy of the priests' intercessions but as a sop to public opinion.

> The Fia of Awuna [Anlo] who is a Christian, would certainly outrage public feeling if he acted on the opinion of the Government and most probably [would] alienate the sympathies of many people including some of his most important sub-chiefs, e.g. those of the old regime like Chief Tamakloe of Huti [Whuti], the Fia of Avenor (who is a fetish priest in the position of Fia over the largest sub-division) and the Fia of Apipe who is also a tronshi.[40]

What was not possible in 1911, however, had become the preferred method by 1920. In that year, the political leaders in the major towns on the northern side of the Keta Lagoon (an area previously associated with the greatest resistance to British colonialism and Christian missionary activity) petitioned the acting governor and commander-in-chief of the Gold Coast Colony to do everything in his power to fill the Keta Lagoon, which was bone dry at the time, with water. The colonial government responded by considering the use of pumps— among other methods—to fill the lagoon. This was deemed wholly impracticable, given the size of the area to be filled (240–300 square kilometers), and nothing was done. Nevertheless, the fact that the leaders of the Anlo resorted to the government for assistance, not just in 1920 but again in 1932, is indicative of the extent to which Anlo understandings of their natural environment had begun to change since the early twentieth century.[41] Spiritual intervention was no longer the normal and assumed means to control the water level in both the Keta Lagoon and in those bodies that supplied the Anlo with their drinking water. New technologies had given the Anlo a different way to manipulate, manage, and understand their inland water resources.

With the Anlo's embrace of these new technologies and understandings of the natural environment, however, came an evacuation of spiritual meaning and loss of memory. The oldest residents of Anlo with whom I spoke in 1996 (all over 92 years old), for example, believed that the spirits continued to exist but had either removed themselves from their former watery abode or simply refused to make their powers evident. Both the abandonment and refusal theories rested on the notion that so much disrespect had been shown the gods by younger generations of Anlos that the gods had become deeply offended and therefore refused to have anything to do with the current population.[42] On the other hand, some younger residents didn't even know that the Keta Lagoon and the potable water bodies in the area had ever been associated with deities. Others knew, but either didn't believe in them or thought they had no power to affect their lives. Profound changes have indeed occurred in the meanings and memories associated with the many water bodies of Anlo since the early twentieth century. Of significance here, however, is the fact that these transformations were neither uniform nor complete.

PHASED FORGETTINGS AND MARVELOUS MEANINGS: BLOLUI AND THE SEA

To the west of Anloga stands a pond called Blolui that managed to defy secularization for more than twenty years after the meanings attached to the Keta Lagoon and the potable water ponds of Anloga were successfully challenged by missionary influence, changing environmental conditions, and the introduction of new technologies. Like those ponds that served as a source of drinking water for the residents of Anloga, the pond Blolui was also associated with a powerful spiritual force. Called Mama Blolui, this god is said to have taken material form in the bodies of crocodiles, dwarfs, and mermaids. Violation of her taboos brought immediate retribution.

> When we were children, we saw a mermaid (*fumemé*) . . . washing something in a gourd. She had lots of hair covering her face. When she saw us approaching she dove back into the pond. . . . The mermaids were sometimes seen [just] lying on the banks of the pond. Their feet were turned backwards. . . . Early in the morning you would see them basking in the dawn light. . . .
>
> There were [also] lots of crocodiles in Blolui. It was believed that the crocodiles normally came out to roam about in the town at night. When we were children [some ninety years ago] we were told not to fish in Blolui if we had eaten leftover food. Women were not to cross or approach the pond when they were on their menses. No one was supposed to enter the pond after having sex. . . . We were told that if we went against these prohibitions, the crocodiles in the pond would drag us to the bottom. . . . They would even chase after you into the town.[43]

It was this imagery which shaped Anlo understandings of the Blolui pond. And although little is remembered about the rituals and rites that were once performed to ensure that Mama Blolui would protect the town of Anloga from spiritual and physical assault,[44] an aura of sacredness is said to have pervaded the site well into the twentieth century. Both the dense and dark grove that once stood at its edge and the fact that, even under the most severe drought conditions, the pond never dried contributed to a sense that Blolui was an impenetrable mystery.[45] That this aura of mystery and danger, of spirituality and power could continue to inspire vivid memories and meanings for at least twenty years longer than could the Keta Lagoon and the potable water bodies in Anloga raises a number of questions.

What was it about this particular pond that allowed these older meanings to persist? Why were these images and meanings not affected earlier by the spread of Christianity and the efforts of Sri II to discredit any beliefs that might hinder the development of Anlo? Answers to these questions can be found in the history of its use and location. Blolui was never used as a source of potable water by the residents in the area. It was too distant. Thus, it never became part of the quotidian rhythms of daily life; it never became normalized and secularized as just another body of water. In addition, the dense, seemingly impenetrable grove situated at its edge; the tales of crocodiles that could and would drag women and children into its waters if they ventured too close; the fact that the deity that occupied the pond was associated with the Ame clan (which was both socially stigmatized because of their origins as war captives and feared because of their association with a number of powerful gods) all contributed to a certain distancing. One did not ordinarily need to venture into the vicinity of Blolui. Efforts to maintain this sacred aura probably intensified in response to missionary activity; the majority of Ame residents did not live on the littoral or in the inland trade town of Anyako where Christianity first took root. Rather, most clan members lived in Alakple, where they—like most others in the scattered villages and hamlets in inland Anlo—clung tenaciously to their traditional beliefs and practices. To champion the power of Mama Blolui and to emphasize the sacred quality of the pond where she manifested herself boosted the Ame's reputation as the custodians of the pond and its deity, but this championing also served as a challenge to missionary notions that Anlo gods did not exist, had no power, and were manifestations of the Devil. Blolui's continued reputation as a site of spiritual power was further facilitated by its location and lack of obvious utility. Blolui was distant from any of the villages in the area and thus never posed a threat even if it overflowed its banks. It was not a source of drinking water and was never vital to the economic activities of the Anlo. In the 1890s, when miasma theories about the origins of malaria still prevailed in the minds of many, colonial efforts to eradicate this disease were directed at controlling the supposedly noxious emissions of gas that caused the disease by draining swamps in such urban centers as Accra and Keta. Nothing was done in distant uninhabited areas such as Blolui. With the scientific discovery in the early twentieth century of the relationship between malaria and the anopheles mosquito, colo-

Figure 7. The pond Blolui and the remnants of the sacred grove, 1996.
Photo by author.

nial efforts in Anlo were again directed at eradicating breeding grounds for
mosquitoes in the major towns and villages of Anlo, not in places such as
Blolui.[46] Thus, this particular pond escaped colonial scrutiny and rather became for the Anlo a site that symbolized both the mystery and the continued
power of their deities, despite the encroachment of "modernity."

By the mid-twentieth century, however, even the aura around Blolui had
begun to dissipate under the pressure of changing times. Urban growth in Anloga took its toll. Most of the trees that once constituted the grove on the edge
of the pond were cut down for firewood, and the grasses and bushes were
cleared to make way for houses and farms. The edges of Blolui pond became
just another marshy area where trash could be thrown. Different perspectives
on the natural environment introduced by Christianity and Western education had become so pervasive by the 1990s that even though no one could
say exactly what had happened to the sacred crocodiles that once lived in
Blolui, residents of Anlo could state credibly and with amusement that they
had probably all been hunted and killed.[47] Only the ocean has been able to
defy complete secularization.

Anlo understandings of the ocean as the home of certain spiritual forces
has a long, if not obscure, history. European travelers' accounts from the eighteenth century say little about Anlo beliefs regarding the sea during this pe-

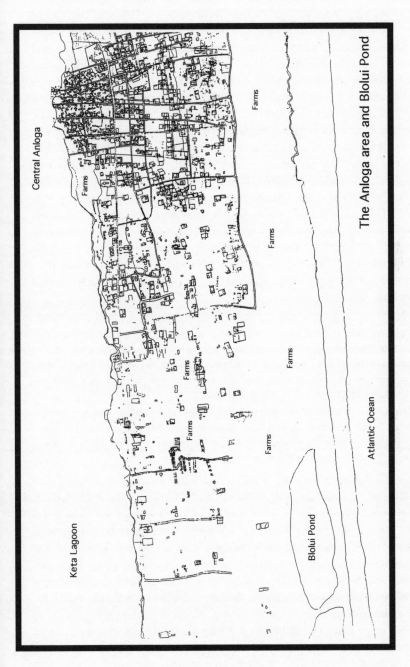

Map 4. Map of Anlo Area Showing the Location of Blolui Pond.
Based on an Anloga city planning map housed at the Keta District Office in Keta, Ghana.
Modified to highlight the noted features by Sandra E. Greene.

riod, and Anlo oral traditions tend to focus on those deities that have more recently come to dominate Anlo religious conceptions of the sea.[48] Farther to the east, among the Hula people of Great Popo, however, accounts dating from the eighteenth century indicate that the residents in this polity believed in a deity called Hu (meaning "ocean" in the Fla language). This deity is said to have had the power, if sufficiently propitiated, to calm the usually rough surf that was so characteristic of that section of the West African shoreline. Robin Law argues that its status rose in importance during this period, when Europeans began visiting on a regular basis for the purposes of trade. The offering of sacrifices to this god calmed the sea sufficiently to facilitate the conduct of trade.[49] An Anlo deity of the same name but called Fumetro (from *fu*, meaning "ocean" in the Anlo dialect of Ewe) was reported by German missionaries to exist in the late nineteenth and early twentieth century. Presumably it had been worshipped in Anlo since at least the eighteenth century, when it is known that Anlo sailors were launching canoes into the sea in order to conduct trade with the Danes, who dominated the commerce on the Anlo littoral at that time.[50] Like its counterpart in Grand Popo, this deity was associated with controlling the high surf and had the power to facilitate trade with Europeans:

> One of the interesting fetishes [among the Ewe] is that of the ocean surf, Fumetro, from *fu*, the sea. . . . The god is represented as a European (with his wife, his employees and boats) sitting on a horse. . . . Anyone who is possessed by the fetish can count on being on good terms with the whites and they believe they can conduct good business with him. With these thoughts, they leave offerings of European goods. . . .

> One of the prayers of the Fume fetish states: May the boat from Europe bring us good things! Even if he is blind, may a white man come and show us goods or may some wise one from Europe come and supply us with sacks [with which to obtain good things].[51]

For eighteenth- and nineteenth-century Anlos, the ocean was associated with more than just deities that could bring wealth from transactions with Europeans, however. The ocean was also occupied by other strange and wonderful entities. Among these were the Fumelokloviwo, sea-persons who built houses, towns, and cities under the ocean. Sometimes at night they were said to emerge from the ocean and could be seen on the beach, only to disappear back into the sea upon discovery. Never worshipped or offered sacrifices, these creatures rather represented the mystery and aura that surrounded the ocean for nineteenth-century Anlos.[52]

Today such imagery and beliefs still pervade the memories and meanings that the Anlo associate with the ocean. In 1996, when I inquired why certain Anlo rituals and rites were conducted at the ocean, I was told:

Has anyone seen the depth of the sea! Nobody knows its magnificent and powerful contents. Most of the *trɔwo* that possess people emerged from the sea. There are lots of powerful *trɔwo, voduwo,* and ancestral spirits in the sea. It is the power of the ancestral spirits that cleanse the spirit of the dead from the widow or the widower. And don't forget that there are lots of mermaids (*fumemé*) in the sea.[53]

Nobody knows its source and its end. . . . We know and we believe God's powers are in it. Therefore we conduct any ritual there; part of its powers will be bestowed on us. For instance, chiefs, including myself, were traditionally enstooled at the seashore. As a result, we believe the gods in the sea will bestow some powers on the chief so that he can rule more effectively. We also believe that the sea contains certain powers that could help a person achieve noble and wonderful deeds. The magnificence and total stillness of the place makes it suitable for prayers. Whenever you are there, it gives you a feeling of not being too far from the gods and ancestors.[54]

Don't you see that it boils on its own, but it is never hot? There are lots of powers in that sea. Nobody can control the sea.[55]

These descriptions of the stillness that one finds on an empty beach, that sense of the sacred, the mysterious, and the uncontrollable yet powerful potential of the sea, are ones that the Anlo also once applied to the Keta Lagoon. Yet, today such perceptions now only apply to the sea. Only the ocean retains today its sacred quality. Why?

Since at least the late eighteenth century, Anlo and non-Anlo residents alike have used both religious and technological efforts to influence and make use of the forces that control the sea. Individuals, families, and fishing companies have regularly offered sacrifices to the gods that are said to inhabit the ocean. Many did so in the eighteenth, nineteenth, and early twentieth centuries to enhance their trade relations with Europeans; others have maintained a relationship with the ocean to ensure bumper fishing harvests and to serve those deities that have called them to their worship; still others use the waters of the sea to separate themselves spiritually from the ghosts of their dead spouses and to cleanse sacred objects and reinvigorate their spiritual character. The most common of these efforts have been performed by and for the benefit of select individuals and groups within Anlo. But on occasion, the religious energies of the entire state have been harnessed and directed at the sea. In the 1960s, for example, Togbui Adeladza II, who succeeded Sri II as *awɔamefia* in 1959, sanctioned the sacrifice of a cow, offered on behalf of all Anlo, to help control the sea, which since the first decade of the twentieth century had been literally eating away at Keta, consuming the sandy coast and destroying everything—schools, athletic fields, houses, churches, cemeteries, homes, and businesses—in its path.[56] Technological efforts to control the sea began in 1923. In that year, "timber groynes [beams] were sunk [by the British

colonial government] at Keta beach . . . with the aim of breaking the force of
the sea and of facilitating the deposition of sand." In 1938 and 1952, the colonial government, and then in 1960 and 1978, the independent government of
Ghana, made similar efforts with different materials after many educated Anlos made strenuous pleas and demands. None of these efforts succeeded in
controlling the ocean. But while these same efforts applied to the lagoon coincided with a loss of the spiritual being associated with this particular body
of water, the same process did not occur with Anlo views of the sea. In the
minds of many Anlo, the ocean has continued to stand as a place of great
spiritual power.[57] The embrace of Western technology and education has done
little to strip the sea of its marvelous meanings.

To understand the ocean's continued spiritual significance, one must take
into consideration the fact that the sea—unlike the lagoon—still commands
the economic attention of the Anlo population. We know, for example, that
while the Keta Lagoon has been seriously overfished since the first decade of
the twentieth century and now provides fish quite small in size largely for
local consumption,[58] the ocean continues to dominate the economic life of
many who live on the littoral. In his study of Anlo fishermen, for example,
Nukunya notes that "those who become fishermen virtually grow up with the
sea. By about age ten, they have already mastered the art of swimming and
acquired the skills to join the fishing expeditions. Those who come from inland areas and are not initially conversant with the sea take to maritime fishing because of its financial rewards and their admiration for the industry and
its practitioners. . . . Fishing is their life."[59] At the same time, the ocean is also
associated with a type of danger rarely, if ever, encountered by adult males on
the lagoon. In much of Tagbamu, the water is normally no more than two me-
ters deep.[60] The crocodiles and hippopotami that once lived in the creeks that
fed the lagoon are long gone.[61] Drowning in the ocean, however, remains a
hazard for even the most experienced swimmers because of the treacherous
undertow. Shark attacks are not unknown. Grave injuries can result from the
handling of the boats. Severe weather conditions are no excuse for not going
out to sea at the height of the fishing season. More significant, it is in their
willingness to face such dangers that men engaged in maritime fishing define
both their masculinity and the power of the sea. One only has to hear these
men "recalling some of their famous exploits at sea, the challenges they faced
and the heroism required to meet them"[62] to understand the extent to which
the very image of the sea is central to fishermen's identities as men. Thus,
when I asked a number of men and women in Anlo why women generally
avoid the sea, many argued that women, unlike men, didn't have the strength
or the courage needed to engage in the business of ocean-fishing. Fishing required both physical and spiritual strength. Women simply did not possess

either of these in ways that would allow them to interact with such a powerful force as the ocean.[63]

The economic importance of fishing and the identities that Anlo men have forged around the sea are not the only factors that have influenced the continued vitality of the meanings that the Anlo have attributed to the ocean since at least the nineteenth century. The rites and rituals that both men and women perform at the ocean shore also rely upon and reinforce this imagery. Many Anlo widows and widowers, for example, whether adherents of traditional religious orders or members of Christian churches, participate in rituals at the ocean as part of the official mourning of their deceased spouse. At the beginning of this mourning period, the surviving spouse bathes in the ocean in a ritual called *ahotsilele*. This is said to cleanse the widow or widower of the spirits of their dead spouse. It is believed that without such rituals the deceased spouse's spirit could trouble the surviving spouse; male spirits in particular might attempt to have sex with a surviving wife, causing—if successful —permanent pregnancy. Women undergo a second cleansing ritual (*zameyiyi*) at the beach after the official mourning period ends. This involves the widow stepping into the ocean. It is believed that if she has engaged in any forbidden sexual activity during her mourning period and refuses to confess, she will be carried away by the spiritual forces in the ocean. She will drown. If she has not engaged in such activity, she is free to remarry and carry on her life with the knowledge that she has been cleansed of anything spiritually associated with her dead spouse that might hinder her from leading a normal and hopefully prosperous life.[64] That Christians and non-Christians participate in these rites is indicative of the extent to which many Anlo have not only retained their traditional beliefs but have also made Christianity their own by attributing far more meaning to the seawaters used in various rituals than the Bremen missionaries would have ever sanctioned.[65]

Adding to the image of the ocean and its waters as spiritually powerful is the belief that the ocean is the home of Awleketi (also known as Agbui), a god associated with Yewe, the most influential traditional religious order in Anlo. During the nineteenth and early twentieth centuries, the power of this deity and its connections to the ocean were regularly demonstrated to the Anlo public. As noted by German missionaries in the late nineteenth century:

> It is not uncommon for a priest to state that a Yewe woman, having become wild [i.e. possessed because she—and by association her god—have been offended], has jumped into the ocean and is living there on the sea bottom. As sure proof of this, they show the offender her clothes and jewels, which they have been found on the beach. . . . A servant initiated into [the religious order] then goes home with his fishing basket and net in hand and says that he has just landed a person in his net instead of a fish. After that, the Yewe

Figures 8 and 9. Traditional religious and Christian rituals at the sea.
Photos by author.

people start dancing and accompany the fisherman back to the shore, where they take the person fished from the ocean back to her home.

After their arrival, they bring the offender face to face with the offended Yewe woman. . . . The "wild one" has a calabash filled with her hair and sea water. The contents are proof that Yewe himself carried her off into the sea and has shaved her hair there. The punishment imposed on the offender includes the payment of 200 marks, two bales of white and blue cloth, and a goat.[66]

In 1915, the colonial government attempted to ban Yewe. This effort failed, but thereafter the religious order came increasingly under the authority of the colonial government. In 1934, Yewe was forbidden to admit any woman into the order who was below the age of 21. In 1937, it again escaped being banned only because it was able to garner enough support among the local chiefs in Anlo to be defined by the colonial government as a "tribal" or "national" religious order that was too central to the culture of Anlo to be abolished. After 1940, however, Yewe religious orders had to pay the government a fee to be licensed.[67] Subsequently, in Dzodze, one of the administrative districts within Anlo, Yewe adherents were banned from being possessed by their deity unless prior permission was obtained. These developments dampened the influence of Yewe in Anlo considerably, but for many Anlo residents, it did not alter their understanding of the ocean as an especially powerful spiritual site. Perhaps in response to the restrictions placed on Yewe, the Anlo embraced another deity associated with the ocean, Mami Wata, by establishing a shrine for the god in the coastal town of Kedzi in the 1930s.[68] Since independence, Yewe in particular has reasserted its influence in Anlo. Yewe members performed in the Ghana independence celebrations held at Keta in March of 1957. Since 1962, they have been seen regularly performing at the Hogbetsotso Festival held in an area that at that time was considered to be on the outskirts of Anloga.[69] More recently, Yewe successfully defied a more than 60-year-old ban that had been imposed on it by the Nyigbla order prohibiting it from the center of Anloga, the spiritual capital of the Anlo polity. In February 1996, Yewe outdoored, that is, introduced to the public, its most recent initiates in the Anloga market, a location that placed Yewe in the very center of Anlo's political and spiritual capital.[70]

The increasing influence of Yewe in Anlo over the last fifty years is especially significant for understanding why the ocean has retained its spiritually charged character for many Anlos. "Modernity" has stripped other sites in Anlo of their spiritual meaning. The deity associated with the Keta Lagoon no longer exhibits its power; the young don't even know of its existence. The deities that once ensured a continuous supply of drinking water for the residents of Anloga have been rendered powerless by technological change and neglect. Blolui, a pond that retained its spiritual aura for longer than many others, succumbed nevertheless to urban sprawl and the advance of Christianity and Western education. The ocean, however, continues to show its power. It "burns," though it is never hot. It can destroy everything in its path and has done just that in Keta. It can drown the most able swimmers, but it is also an important source of potential wealth. Its mysterious depths are the home of ancestors, strange creatures of the sea, and Awleketi—a member of the Yewe religious order that has not only withstood the onslaught of Christianity, colonialism, and opposition from the Anlo's war god, Nyigbla, but has come to thrive in the towns and villages of Anlo. The ocean represents all this in the minds of many Anlo, Christian and non-Christian alike. And thus it continues to retain an aura of spirituality, drawing to its shores some who offer prayers and others who seek spiritual fortification, ritual cleansing, and the rewards that only the gods, ancestors, and mysterious creatures of the sea can provide.

REVIEWING THE PAST/UNDERSTANDING THE PRESENT

In reviewing the ways that certain spiritually significant water bodies in Anlo have been affected by phased forgettings while others have experienced a continued vitality in memory and meaning, it becomes clear that Anlo understandings of their watery environment have been affected by a variety of factors: specific historic events, changing patterns of usage, and Anlo understandings of the spiritual. We know, for example, that from at least the nineteenth century (and certainly much earlier for some) the Atlantic Ocean, Tagbamu, and the potable water bodies in Anloga were central to life on the Anlo littoral. For hundreds of years, Klalavime, Welifome, and Tsivume provided the drinking water for Anloga, the largest settlement on the coastal sandbar until the growth of Keta in the nineteenth century. From at least the mid-seventeenth century to the nineteenth century, it was the Keta Lagoon that served as the principal source of fish for both local consumption and the exchanges made with those in the interior that made many in the littoral communities wealthy. As the nineteenth century progressed, economic activity shifted from the lagoon to the ocean, and the ocean began to assume an especially important place in Anlo society. It was a site of employment, a source for wealth accumulation and a symbol that was used by Anlo men to define their masculinity as the age of warfare gave way to an age of commerce and monetary accumulation. Dependence on all these waters as resources and the desire to ensure that the spiritual forces which occupied these waters continued to make the resources therein available characterized the meanings and memories that structured Anlo understandings of these water bodies. But it was this very dependence that made these waters vulnerable to new understandings.

When the desire for more convenient sources of potable water encour-

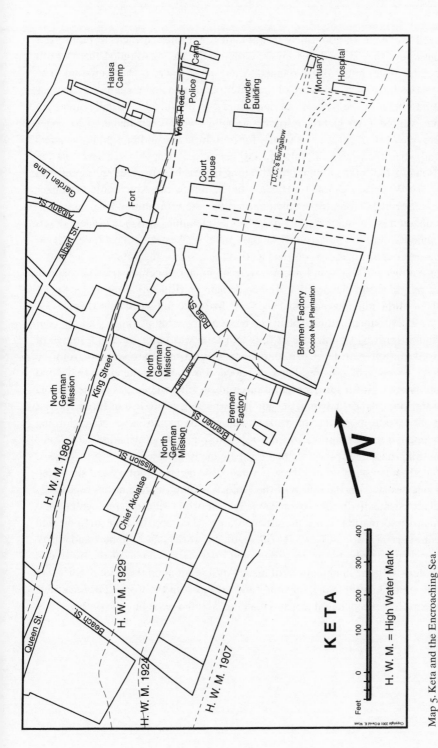

KETA

Feet 0   100   200   300   400

H. W. M. = High Water Mark

Map 5. Keta and the Encroaching Sea.
Based on Gold Coast Map No. 145, housed at the Survey Department, Accra, Ghana. Modified to highlight the noted features by David K. Wyatt.

aged the Anlo to adopt new technologies that allowed them to build wells anywhere they wished, the mystery that had once surrounded the ever-full potable water ponds of Anlo faded. Attention to the gods that were said to be responsible for the existence of the water ponds was no longer as necessary as it had been in the past. Water could and was obtainable virtually anywhere one wanted if one had the resources to build a well. When Tagbamu no longer provided fish in sufficient quantity for both local use and profitable exchange and when the priests of Anlo proved themselves incapable of alleviating the droughts that made even minimal fishing impossible, the Anlo were prepared to try Western technology. This too failed, but as the Anlo could no longer count on the lagoon for supplying fish other than for limited local consumption, interest in and memories of its former meanings also faded. These developments were of course aided by the spread of Western education and technology, but ultimately it was the fact that these sites—the potable water ponds of Anloga and the Keta Lagoon—were no longer of demonstrated economic or religious significance that rendered them spiritually vacant and stripped them of the religious aura that the Anlo had once felt when near them.

These same factors explain the phased forgetting of Blolui and the continued spiritual significance of the sea. Blolui was never used as a source of drinking water. It never had an economic function. It stood apart from the town, rarely visited by residents, shrouded in mystery by the grove that stood on its edge. But it too eventually succumbed. Like the deities in the potable water ponds and Tagbamu, the god that was believed to live in Blolui did not demonstrate its power when urban sprawl threatened its sanctity. Nothing happened when its grove was destroyed to make way for homes and farms; nothing happened when women on their menses passed close to its edge. It failed to demonstrate its power. For many, the deity of Blolui pond simply no longer existed. In the minds of the Anlo, it is only the ocean that repeatedly demonstrates its power. It serves as an important site for employment and identity formation. It has literally consumed the once-thriving surf port and commercial town of Keta. It still regularly washes away homes and roads. It devours the bodies of fishermen and exists as the home of the Yewe god Awleketi. In the imaginations of many Anlo resident on the littoral, Christian and non-Christian alike, spiritual forces do exist in the world. They manifest themselves through that which is material, and the sea is but one of these sites.

3

Placing and Spacing the Dead

PRIOR TO THE mid-nineteenth century, Anlo perceptions of their built environment[1] were based on the notion that their homes, the physical layout of their villages and towns, and the placing and spacing of the dead served many purposes and had multiple meanings. Houses provided shelter and comfort and symbolized one's social status. But they also constituted one of the sites where living family members maintained spiritual connections with the dead. They contained shrines and charms to protect the residents from harm. They represented for most born in these houses the spiritual center of their social lives. The priorities that informed Anlo ways of organizing their towns and villages were also based on both practical and religious concerns, through which the physical and the spiritual were so intertwined as to be inseparable. Access to drinking water and good agricultural land and the desirability of having a large household whose members were close at hand influenced Anlo settlement patterns. But efforts to maintain one's health and wealth within the many homes and towns and villages of Anlo also influenced the way the residents used their houses and spatially organized their communities. The Anlo believed that by burying the aged in the floors of their own homes, by building one's house on the foundation of an ancestor's dwelling, by establishing the boundaries of towns and villages and then disposing the bodies of those who died in war at the edge of settlements in shallow graves, they could maintain relations with the dead, who in turn were able to influence both the physical and spiritual health of their families and communities.

By the late nineteenth century, however, the Anlo's understanding of their built environment and its interconnected spiritual and material characteristics had come under serious attack. In their ever-expanding network of schools and churches, the Bremen missionaries encouraged their parishioners to understand the physical as something quite distinct from the spiritual. If constructed for and by true Christians, homes, cemeteries, and places of worship represented the refining power of the religion because it encouraged believers to renew not only their inner spirits but also their surrounding physical environment. But such places had no spiritual significance beyond the symbolic. The Bremen missionaries rejected completely the notion that the location of one's home or the graves of one's relatives could have a direct impact on the spiritual and physical health of the living. To them, the Anlo's built environment—insofar as it was deeply influenced by "idolatry and heathenism"—was a direct reflection of the darkness in spirit that also characterized their indigenous religion. Both were primitive. Both were physically and spiritually unhealthy. Comments like the following made by a number of missionaries between 1872 and 1907 were typical:

> If you climb onto the roof of our house to take a look at Keta, the impression is no different from the view you get when you examine a ... village. Straight rows of houses, an even-ness in the lay-out and decent streets on which you could walk with some pleasure are out of the question. You have to be glad if only a path leads to every front door; and you don't see anything of cleanliness and order either.[2]

> [In] the notorious Anglo-ga ... the streets (or more precisely the paths) are so narrow that the thatch roofs of the houses very often meet.[3]

> One cannot pass another on these streets shoulder to shoulder, but must pass by sideways. Fearful children or women often turn their heads to face the wall or suddenly turn around and run hastily away when they meet a white man in such a street.... [Only after we left this place] could we breathe more easily after the long stay in the humid and unhealthy atmosphere of the confined town.[4]

> The shrines for the idols tend to be the worst in the village ... [as] idolatry and heathenism pull the human spirit deeper and deeper into the depths ... allowing no higher thoughts of wonderful accomplishments.[5]

Not all Bremen missionaries viewed the Anlo built environment and the beliefs that influenced its organization in these terms,[6] but the vast majority did. More important, this majority was able to take comfort in the fact that they were not alone in their views.[7] In 1875, when Britain began administering Anlo as part of the Gold Coast Colony, those officers posted to the district also viewed the Anlo built environment as wholly unhealthy. As officials of a reportedly secular effort, however, they focused less on trying to explain the situation in religious terms and more on the need to impose on the Anlo built environment their own notions of what they believed would promote greater public health. Armed with the latest scientific principles, they widened a number of the paths that wove circuitously through Keta, creating a road to supplement the older, just as wide and open, path on the ocean beach. They required every house-owner to keep his compound clear of debris on pain of punishment, even though the political and religious leaders of Anlo periodically ordered their own mass communal cleansings of the entire polity.[8] No one was allowed to erect a house according to local social or religious interests; each person had to receive prior permission from the British commander "to guarantee that the streets [remain] straight and unrestricted."[9] By 1910, the British colonial government had opened or ordered the opening of public cemeteries in every town and village in Anlo. They held regular inspections to discourage the burial of the dead in places not approved by the government. They prosecuted anyone found in violation of the burial ordinance.[10]

Resistance by the Anlo to the imposition of these different understandings of how to organize and relate to the built environment was ongoing and included both direct and indirect, passive and active responses. Of particular concern here, however, is the fact that despite this resistance, the Anlo did eventually alter some aspects of those beliefs that had influenced the way they organized their homes and communities. This led to significant changes in their built environment. Prior to the mid-nineteenth century, for example, virtually all Anlo homes had separate bathing facilities for men and women. Such separations were deemed absolutely essential if men were to make effective use of the physical and spiritual forces at their disposal when protecting themselves and their families from harm, for it was believed that if a man had contact with a women during her period or if he was unwittingly exposed visually to a woman's menstrual cloth, he would be weakened physically and spiritually.[11] Separate bathing places helped ensure that such contact would not occur. Today, however, virtually no one maintains this particular form of separation. Most men and women who live in the same household use common facilities. They no longer believe that menstrual blood has the power to influence through the human eye. And although many remember the reasons for such practices, they no longer find them meaningful. The same, however, cannot be said for other spiritually informed material practices. Today, cemeteries have largely replaced burials in the home or on the outskirts of town, but many families still keep separated within the confines of these cemeteries those who died "good" deaths and those who suffered "bad" deaths. The meanings associated with these burial practices are remembered and retained, but they have been displaced to the modern cemeteries established by order of the British colonial government.

The purpose of this chapter is to examine more fully the nature of early-nineteenth-century Anlo understandings of their built environment and the ways in which the Anlo adjusted these understandings in response to late-nineteenth-century British colonialism and Christian missionary influence. This built environment included any number of structures and spatial arrangements: houses, farms, shrines, burial grounds, and marketplaces; each a separate location but all positioned in relation to the other. Of particular interest in this chapter is the placing and spacing of the dead. What was the spiritual significance of burials, and how did the interment of the dead in the various locations in which they were buried influence how the Anlo perceived those locations? Did the burial of elderly residents in the floors of their houses generate a sense of sacredness around the notion of home? Did the interment of those who died "bad" deaths on the edge of Anlo towns and villages give those places a certain aura? How did the spread of Christianity and the imposition of European colonial sanitation laws impact not only the placing and spacing of dead bodies and body parts but also the spiritual significance of these burial patterns? To answer these questions, this chapter explores early-nineteenth-century Anlo notions about death and rebirth and the nature of the human soul and the significance of these beliefs for understanding how the Anlo perceived their built environment. It also examines how and why European influences resulted not in the erasure of the meanings and memories associated with burial places and spaces but a displacement of meanings to new locations. While most Anlo came to accept Western scientific notions about the importance of engaging in particular burial practices to ensure the physical health of their families, many also continued to believe in the power of the dead to affect the living. This, in turn, prompted some to retain but displace the material aspects of these beliefs. Notions about reincarnation— once given physical meaning through the burial of the individuals in specific locations—were redirected onto the body, where ritual marks were made to recognize the power of the dead to influence the living. Others displaced these same meanings (those that had informed the placing and spacing of the dead) onto the body of the modern cemetery, burying those who died prematurely on the edge of the cemetery and using the center only for those who died in old age. And still others shifted their belief in the power of the dead onto the notion of disembodied ghosts, spirits that were defined as much by their disembodied state as by their disconnection from the ritual significance of place and space. Thus, older beliefs that had once informed the placing and spacing of the dead were reconfigured and, in some instances, displaced to form a unique set of Anlo modernities about the proper material and spiritual handling of the dead.

BURYING THE DEAD IN
EARLY-NINETEENTH-CENTURY ANLO

Early-nineteenth-century burial practices were informed by a number of beliefs and concerns, but perhaps the most important was the notion that the spiritual aspect of human beings was a complex entity that existed separately from the body and could influence human affairs through a variety of mechanisms. Spirits could enter one's dreams and warn an individual of impending danger. They could manifest themselves at night as ghosts (*noaliwo*). They could physically assault individuals, causing sickness or death. They could also be reassuring and supportive, bringing joy to their families by returning from the spirit world through reincarnation (*amedzodzo*) and being reborn in newborn infants. According to Anlo thought, this was possible because the human soul consisted of two entities, the *gbɔgbɔ* and the *luwɔ*. The *gbɔgbɔ,* or life soul, was bequeathed to a person by the Supreme Deity on their birth. The *gbɔgbɔ* was evident in humans through their drawing in and expelling air as breath and flatulence. It was also in the *gbɔgbɔ* where one found a person's conscience. Once the *gbɔgbɔ* exited the body to return to the Supreme Being, death ensued. It was the *luwɔ,* the personality soul, however, that moved through the world in a disembodied form affecting the material world. And it was the *luwɔ* that was central to the notion of reincarnation. The *luwɔ* was believed to join the *gbɔgbɔ* in forming the soul of the living person upon their birth. It came into the material world (Kodzogbe) not from the Supreme Being, however, but from the spirit world (Tsiefe). In this particular world lived the spirits of deceased ancestors and the spiritual relatives and companions of the living. When the *luwɔ* left Tsiefe to enter Kodzogbe, it was often not just any spirit but one that had lived in the material world before as a child who was born, had died, had been reborn, and had died again or as the spirit of a person who had lived a relatively long life in Kodzogbe. Thus, when a child was born in the material world, it was part of the expected routine after childbirth among the Anlo for the new mother to consult a diviner shortly after the birth of her child to determine if the spirit of the child intended to stay and whether the spirit that had entered her newborn infant was that of a deceased relative.[12]

Central to this belief in reincarnation was the notion that where one buried the dead influenced who would and would not reincarnate and that the location of a particular burial should be based on how the deceased had died. As a number of Bremen missionaries observed between the mid-nineteenth and early twentieth century:

> [Among the Anlo] here are two types of [acceptable] deaths: the good death and the fast death. If one lies on one's mat and is sick before one dies, one dies a good death. If one is not sick before one's death, one dies a fast death. Perhaps one was walking back from the field and suddenly died after entering the house. These are the best ways to die because they involve no suffering. . . . The same is said about a child that dies during or directly after its birth. This death is not as painful for the relatives because the child had not lived before its death.[13] [In addition], children who die [do so] . . . because the spirit that should have animated this person disdained our way of life and therefore killed the child after he saw how he would have lived in this world.
>
> The normal custom . . . is [burial] in the house. . . .[14] If the person has died a good death, he is buried in his room . . . [but] children are always buried behind the house.[15]
>
> If a married couple lives together very well, and the wife dies, the relatives of both sides unite to bury the dead woman. The burial, if possible, is in her father's hut or in a paternal ancestor's hut.[16]

"[Those] buried in the hut . . . don't need to be feared, but the ones who have died from contagious diseases like smallpox or have died a sudden death . . . have to be buried out in the wilderness, far away from any human dwelling.[17]

Interviews in 1996 with many elderly residents of Anlo about past practices indicate that these missionary renderings of Anlo burial patterns were quite accurate.[18] A man who had married, built his own home, and died an "acceptable" or "good" death (*e ku nyui*) was interred in his own home. An adult woman who had given birth was buried in a room in the house of a paternal relative. Firstborn children were also buried within their paternal family's compound, usually in the floor of the bathhouse.

These documentary and oral accounts also provide insight into the meanings behind these particular burial practices. Togbui Awuku Dzrekey of Whuti indicated, for example, that in the past if a man was able to build his own house, it only made sense that he should be buried in it. By doing so, the relatives of the deceased acknowledged the accomplishments of the one who had died, since such an individual had fulfilled the expectations of an adult male by marrying, building his own house, and then producing many progeny.[19] A woman who had become a mother—one of the most important accomplishments for females in nineteenth-century Anlo society—was similarly honored by her patrilineal family by having her body returned and interred in her family home. Burials did more than reinforce societal norms that valued the productive and reproductive capacities of adults, however. They also reflected beliefs about the relationship between the material world (Kodzogbe) and the world of the dead (Tsiefe). In his account of nineteenth-century burial practices in Anlo, Bremen missionary J. Spieth noted that the Anlo "worship the dead through the choice of building location." He observed that "the normal residential house of the Anlo is built on the ruins of a paternal ancestor's house. . . . This is done so that the dead ancestors in the underworld have nothing to complain about. Everyone then knows that the son is at home so that the father will have something to eat and drink from him. The father also knows that his house will not decay."[20] In other words, by burying the adult individual who died an "acceptable" death in a room in his own house, this person's relatives could more easily maintain excellent relations with the deceased whose spirit had the ability to influence, for better or for worse, the lives of the living family members. Burying such relatives in the rooms of the house and continuing to live in and build upon the deceased's home also served to signal to the deceased that his spirit was welcome to return in reincarnated form to the family. Firstborn children who died before other infants were born were buried within the family compound and with little ceremony for similar reasons. Little mourning was allowed because they had died prematurely and had accomplished nothing. But their burial within the family compound, usually in the bathing enclosure, reinforced the significance of their ties to the family and the importance of strengthening the family through the generation of new members. They too were encouraged to return again to their families from the spirit world in the form of a newborn infant. To emphasize the religious significance of burial location, Mama Dzagba asked rhetorically in 1996 "If something precious fell from your hand, would you throw it away? No. It must be kept at a place where you can easily go for it when you need it."[21]

Notions about the ability of the dead to affect the lives of the living not only influenced the definition of those who should be buried in homes and family compounds but also determined who should *not* be buried there. Among those barred from house interment were individuals who died "in blood" (*wumekukulawo/ametsiwumewo*). This group included those who had died as a result of war, snakebites, fatal accidents, and diseases such as smallpox and tuberculosis. Adult women and men who died before they were able to reproduce and hunchbacks were also said to have died a "bad death (*wo ku voe*)." Such individuals were not buried in the home for fear such loving treatment would encourage them to return through reincarnation and die again in the same way. Instead, they were interred on the outskirts of town in an area one might term the transition zone, an area located between the built environment of the town or village and the much-less-developed environment of the bush. Often conceived of as an extension of the built environment, the transition zone[22] contained farms, latrines, and shrines for the gods that protected the entire community and the graves of those who died "bad" deaths.[23] It was here that families interred the bodies of those whose lives had ended prematurely, most often at night in hastily dug shallow graves.[24]

The ways in which nineteenth-century Anlos handled burials did more than reflect a particular understanding of how the worlds of the material and spiritual should be mediated through the handling of the dead. The same understanding that guided burial practices also imbued the built environment with spiritual meaning. The rooms of the house in which individuals were buried brought family members into daily contact with those ancestors. So did shrines (*legbawo*) erected at the entrance of family compounds. Some served as charms, protecting the residents from fires or alerting a male household head if a wife was having an adulterous affair.[25] But others were used to communicate with and honor those ancestors who had died "bad" deaths but who had refused to leave the family alone by demanding through spirit possession or the sending of an illness that a living relative recognize their power to influence the living.[26] Families used the floor of the woman's bath enclosure to bury the placentas and umbilical cords of all babies born in the home. This was done in acknowledgement of the notion that the spirit of each child born into the family had a spirit mother (manifested in the umbilical cord and placenta) in the world of the dead (Tsiefe) who could call the child back to that world. By burying the child's placenta and umbilical cord in the house's female bathing area, the family connected the child spiritually to the family through the family house. This provided a site from which the family would be able to communicate with the spirit mother if it proved necessary because the newborn had begun to exhibit a desire (through sickness) to return to its spirit mother.[27] The walls of rooms within the house and the fences that surrounded family compounds were similarly imbued with spiritual significance. Nineteenth-century Anlos used to hide hair-cuttings and nail-clippings there. Both were items the Anlo believed contained elements of one's soul (*luwo*). If they fell into the wrong hands, they could be used to harm the owner, so most took special care to hide them within the home. If a family member died a "good" death, but far from home, it was this same form of *luwo* (hair-cuttings and nail-clippings) which the deceased's family would remove and inter in the family compound (or on the outskirts of town, depending on the type of death) if they were unable to return home with the entire body.[28]

Streets constituted yet another site within the built environment that the Anlo associated with the dead. According to nineteenth-century Anlo belief, people used streets to move about the town during the day, but it was spirits (and those individuals especially knowledgeable about spiritual matters) who used them at night. The smallpox deity, Sakpana, is said to have periodically made his appearance, usually after dark, by emerging from the earth and roaming through the narrow paths of the residential zone, infecting those whom he encountered. Ancestral spirits did the same.[29] Thus, if a stranger happened to enter an Anlo village at night requesting refreshment or accommodation, the person was usually welcomed so as not to offend them if they, in disappearing before the morning, had actually been an ancestral spirit. Specific areas within the transition zone were similarly imbued with spiritual significance. In Anloga's Gbaakute (an execution ground) one could encounter the unhappy ghosts of those whose lives the government had deliberately ended. In Avevoeme, the transition zone where Anloga families buried those who committed suicide, ghosts were thought to emerge (most often at night) and throw sand at passersby.[30]

That nineteenth-century Anlos associated spiritual forces with the material reality of their built environment is, of course, consistent with how they viewed the world around them more generally. They believed that spiritual forces were capable of manifesting themselves not only in houses and in shrines, in streets and cemeteries but everywhere: in the air, in water bodies, in distant towns, in the earth, in the groves that dotted the Anlo landscape. Whether these places were encountered rarely or formed part of the quotidian rhythms of daily life, all were viewed as sites with multiple meanings, as both material objects and as containers of the sacred.

Yet the built environment of town and transition zone was defined by more than just its individual elements. Spatial positioning was equally meaningful. The places of village, wilderness, and transition zone were also defined in relation to each other. Movement between the three was normal and necessary, but such movements also required spiritual mediation. When hunters and soldiers returned to the village from the wilderness after engaging in war or the hunt, Anlo beliefs required that they spiritually cleanse themselves to leave the angry spirits of the humans and animals they had killed in the bush or in the transition zone.[31] When spiritually knowledgeable men sought to harness powerful forces of the bush, they most often entered the wilderness at night, naked, wearing not a shred of clothing, so as to limit the possibility of bringing back into the village unwanted and unseen forces that could wreak havoc on their families and friends.[32] And when the Anlo buried their dead in the transition zone on the outskirts of town, they made sure that on their return they never glanced back in order to prevent their gaze from inviting all that had been thrown out of the town to reenter the community. All this they did in accordance with a larger cultural logic which defined places and spaces as spiritually significant because of their ability to be simultaneously material objects and containers of the divine.

THE MISSIONARY AND COLONIAL CHALLENGE

Christian missionary understandings about places and spaces and their spiritual significance differed considerably from Anlo understandings. The Bremen Mission, for example, as a product of the European Enlightenment, the Protestant Reformation, and an Awakened Pietist tradition, emphasized the notion that the physical was defined exclusively by its materiality. Houses, burial grounds, and streets were just that, dwellings for the living, resting places for the dead, and constructed pathways to facilitate the healthy movement of man and beast from one place to another. The souls of the dead could not communicate with the living and the living could not communicate with the souls of the dead. Ghosts did not exist, and any apparitions, dreams, or visions that one might have were interpreted as signs that the Devil was attempting to steer that person away from God's path.[33] Such beliefs did not preclude the notion that there did exist a relationship between the spiritual and the material. But this relationship was defined exclusively by its symbolic characteristics. The building of a church, for example, did not in itself bring one closer to God simply because one physically worked to facilitate his worship. Rather the building of a splendid chapel—and it necessarily had to be so to distinguish it from "heathen" shrine houses—symbolized an inner Christian faith, one that "renewed and refined the human spirit" in ways that manifested itself in superior physical structures.[34] In the establishment of Christian cemeteries in Anlo, the Bremen missionaries emphasized as well that these spaces did not constitute sites where the dead and the living could communicate with one another. Instead, Christian cemeteries were places that had spiritual significance only if one understood them as locations where one could quietly contemplate the meaning of death and then renew one's faith with the knowledge that on Judgment Day Christian souls would awaken and ascend into heaven.[35] Thus, when Anna Toepfer—the Bremen Mission's first female missionary to work in Anlo—described the Bremen Mission cemetery in Keta, she noted that it "resemble[d] a lovely grove with its palms, eucalypti, acacia and oleander" that gave her a "miraculously heart-moving feeling" when she walked among the graves.[36] It was a place for contemplation, a place to renew one's faith.

This focus on the spiritually symbolic significance of place led the Bremen Mission to develop specific guidelines about exactly who was and was not allowed to be buried in their cemeteries. Only Christians, for example, were given the right to such interments. And to be considered a Christian, one had to abide by an extensive set of rules and regulations that governed every aspect of daily life.[37] Anlo converts were not to participate in any ceremonies (the outdooring of newborn infants, the funerals of relatives and friends, the weddings of nieces and nephews) that involved "heathen" rituals. They were to abandon altogether any involvement with "pagan" ritual devices, such as the beads used in communicating with the spirit world to divine the future or protect one from harm. The use of local musical instruments was also forbidden since they were used by "pagans" in their "heathen" worship services. The dead were to be carried in coffins, not in mats as had traditionally been the practice in nineteenth-century Anlo. And such coffins were to be carried not on the heads of mourners but on a wagon that would be wheeled solemnly to the cemetery.[38] Persistent and conscious violations of these rules and others could result in one being expelled from the church. This meant that after death, one's remains would also be forbidden burial in the church cemetery. While the notion of sacred ground had little meaning for the Bremen Mission, and theoretically the location of one's burial meant nothing,[39] the interment of Christians together in their own cemetery did have symbolic spiritual significance. Those who willingly gave their lives to Christ and worshipped as Christians while alive should also—according to Bremen Mission understandings—be together symbolically (through their burial in a Christian cemetery) on Judgment Day. All others, heathens in particular, were to stand alone before God, for the moral (or, more accurately, the supposedly immoral) status of their souls required their separation from the Christian community of the dead.[40] Other Christian denominations that entered Anlo later (the Roman Catholic Church in 1890 and the African Methodist Episcopal Zion Church in 1899) did the same, erecting their own cemeteries for the exclusive use of their members. None of these Christian missions, however, cared where they situated their cemeteries, for this was believed to have had no spiritual significance at all. Instead, they based the siting of their grave-yards on more mundane, secular concerns, erecting them only on those lands they controlled and, if possible, at some distance from human inhabitation, since according to nineteenth-century scientific understandings, "vapours and mists arise from the graves to pollute the air."[41]

When Britain began administering Anlo as part of the Gold Coast Col-ony, they wasted no time in imposing on the district their own conceptions about the proper disposal of the dead. Following practices developed in mid-nineteenth-century England,[42] the colonial government assumed responsi-bility for ensuring that the bodies of all deceased persons in Anlo, whether Christian or non-Christian, were disposed of in a sanitary manner.[43] They did so because they too believed that "the exhalation of the gases and the ema-nations of the dead into the air posed a serious threat to public health." In addition, they had learned from experience in England that to leave the issue of burial to parochial authorities was inefficient and dangerous, as was evident in the following report provided to the Parliamentary Select Committee on Interment in 1842 by Robert Baker, a sanitary reformer in Leeds, England:

> I was in the ground last Wednesday collecting information and the sexton took me to a grave which they were digging for the interment of a female; two feet below the surface they took out the body of an illegitimate child, and it had been buried for five years; below that and two feet six inches be-low the surface were two coffins side by side, the bones were in a state of freshness; the matter had putrified off the bones, but they were perfectly fresh; they were thrown on the surface and at that time the person came in who was going to do the interment; he spoke to me about it and made use of the expression, "Look! These are the skulls of my father and brother and the bones of my relations—is not this a bad business."[44]

Reports such as these prompted so much moral outrage and concern about the health hazards of shallow burials where bodies were also simply piled one on top of the other that the British government passed national legislation (known as the Burial Acts) in 1852 and 1853 empowering local authorities to establish public burial grounds.[45] In 1878, the Gold Coast colonial govern-ment passed similar legislation, known as Ordinance No. 10. It did so not be-cause of overcrowded church cemeteries, however, but rather to combat the spread of those diseases it thought were caused by noxious odors emanating within the houses of the local population due to the practice of burying the dead in the floors of homes.[46] Twenty-three years later, in 1911, the colonial government expanded the coverage of the laws concerning burials by amending the bylaws of the 1883 Native Jurisdiction Ordinance. This change extended the burial laws beyond the previously covered major towns in the Gold Coast Colony by requiring all villages and hamlets under the authority of a chief or headmen to establish cemeteries. Each chief or headman was required to "select a site . . . not less than 100 yards from any house or water supply and [to] fence it in." In addition, they were authorized to fine anyone found burying a body outside the cemetery.

Enforcement in Anlo began immediately but was made difficult—especially in the villages and hamlets of Anlo—because until 1911 sanitary inspections occurred only in the major towns on the Anlo littoral.[47] Coverage elsewhere had to be handled by periodic visits of the medical officers assigned to the district. Resistance could also be considerable. Many buried empty coffins in the cemeteries and then secretly interred the dead in their homes or elsewhere.[48] Some traditional religious orders attempted to maintain their influence over the lives of former members who had converted to Christianity by threatening anyone who attempted to bury them in the Christian cemetery.[49] A number of chiefs offered resistance by delaying as long as possible the requirement that they establish cemeteries in their towns and villages. Others complied but offered no further encouragement to their people to actually use them.[50]

Progress in altering Anlo burial practices came only as mission education (the only form of Western education available in Anlo until 1935)[51] grew and expanded within the district. While the Christian missions in Anlo gave principal attention to the spiritual meaning of burials, operating cemeteries that were to be used exclusively by their members, they shared in common with the British colonial government concerns about the health risks associated with "improper" burials. They willingly agreed to follow government educational regulations which required, after 1905, that lessons on sanitation be included in the curriculum for all schools that received government assistance.[52] In the initial years after this legislation was passed, teachers were encouraged to use either the text on tropical health by Dr. Prout or "Mrs. Deacon's Lectures on Hygiene" as a basis for their lectures. By 1913, however, Henry Strachan's *Lesson in Elementary Tropical Hygiene* was adopted as the text to be used by students.[53] This book emphasized the following with regard to burials:

> Air contains a certain amount of water-vapour . . . also the nasty sulphuretted hydrogen we smell in the horrible odour given off by swamps and cesspits and sewers [and] badly made graves. . . .
>
> There are also other gases, which you need not trouble about now, as you need only to remember the most important of the impurities of air.
>
> From what you have learned as to the poisonous gases that come up from graves, and the equally poisonous stuff that passes from them into the soil and so, by the ground-water, into wells near them, you will see how bad it is

Figure 10. A late-nineteenth- to early-twentieth-century Bremen Mission photo
of "unsanitary" conditions near Keta.
Photo entitled "Eingeborenen gehoeft in der Naehe Keta," Staatsarchiv
Bremen, 17, 1025/106).

to have graveyards in towns and especially how bad is the custom prevailing
in some parts of Africa of burying bodies in houses where people live.

This is very wrong; and now you know why it is so.[54]

Widely read by students in Gold Coast government-assisted schools, this text
emphasized the importance of adopting "modern" approaches to burials. But
the way in which it was used by teachers also encouraged students to do more
than learn about sanitary practices in order to pass an examination on the
subject. They were also urged through participation in dramas to use this information to revise their views of their own home environments and to encourage others to engage in more sanitary practices. In some schools, for example, the students constructed clay models of two villages, one that had poor
sanitary conditions and another where such conditions were excellent. One
child would then play the part of the village chief. A second child acted as a
sanitary inspector and a third as a traditional linguist, while the rest of the
class formed "a chorus of villagers." The "sanitary inspector" would explain
to the "chief" through the "linguist" how defective his village was (represented
by the unsanitary model) and would practice countering all the "chief's" ob-

jections. The "sanitary inspector" would then produce the model of the more sanitary village, explain how it was "more correctly" planned and then discuss all the advantages associated with a village organized along more sanitary lines. Armed with both the appropriate scientific knowledge and experience in applying this information in the classroom, the students were then charged with the task of taking this knowledge into the real world of their homes and villages.[55] By 1930, the colonial government in Anlo had expanded their sanitation education campaign yet again. In addition to the school lessons introduced in 1905 and the monthly lectures on tropical hygiene that had been held at the Keta Hospital since 1911,[56] the government also began sponsoring Health Weeks, where prizes were awarded for, among other things, the most sanitary compounds.[57] The colonial government and mission schools were not alone in their efforts. They gained additional assistance in altering Anlo burial practices from the individuals whom the Anlo began to select as their chiefs. Many came increasingly from the mission-educated community. Awoamefia Sri II, for example, who was based in Anloga, was one of the early graduates of the Bremen Mission. He, Togbui Sokpui of Dzelukofe, and Togbui Agbozo and Chief James Ocloo, both of Keta, and others embraced Western notions of sanitation and supported government efforts to prevent the spread of disease by, in part, encouraging the use of cemeteries located some distance from human habitation.[58]

ANLO ADJUSTMENTS/ANLO DISPLACEMENTS

Although the evidence is limited, the resistance by many Anlos to the burial of their dead in government-approved graveyards, especially in the smaller villages, continued through at least the 1940s.[59] Nevertheless, change did eventually occur. Non-Christians in Anloga developed their own cemeteries—usually for fellow clan members—since they were barred from burial in the Christian graveyards in the town. Those villages that had been bringing their dead for burial to Anloga since the late eighteenth century stopped doing so as they too established their own local cemeteries. Directives from both the colonial government and Fia Sri II facilitated these changes, but educational campaigns also were of tremendous importance, for the information disseminated in these campaigns became the basis for a new understanding about the relationship between burial practices and the spiritual world. In 1996, for example, when I conducted interviews about the changes that had occurred with the adoption of Western-type cemeteries, I was continually informed by those who had limited Western education that the elimination of house burials brought an end to the potentially fatal respiratory disease known as *alokpli*. This was a disease associated with a type of coughing that ultimately led to death. Of particular interest, however, is the fact that in the

Figure 11. A modern cemetery in Anlo, 1996.
Photo by author.

past the Anlo had made no connection whatsoever between this disease and house burials. Rather, *alokpli* was believed to be a spiritual disease caused primarily by immoral behavior:

> When two men sleep with the same woman, they are said to have mixed their blood (*wo toto vu*) and this is said to expose them to a fatal pulmonary disease not unlike tuberculosis called *alokpli*. *Alokpli* comes about when these two men come into contact under certain conditions, such as when one of them is sick and the other pays him a visit or when they eat together from one bowl or even when one eats from a bowl [or drinks from a] cup previously put on a bed or seat used by the other. When [one of the men dies] the other, it is believed, may not see his corpse or drink at his funeral without contracting the disease. On the battlefield, it was believed that should one touch the body of a fallen comrade with whom one has mixed blood, one would also immediately fall prey to enemy bullets.[60]

Alokpli is also said to have attacked parents who failed to observe those rules and regulations they were spiritually obligated to follow because they had given birth to twins.[61] Because the symptoms associated with this disease are most often described in such general terms, it is impossible to determine if *alokpli* is the name of a single affliction or is the same term for a variety of conditions, all of which involve coughing and ultimate death. What we do know, however, is that the late-nineteenth and early-twentieth-century Western notions that bad air caused disease constituted a central theme in the sanitation education introduced into Anlo by the colonial government. Anlo residents were enjoined, on the basis of this theory, to plan accordingly when developing any new residential districts or when rebuilding older sections of town that may have been destroyed by fire. "Noxious emanations" from the shores of the Keta lagoon or from gravesites were to be rendered harmless by designing towns that had ample space between the individual homes and had at least 100 feet between residential areas and cemeteries. And this is precisely what happened when Anloga burned to the ground in 1911 (an event known locally as Fuifudzidzo).[62] The entire town was rebuilt on a grid pattern, in part to facilitate the healthy flow of air through the community. And while it took some time for Anloga residents to embrace burial within the cemeteries, they did do so at a time when the government and the mission schools were promoting the notion that where and how one buried the dead affected both air quality and the prevalence of disease. The belief that interment in cemeteries coincided with a decline in deaths caused by the lung malady known locally as *alokpli* suggests that a certain adjustment began to occur in the meanings of home burials. Such burials were no longer associated solely with honoring those who fulfilled the obligations of adulthood and died "good" deaths; now home burials could also cause the spiritually induced disease known as *alokpli*.[63] In making this connection, some, no doubt, continued to view the disease as one caused by spiritual forces. Others began to view it as only a physical malady caused by "bad" air. Of greater significance, however, is the fact that the connection the majority began to make between burial practices and *alokpli* (whatever its ultimate origins) brought in its wake a much wider acceptance of the use of government-approved cemeteries and a significant decline in home burials.

The meanings attached to the areas where those who died "bad" deaths also changed under the pressure of colonial regulation. Individuals who died "in blood," as a result of accidental death, drowning, disease, and so forth were buried in shallow graves in the transition zones that surrounded every town and village. In Anloga, these zones were known as Gbaakute and Avevoeme. Both were associated with the ghosts of unhappy, potentially dangerous spirits. Mission-educated Fia Sri II, with the strong backing of the colonial government, challenged the meanings associated with these sites by insisting after Anloga was destroyed by fire that the once extremely congested town be rebuilt along "modern" sanitary lines. This could only be achieved, however, by expanding residential development into Avevoeme. Many objected to the relocation. The enormous effort needed to build the foundation of a completely new house alone deterred many. Others refused to relocate the shrines they maintained to communicate with particular deities and ancestors because of objections by the spirits themselves to the move. Still others feared

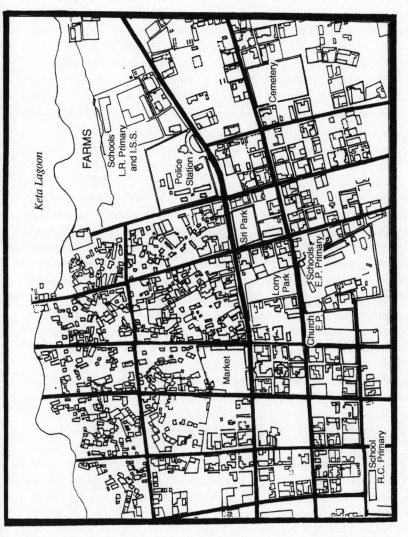

Map 6. The Grid Design of the Rebuilt Center of Anloga.
Based on an Anloga city planning map housed at the Keta District Office in Keta, Ghana. Modified to high-light the noted features by Sandra E. Greene.

building on land that had been used to bury those who had died "bad" deaths and whose spirits were known to throw sand at passersby at night. Such objections were generally short-lived, however. Fines imposed by the colonial government on recalcitrant priests eliminated opposition in that quarter. The sheer necessity to move forward quickly with building new homes prompted others to accept the government plan. So after conducting rituals to pacify the spirits of those who had been hastily buried there, the vast majority built their new homes in Avevoeme or in the surrounding area.[64] Other towns followed suit when they too faced the need for more land on which to build housing. Thus, prompted by government regulation, educational campaigns, and the need for additional land on which to accommodate a growing population, most Anlo towns had established cemeteries where the bodies of those who died "good" and "bad" deaths were both interred by the 1950s.

This embrace of the notion that it was best to situate the dead in locations that encouraged better health occurred not, however, because all Anlos (Christian and non-Christian alike) had abandoned their beliefs that the world of the dead could influence the lives of the living. Many continued to adhere to traditional beliefs that explained a newborn's unusual birthmark or physical resemblance to a deceased ancestor as physical proof of reincarnation. The spiritual meanings that had previously been associated with burials in Anlo were simply displaced to a different site. Christian converts were expected to accept fully the notions that with death the soul remained asleep until Judgment Day and that as Christians they should be interred with other Christians according to Christian principles. No separation should occur in such graveyards between those who died "good" and "bad" deaths. And many Christians did indeed embrace this approach as a fundamental aspect of their faith. Other Christians, however, found the change more difficult or were simply unwilling to sever themselves from the beliefs held by their non-Christian friends and relatives. They identified themselves as Christians and expected to be buried in Christian cemeteries where all were interred together no matter how one died, but they also continued to believe in the power of the dead to influence the lives of the living through reincarnation. In blending these two belief systems, they upheld the spatial practices that governed Christian cemeteries but displaced their belief in reincarnation from the graveyard to particular ritual practices applied to the body. Pastor Elia Awuma of Anyako described such a situation in 1927:

> One of the things here that may come across as strange and conspicuous to an outsider . . . is the funeral rites of the Christians and the heathens. There is no difference between either group. After a Christian is buried in a Christian manner, he is still given a wake by his heathen relatives exactly as is done after the death of any other heathen. Worst of all, many Christians also

participate with the heathens in these wakes. They booze and dance together with the heathens. . . .

Very many Anyako citizens [also] reside in Keta. . . . One of the many parish mothers, for example, came here last year on a beautiful Sunday with her daughter (who is said to be a teacher at the Keta School for Girls) and her grandson. They only came in order to have the child (who was of course baptized) partake in a very heathen rite. The belief that after death a man will return to the world through a second birth has been rooted in our people for a long time. If perchance a child resembles someone in his family who is already deceased, it is said that the deceased member has returned to life. A particular string of beads is wrapped around the arm of such [a] child. This is done by praying to the deceased member and participating in special heathen practices.

This is what our poor parish mother and her daughter were doing here. Not even the gravely threatening admonitions of our dear church elder Josef Tosu could stop her.[65]

The determination of this Anyako woman to blend traditional beliefs with her Christian faith was probably promoted when her grandchild became ill. The beads Pastor Awuma observed were probably those known as *amedzodzo dzonuwo.* Always worn on the wrist, these beads represented recognition of the belief that a child's illness was being caused by the spirit of the ancestor of whom the child was a reincarnation. By insisting on her course of action—despite the protests and admonitions of the church elders—the grandmother was seeking to protect her grandchild in the only way she thought would be truly effective.[66] Such determined efforts were not uncommon in Anlo in 1927. But it was not until the 1930s that these individual acts developed into a larger, more organized collective effort on the part of many Anlos to develop a Christianity that was more receptive to their culture. In 1934, several teachers associated with the Keta Roman Catholic Mission resigned in protest. The issue that precipitated their resignation was a dispute over a delay in the payment of their salaries, but simmering underneath were the teachers' concerns that while Anlo youth were encouraged to embrace Christianity and Western culture, they were also taught to despise their own culture. The Catholic Church—as had the Bremen Mission—forbade members to be involved in anything that was associated with traditional Anlo beliefs. The teachers who resigned gave voice to these concerns by establishing—with the blessing of mission-educated Fia Sri II and his advisors (many of whom were also mission-educated)—the Anlo State School at Keta. The subjects taught were the same as those found in the mission schools, but as a locally supported institution, students were also encouraged to embrace their own indigenous culture. They were encouraged to see themselves not as a group culturally and religiously apart, but as part and parcel of their communities despite their Western education. Drumming and dancing were not only allowed but encouraged through formal instruction. A much more tolerant attitude was fostered toward local cultural practices.[67] The results of this effort are perhaps most evident in the fact that today many Anlos maintain their Christian faith in a form close to that found in mainstream Christian churches elsewhere in the world, but some also retain the memories and meanings associated with traditional burial. In affirming their belief in reincarnation, for example, these individuals no longer spatially separate the bodies of the dead based on how and when they died, but they do affirm their belief in the ability of the dead to influence the living through the application of beads and ritual workings onto the human body. Ghosts—disavowed by the missionaries and mainstream Christians—are acknowledged to exist but have been rendered rootless, defined in terms of their power to influence the living but unaffected by how one buries the corpse. Some Christians also both participate in and officiate at important occasions where offerings of libation are made to ancestors.

In embracing the health benefits of cemeteries, traditional believers have managed "modernity" by effecting their own displacements of meaning. The demise of transition zones has meant that most[68] non-Christians no longer bury those co-religionists who died "bad" deaths in shallow graves outside of town.[69] Colonial Gold Coast and independent Ghana government laws (where observed or enforced) and new local understandings about the relationship between older burial practices and *alokpli* no longer allow such interments. The population growth in many Anlo towns and villages has resulted as well in the transformation into residential areas of those areas once reserved for the interment of *ametsiwumewo*. The memories and meanings associated with the practice of separation according to type of death do continue, however, through displacement. Where once the bodies of those who died "good" and "bad" deaths were physically kept apart by interment in the home and the bush, respectively, now this same apartness is maintained in clan or "pagan" cemeteries. The old and respected are buried in the central sections of such graveyards, and accident victims, suicides, and those who died before coming of age are consigned to the margins. The physical separations that the Anlo used uniformly in the nineteenth century to organize spiritual understandings of their built environment were simply displaced and reproduced by traditional believers onto the body of the modern cemetery. The opposition between town/home and wilderness/transition zone became cemetery center and cemetery edge.

But why displacement? In the previous chapter, we saw that by the end of the twentieth century Anlos had simply forgotten many of the beliefs held in the nineteenth century about their watery environment. The advent of "mo-

Figure 12. A reincarnation ritual, 1996.
Photo by author.

dernity" did not displace beliefs. Rather, it fostered forgetting. And where
memories and meanings did remain strong, it was because Anlos could point
to seemingly undeniable evidence that, in this case, the ocean continued to be
the site of spiritually powerful forces. It has continued to devour the bodies of
fishermen; its destructive waves wreak havoc on the town of Keta; and it serves
still as a critical site of employment and identity formation. But what of Anlo
beliefs about the dead? Why has "modernity" displaced belief in the ability
of the dead to influence the living for many rather than simply erasing or re-
taining such beliefs through previously normal markings on the built environment? What keeps this notion active in the minds of so many even as the practices informed by this belief are transferred to different sites? Answers to this
puzzle seem to lie in the fact that while many Anlos have embraced the "modern," the approach they take to their faith (whether as Christians or as traditional believers) is one that blends the new with the old. Many Anlo Christians have accepted as their own, for example, the notion that it is wrong to
"discriminate" against the dead based on the circumstances of their death.
Such individuals should not be held accountable for that over which they have
no control. Yet many other Christians also believe that there is much in the
world that their religion and Western education does not address or explain.
In such circumstances, recourse to those beliefs and practices that make the

seemingly inexplicable comprehensible and controllable is only sensible. They combine the old with the new in ways that admit no contradiction but satisfy the desire to harness the power of the spiritual world in support of the interest of the living. Non-Christian Anlos embrace "modernity" and the health benefits associated with extramural burial, but they, too, do so in ways that have allowed them to continue to acknowledge the power of the spiritual world to influence the lives of the living. Displacement is a result of such combinations. Older beliefs that had once informed the placing and spacing of the dead were combined by some with the new and reconfigured into a set of Anlo modernities whereby the memories and meanings of death were retained but were also displaced through ritual enactments onto the bodies of individual Anlos, onto disembodied rootless spirits, and onto the sites of modern cemeteries.

4

Belief and the Body

IN PREVIOUS CHAPTERS, the sacred sites examined have all been geographical locations, those places and spaces that the Anlo once—and in some cases still do—imbue with spiritual significance. But what of the human body? Did the Anlo think of this site as sacred as well? It would seem so, given the fact that in the last chapter we saw that nineteenth-century Anlos conceptualized the body of a living human being as an entity that contained two distinct souls, the *gbɔgbɔ,* or life soul, which was evident through the body drawing in and expelling air; and the *luwɔ,* sometimes called the personality soul, which entered the body upon birth as a soul that had once lived before but which could be reborn into the body of a newborn. This belief influenced the placing and spacing of the dead. It informed the ritual practices associated with the belief in reincarnation. But how did this belief inform Anlo notions about the body itself? What was the relationship between the corporeal self and its spiritual components? Were the *gbɔgbɔ* and the *luwɔ* simply animating principles, or was the body understood to be a fusion of the material and the spiritual, components that were separable upon death but even then still intimately linked to one another? As this chapter demonstrates, it was this latter conception that characterized Anlo understandings of the body, an understanding that also allowed the Anlo to believe that if they took action on one aspect of the self (whether the physical body, the *luwɔ,* the *gbɔgbɔ,* or any external spiritual force added thereto), they could also influence the other. But how were these beliefs connected to Anlo notions about the health of the body? What causal factors did nineteenth-century Anlos associate with various illnesses, and what part, if any, of the spiritual aspect of the body influenced one's own health or the health of another?

We know that like other African communities, most in Anlo deemed illnesses to be of either spiritual (*gbɔgbɔmedo*) or non-spiritual origins (*dɔtsoafe*). They also believed that naturally induced diseases could be redefined as spiritual if they were particularly difficult to cure or life threatening. Maladies such as measles (*agbayi*) and yaws (*dzobu*)—rarely fatal and almost always contracted in childhood—were believed to be naturally caused, for example, by too much sun, by exposure to bad water, or because one was simply born with the disease that emerged only later in life. In such cases, no one saw the need to consult a diviner, since these were not spiritually induced diseases. Rather, families employed purely herbal remedies that were commonly known within their communities.[1] Other diseases, such as smallpox, leprosy, and certain forms of respiratory illness and insanity, were defined, however, as spiritually induced. Smallpox was thought to be caused by the deity Sakpana calling the infected person to its worship. Leprosy was attributed in some instances to the work of a witch (*dzoduametowo* or *adzetowo*). The respiratory disease known as *alokpli* inflicted people when they violated certain spiritually sanctioned rules of behavior.[2] But were all spiritual illnesses caused by agents external to the body? Given the fact that nineteenth-century Anlos believed the body contained its own spiritual elements, did they also believe that the spiritual self could induce illness within the physical body? Evidence from the nineteenth century suggests that yes, they did believe that one's own spiritual self could induce illness in the physical self. But then how was the body conceived? What was the relationship between its component parts? And equally important for this study, how did the coming of Christian missionary influence and British colonial rule affect Anlo notions of the body and the nature of bodily illnesses?

This chapter addresses these questions by exploring nineteenth-century Anlo beliefs about the body. It argues that most conceived of the body as a spiritual site of embodied power that had the ability to affect and be affected by the spiritual self and others. It also argues that it was these beliefs that the Anlo used as a basis for understanding the nature of illness. I then examine the ways in which late-nineteenth- and early-twentieth-century European conceptions of the body challenged Anlo beliefs about the body and how the Anlo reconciled these very different conceptions by constructing new synthetic notions about the body and illness by the late twentieth century. This chapter argues that the meanings the Anlo had once attributed to the body were not simply retained, forgotten, or displaced to new locations, as was the case with other sacred sites. Rather, the Anlo significantly modified their notions about the body, in some instances abbreviating their beliefs and in others amending them to take into consideration new knowledge introduced by missionaries and British colonial officers. For example, they increased significantly the number of diseases and calamities that they recognized as naturally induced, but they both abbreviated and amended their belief in the existence of spiritually induced calamities by attributing such illnesses to the work of the Devil and/or other spiritual forces. As a result, by the end of the twentieth century, the Anlo no longer considered the body spiritually potent in and of itself. Rather, the corporeal self had become a largely material entity that could still be affected by spiritual forces, but only by those external to it.

THE BODY AS SACRED SITE: NINETEENTH-CENTURY
ANLO BELIEFS AND PRACTICES

In nineteenth-century Anlo, recognition of the body as a site of spiritual significance focused, in part, on the corporeal self as inherently powerful because it contained the very force, *gbɔgbɔ,* that gave human beings life. The term *gbɔgbɔ,* however, meant not only life soul but also breath. Breathing constituted the material manifestation of *gbɔgbɔ,* and as long as one was breathing, it was believed that a person continued to exist as a living human being. Breath, however, was more than simply a sign of life. Breath itself had power, and in using one's breath to produce sounds, language (*gbe*), individuals had the ability to use their *gbɔgbɔ* to affect the world around them. Words could create and destroy. They could both inspire and demoralize. They were also part of the quotidian rhythms of everyday life. A mother's admonition to her child did not necessarily lead to a spiritually induced illness. A husband's kind words to his wife were not necessarily seen as a sacred blessing. Yet, in some instances, it was believed that in using the body's *gbɔgbɔ* to produce words, one could do more than simply influence the actions and thoughts of others. One could also give materiality to the spiritual. In his study of Anlo oral culture, for example, Kofi Anyidoho observed that in the past, the Anlo handled bad dreams in very particular ways. One was not to recount such dreams at all. But if one felt impelled to speak about the experience, it was important to leave the house immediately after waking and proceed to the outskirts of town. Only there should one then recount the dream, speaking of it over a garbage heap. In giving word to the nightmare, it was believed that one brought the vision into existence. Doing so on the outskirts of town over a refuse dump was deemed necessary because this relocated the materialized nightmare to a place where it could do no harm. It was deposited away from human habitation and near those deities that protected the community from external malevolent forces. At the same time, the preferred approach to handling bad dreams was to take no action at all. By not speaking of the nightmare, one could deny its existence altogether.[3]

That this belief was also dominant as far back as the nineteenth century is evident from an account by A. B. Ellis, a British colonial officer and amateur anthropologist who was stationed in Anlo as a British colonial officer in 1878. In noting the power that the Anlo and other Ewe-speaking communities on the coast attributed to the spoken word, he observed that

the Ewe-speaking natives believe that there is a real and material connection between a man and his name, and that through the name injury may be done to the man. An illustration of this has been given in the case of the tree-stump that is beaten with a stone to compass [*sic*—that is, effect] the death of an enemy; for the name of that enemy is not pronounced solely with the object of informing the animating principle of the stump who it is whose death is desired, but through a belief that, by pronouncing the name, the personality of the man who bears it is in some way brought to the stump.[4]

In this account, Ellis emphasizes the use of words to harm others. But the spoken word could also protect. If, for example, a child was believed to have come into the world only to die and then be reborn again, thus tormenting his or her family, such a person upon birth would be given an "ugly" name such as Sewugbee (Se, or God threw him away), Adudo (feces), or Hato (pig trough). Such names in nineteenth-century Anlo were "supposed to protect the child during its life [because] . . . these names [were believed to] have a certain power and could keep the child alive." Those spirits that might cause the child's death were "supposedly tricked by these names into believing that these children were not human."[5] The power of the word, the power of naming, however, was directly related to the fact that such words were produced using the body's *gbogbo*, its breath, its life soul. It was the *gbogbo* as a source of spiritual power within the body which gave the body itself (by using the mouth to speak) the ability to influence the physical and spiritual well-being of both self and others.

While powerful, the *gbogbo* was not the only spiritual aspect of the body which infused the self with inherent power. The *luwo*, sometimes known as the personality soul, was also believed to provide the body with great potency. It was the *luwo*, for example, that nineteenth-century Anlos believed could leave the body and return with no ill effects. Individuals could turn themselves into animals, transform themselves into birds, and occupy the bodies of snakes if they had the knowledge to do so.[6] Upon death, it is the *luwo*—called the *noali* when separated from the body by death—which returned to the land of the dead (Tsiefe) or wandered about the landscape if proper funeral rites were not performed. If a person died a bad death and was interred on the outskirts of town, that individual's soul had the power to harass passersby and demand recognition by possessing the body of a living relative and causing illness. If the *luwo* of a newborn was determined by a diviner to be the reincarnation of a deceased relative, recognition of the *luwo* was deemed absolutely essential, since this reincarnated soul had the power to cause illness in the body of the individual to which it was attached.[7] Recognition of one's *luwo* in nineteenth-century Anlo also entailed performing rituals to acknowledge its entrance into the body on the weekday in which the person was born. Thus, Ellis noted:

The Ewe-speaking native offers worship and sacrifice to his in-dwelling spirit [*luwo*] in much the same way as is done on the Gold Coast. In both cases the natal day of the man is the day kept sacred to the in-dwelling spirit, and is commenced by a sacrifice, either a sheep or a fowl, according to the means of the worshipper.... The procedure on the Slave Coast ... varies somewhat. The worshipper, having provided a fowl, some kola-nuts, water and rum, seats himself on a clean mat, and a woman, dipping her hand in the water, touches with the fluid on the forehead, crown, nape of the neck and breast. This process is repeated with the rum, then with chewed kola nut, and lastly with the bleeding head of the fowl, which is torn from the living body.[8]

Ellis's account does not indicate under what circumstances or how often individuals engaged in ritual recognition of their *luwo*. It is unlikely, however, that it was very frequent, given the expense. Such rituals probably took place only when a diviner (*bokono*) determined that a person's illness was caused by her or his *luwo*, which was demanding recognition of its power. Much more important is the fact that for nineteenth-century Anlos, the body was a site of inherent spiritual power because of its connection with the spiritual force known as the *luwo*. The body had the power, through that which gave it life, the *gbogbo*, to influence self and others through the spoken word, a power that was directly connected to the use of one's breath (*gbogbo*). The *luwo*, too, infused the body with spiritual power, demanding from self and others recognition—through rituals on the physical body—that it had the power to inflict illness on the physical self.

An equally important aspect of nineteenth-century Anlo understandings of the human body involved the notion that the body and the spirit were understood to be one. They could be separated from each other, for example, in death, but even in death the actions involving the one necessarily impacted the other. Thus, if someone died a "bad" death, burial of the body on the outskirts of town impacted that person's soul by limiting the *luwo*'s ability to reincarnate into the body of a newborn infant. To recognize the spirits of those ancestors who did reincarnate into the body of an infant, action was taken on the body. Beads were applied to the wrist of the child. Water, alcohol, kola nut, and the bodily fluids from strangled chickens were applied to those who had failed to ritually acknowledge the power of their own spirit to inflict illness on the physical self, as demanded by their *luwo*. No distinction was made between the material body and the spirit self in the minds of nineteenth-century Anlo. Actions on the physical self necessarily involved the spirit, and actions of the spirit necessarily involved the body, since one's spirit was understood to be not simply "that ... which dwells within its physical manifestation" but was "the whole and the peculiar characteristics of a person."[9] Thus, in 1896, when an enslaved woman from the Anlo town of Weta was murdered after she attempted to free herself, her prepubescent daughter, and her infant child from slavery, the murderers drove a stake so deep into the woman's ear after killing her that those who later discovered her skeleton found it impossible to remove it. Their purpose: "To prevent the murdered woman's spirit from troubling them. . . . To prevent the woman's ghost from walking; by damaging its sense of balance."[10] Similarly, it was common in nineteenth-century Anlo for those who were repeatedly admonished by others for bad behavior to respond that it was their spirit (dzogbe or luwo) that was responsible: "God has given me a bad dzogbe. Is it my fault?" Yet family, friends, and community members did hold them responsible if they committed a crime, and they were punished accordingly through actions on the body.[11] These examples illustrate yet again the fact that in nineteenth-century Anlo, the spiritual and the material were one, in life and in death. Actions taken on the body (whether living or deceased) necessarily affected the spirit, and actions taken by the spirit necessarily impacted the entire self.

Another aspect of nineteenth-century Anlo understandings of the body as an inherently powerful spiritual entity that could influence self and others (as manifested in their health) had to do with the gendered character of the adult human body. Fluids produced by men (semen) and women (menses), for example, were thought to be powerful substances, giving sexual identity to the individual and making them capable of harming others. It was believed, for example, that if two men slept (i.e., had sexual relations) with the same woman, they "mixed their blood (wo toto vu), the results of which could be fatal. Either could contract alokpli."[12] Women's menses was likewise thought to have the power to strip a male of his sexual potency, to disempower spiritually infused objects, to make the sick even more ill.[13] Thus, the human body, especially the adult human body, as a gendered entity, was thought to be inherently powerful.

This same body, whether male or female, was also subject to external interventions that could infuse it with additional spiritual power, a power which, if handled correctly, could effect certain spiritually induced results. It was this belief, for example, that helped the Amlade clan (hlo)—ethnic outsiders in late-eighteenth- and early-nineteenth-century Anlo—gain access to the political and ritually powerful position of offering prayers to the gods on behalf of the entire Anlo polity. Believed to be invested with great power by their clan deity, members of this hlo not only interacted with some of the most powerful gods in Anlo, they were also said to have had the ability to use snakes to strike at their enemies and at any others who discussed their non-Anlo origins.[14] This same belief in the ability to be spiritually fortified also guided the investiture rituals used by the Anlo when installing the political and religious leader of the polity, the awoamefia. Rituals enacted on the body of the person being installed included a purification ceremony (_eflaxǫxǫ_), treatment with certain leaves, and the marking of the body with both temporary and permanent markings. These actions were designed to rid the candidate of any malevolent forces that might be lurking within the body. They also fortified the person against external threats and infused him with such spiritual power that the body was remade into a force so potent that to look into the face of the ritually prepared _awǫamefia_ was to risk death. Thus, in nineteenth-century Anlo, the _awǫamefia_ remained secluded. He was forbidden to engage in ordinary movement throughout the town, since his very person had been transformed spiritually in ways that could bring life and prosperity to the polity, if properly managed, or death to those who themselves were not strong enough (usually women and children) to withstand the spiritual power of his physical self.[15]

Spiritual fortification also constituted the principal means by which the Anlo explained the existence of witches (_adzetǫwo_). According to nineteenth-century Anlo thought, such individuals were not born with the power to harm others through witchcraft or the interest in doing so. Rather, they, like the _awǫamefia_, were given this ability, but in this case by other witches, most often without their conscious knowledge.[16] Thus, in recounting the witchcraft beliefs that existed among the Anlo and other Ewe-speaking peoples in the region, German missionaries emphasized the unwitting acquisition of a power that could act on its own, but which necessarily, nevertheless, implicated the entire self.

> Witches . . . are humans who carry a mysterious power in them[selves] which sometimes can leave their body and hurt others, even kill. . . . Dreaming specific dreams, believing oneself to be a dog and eating piles of garbage, believing oneself to be a bat, [seeing oneself] jump fences . . . are some of the signs. . . .
>
> If one notices this, someone with spiritual power can free the person from this witching spirit, but only if the person has yet to kill. Otherwise it is too late.
>
> A witch murders someone usually by taking the form of a flame and then lying on the chest of the victim while exerting great pressure. The victim can neither scream nor move, and the witch then sucks out the person's blood. The result is death by blood loss. The blood is then spat by the witch into a pot which he or she hides.[17]

In having such additions to the body, individuals emanated power whether they consciously wished it or not. Yet, like those who claimed to have had a "bad" _dzǫgbe_ or _luwǫ,_ they were still held responsible for controlling that power. The _awǫamefia_ was expected to avoid contact with those vulnerable to his acquired powers. Those unwittingly infected with the witching spirit were expected to manage their situation once they became aware of it by seeking the assistance of those who could help rid them of this witching spirit. Thus, whether consciously or unconsciously acquired, whether obtained from outside the body or by having only that spiritual power that was inherent in every individual, nineteenth-century Anlos understood the body to be a spiritual site where the self could be enhanced spiritually through both conscious and unconscious workings on the body, but where such workings also brought added social responsibilities to the individual.[18]

Nineteenth-century Anlo beliefs also understood the body to be an object that could be both possessed and affected by spirits external to itself in ways that did not necessarily enhance the spiritual power of the body but which certainly affected it physically and spiritually for good or ill. When, for example, an individual began to act oddly but behaved in ways that precluded deeming the person insane, when someone became ill and all the usual remedies proved useless, when a dreaded disease known to be spiritually induced afflicted an individual, most understood such maladies to be caused by either a sorcerer (who sought to harm others out of jealousy or sheer meanness), the spirit of a deceased ancestor, or a deity (who was using the illness as a means to call that person to recognize its power to influence their lives). In some instances an individual actually sought to establish an intimate relationship with an external spiritual force; but whether it was seized or sought out, the relationship between self and external spirit had important implications for how the Anlo managed the body. Recognition that a spirit (whether it was internal or external) or a deity had caused the illness often involved making an offering to the deity or becoming its priest. This, in turn, meant that the person had to follow a regime that directly implicated the body. One had to avoid particular foods because the deity or spirit (which had entered that person's very being) did not consume such items. One was required to abstain from certain acts (the eating of leftover food or having sexual relations) shortly before interacting with the external spirit in order to be ritually pure. Violation of these rules and regulations could bring additional spiritually induced illnesses or death. Those afflicted by the witchcraft of others most often sought assistance from a healer (*nuwǫlawo*) who would remove the spiritually induced illness that might be manifested in the body as "magic strings" or cords, worms, cowry shells, or small stones.[19] Failure to even acknowledge the fact that a spirit was calling one to its worship (whether it was an external spirit or one's own reincarnated *luwǫ*) or that a witch was the cause of one's illness brought similar consequences to the body.[20]

Not all illnesses, of course, were thought to be caused by spiritual phenomena. And not all spiritual influences on the body (whether generated from an internal or external source) caused illness or near death. When someone who had already accepted a deity as an integral part of themselves experienced spirit possession, for example, this person was not considered ill when in possession. Rather, it was believed that their bodies had simply been taken over temporarily by the possessing spirit.[21] Only when one was first called by a spirit to recognize its existence or when one had violated spiritually enforced rules and regulations did these forces then use illness as a means of alerting the individual to the spirit's concerns.[22] That so many illnesses in nineteenth-century Anlo were deemed to be spiritually induced, however, is evident from nineteenth-century accounts about how the Anlo perceived their own medical conditions. The majority saw themselves experiencing the very kinds of illnesses (long-lasting maladies and epidemic diseases) that were understood by the Anlo to be spiritually induced: smallpox, dizziness, syphilis, elephantiasis, headaches, skin rashes, certain childhood illnesses, bad accidents, scorpion stings, and snake bites.[23] In the early 1900s, for example, Bremen missionary J. Spieth wrote the following after having already spent several years among the Anlo and other Ewe-speaking peoples in the area:

> One sees many strong people and one enjoys looking at their beautiful body structures, strong muscles and supple forms. If one then has the opportunity to meet individuals, however, the enjoyment is spoiled for they have many tales to tell of illnesses. Among the Ewe, to whom I have developed a close relationship, the life stories of the majority seem to be made up of a long sequence of illnesses. Even the stories of individual polities reinforce this observation. For in the first half of the last century smallpox was widespread.[24]

Western medical observations made at the same time confirmed the ways in which the Anlo viewed their own bodies. As Missionary A. Knuesli recalled:

> Missionary Spieth once spoke with the Basel missionary doctor about the great number of sick among our Negroes. The doctor's observation [was that] among one hundred people, only twenty were relatively healthy.[25]

These observations indicate the extent to which spiritually induced illnesses were considered all too common among nineteenth-century Anlos. But more important, they also reveal the underlying principles behind Anlo understandings of the body. Illnesses could be spiritually induced because the body itself was not simply a physical shell animated by the *gbogbo* and the *luwo*. It was a fusion of the physical and its two spiritual components: inherently sacred, a site that could be influenced spiritually from within by the spiritual self and by spiritual forces from without, where distinctions between agency and passivity, physical self and spirit, the conscious and the unconscious had meanings quite different from those found in contemporary Western societies. Whatever the spirit did, whether it was willed or not, this action necessarily implicated the entire self. And whatever actions were taken on the body by spiritual or physical forces, these too could—depending on the situation—affect the entire self and called for a management of the body that recognized its complex characteristics. The bodies of those who died "bad" deaths had to be buried on the outskirts of town in order to prevent the *luwo* of such persons from reincarnating into the bodies of newborns. Despite these precautions, such spirits could still enter the bodies of the living, and this, in turn, required performing certain rituals on the body. Recognition of the power of one's own *luwo* required one to acknowledge this power through the holding of rituals that were done to the physical self on the weekday of one's birth, for this physical self and the spiritual self were inseparable and could only be understood in relation to each other.

Reminders of this understanding existed everywhere in nineteenth-century Anlo life. Illnesses diagnosed as spiritually induced could be cured in some instances only by extracting the physical manifestation of the spiritual force that had entered the body: small stones, cords, and cowries. Such healing practices reminded all present that just as a spiritual force that caused illness could take physical form (and be removed), so too, the physical self was both material and spiritual and could also be both physically and spiritually affected.[26] Few dared to gaze at the face of the *awoamefia,* for to do so was to not only see him as physical form but also to experience his spiritual power. Priests and the devotees of deities wore raffia cords around their necks, styled their hair in particular ways, and decorated their bodies with specific cosmetics, beads, and the red tailfeathers of gray parrots; they applied to their physical selves temporary or permanent markings and wore special hats to signal symbolically the fact that they were intimately linked to particular spiritual forces.[27] Thus, nineteenth-century Anlos managed the body—its burial, its consumption patterns, its physical adornment, its health, its location in relation to others and to particular geographical sites—in recognition of the fact that the body was both a material and spiritual site which could affect and be affected both spiritually and physically by itself and by others.

CHALLENGING BELIEFS

Beliefs about the body held by the Bremen missionaries who came to work in Anlo between the mid-nineteenth century and the early twentieth century differed markedly from nineteenth-century Anlo views, yet both groups shared certain concerns. For example, both understood the body to be more than a mechanical entity composed of blood, organs, flesh, and brain. For both, it was also a site associated with the spiritual. Anlos understood the body as intimately connected to its spiritual components, the *luwo* and *gbogbo,* which imbued the physical with life and a personal self. Bremen missionaries, as evangelical Pietists, understood the body to be animated or enlivened by "the guiding purposive power of a soul. This soul or *anima* was the agent of consciousness, God-given and the prime mover of human actions."[28]

Figure 13. A man wearing a hat that identifies him as a priest.
Photo entitled "Ein Fetishpriester," from G. Muller, *Geschichte der
Ewe Mission* (Bremen: Bremen Mission, 1904), p. 41.

Profound differences did exist, however. For the Anlo, the soul was an inherently powerful entity. It could induce illness in the physical self if its power was not recognized in those ceremonies associated with the belief in reincarnation; it could influence others even after the body's death by possessing and causing illness in the bodies of living relatives. As a power in itself, it was the *luwo,* the personality soul, that the Anlo blamed if a person had certain character flaws. According to Bremen missionary Jakob Spieth, nineteenth-century Anlo notions about this spiritual aspect of a human being were based on the understanding that

> a stupid person brought his stupidity along with him [at birth], an impatient person brought along his impatience, a liar brought along his lies, a coward brought along his cowardice, a hero brought along his bravery. . . .

> For example, a fool was someone who differentiated himself from others by his foolishness. He believed himself to be correct. If someone gave a person a basket with which to fetch water [and they actually tried to accomplish

this task] that person was a "sheep" [that is, stupid]. But that was how he arrived from the home of the souls.

Such people were admonished for their behavior, but if the person did not learn or could not change one said that he [came that way] from the home of the souls.[29]

This understanding meant that it was the _luwo_ that was held responsible if someone continued to behave in a way that fell outside the boundaries that defined normal and acceptable human behavior. The total person was not held responsible since they could not control this aspect of their selves. Rather, it was only when one's actions resulted in harm to others that the Anlo imposed sanctions on the entire self. Thus, fools and idiots were most often ignored, while thieves, murderers, unrepentant debtors, and adulterers were fined, exiled, or, in extreme cases, sentenced to death.

The Bremen missionaries, in contrast, tended to hold a very different understanding of the inherent power of the soul. Most believed that it was absolutely necessary to reject the notion that one did not have control over one's actions. While they believed that the status of one's soul (a single entity rather than the double entity of the Anlos) determined the nature of one's actions, they also believed that it was possible not only to influence the soul (as the Anlos believed) but also to control it. The individual, in fact—as defined in the Pietist tradition which informed the beliefs propagated by the Bremen Mission—was responsible for the state of their soul. According to this perspective, people should—but more important, could—choose the path that their lives took. If they chose to follow a righteous path that was pleasing to God, they were expected to control (as the Anlo believed) those impulses that might harm others, but they were also expected to exercise mastery over those personality traits thought by the Anlo to be unchangeable aspects of one's character: an excessive love of alcohol,[30] the tendency to lie repeatedly, self-centeredness, greediness, and a love of display. Control was possible, according to the Pietist missionaries. And it was to be achieved by practicing an "inner-worldly asceticism" that involved not simply engaging in certain rituals and performing good deeds but in continuous self-examination, prayer, and refusal to indulge mentally and physically in the temptations of carnal pleasures. Control over one's impulses, the actions of one's soul, was important and possible. It was also necessary if one was to direct and then maintain the soul on the path of righteousness.[31] Thus, in their exhortations to the Anlos whom they were attempting to convert and in their preachings to those who did convert to Christianity, they continually emphasized the importance of the power to choose, to control the path taken by one's soul.[32]

Differences also existed in how the Anlo and the Bremen missionaries understood the relationship between the body and the soul. The Anlo believed that the soul and the body were intimately connected to one another in ways that meant actions taken by and on the body implicated and influenced the soul while actions taken by the soul necessarily implicated the physical self. In contrast, the Pietists believed these two—the body and the soul—to be separate.[33] One could not speak of the soul as the Anlo did, as if it were an entity that operated as a consciousness separate from yet intimately linked to the physical self. Pietists believed that the soul could not directly influence the body in which it was situated and that it could not influence the health of anyone else, that witches did not exist, that sickness was caused largely by natural causes.[34] They believed that the body only reflected the extent to which one successfully guided the soul onto the path of righteousness. Thus, when many of the missionaries who worked in Anlo wrote about what they considered to be the deplorable ways the Anlo and other Ewe-speaking peoples in the region handled the body, they invariably (and erroneously) attributed this situation to a lack of inner spirituality and self-control, a lack that manifested itself on the body.

> A truly shocking witness . . . to the moral misery of heathendom . . . is how much [one sees] insincerity, anger, quarrelsomeness and hate . . . lack of energy, spiritual apathy and bodily misery. . . . [35]

> Young women are not ashamed to go around only wearing a small loincloth when talking to people or even going out into public. The men are not dressed much better.

> There is a place to bathe at every house, but there is a woeful lack of manners. . . . Often young and old bathe in the middle of their homestead without any sort of barrier.

> Their body care . . . leaves much to be desired. Men, women and children should bathe often. The men give more care to cleaning their hair than the women, who often clean themselves of lice in their huts or even in the public streets. One can often observe women wearing head cloths, and instead of scratching their head where they are being bitten, they hit themselves with the knuckles of their left hand. This results from a lack of proper hair care.

> The care of the mouth is often done to embarrassingly extreme levels.[36]

> [This is because the Anlo's] religion leaves their hearts empty and cold. Their heavenly and earthly gods represent themselves to them as sinister forces of which they are afraid and whose anger they seek to appease, whose favor they seek to obtain for themselves in order to gain earthly profit for house and field. They serve them with many sorts of sacrificial gifts, but no sanctifying breath, no inner revival comes over them from this worship. . . . Only natural, naked selfishness governs.[37]

> The highest goal of [the Anlo's] religion is [to satisfy] the belly.[38]

> To recognize how dark it is when one is separated from the life of God one only has to go the heathens, who continue to walk away from God, empty in heart, with darkness in their thoughts and directionless in their actions.

[They] shamelessly face the winds of excess [as manifest in their] unclean-
ness and greed.[39]

Not all German missionaries subscribed to these views all the time,[40] but
most did. And in so doing, they defined and then maintained the standards
which all Anlo Christians were expected to uphold with regard to the proper
approach to the Christian faith and the ways in which their faith should be
symbolically evident on their bodies. They were instructed, for example, to
"refrain from the usual exaggerated jewelry worn by their heathen sisters"
and instead to reach for heaven by focusing on the decoration of their inner
souls. Christians were to "eat and drink simply," maintaining control over
their bodily desires, for gorging and drunkenness, drinking brandy and in-
dulging in other pleasures would "rot the body and the spirit." They were
not allowed to "walk around totally or half naked and should also not allow their children to go around naked as the heathens [did]."[41] According to
their understanding of the relationship between the body and the soul, only
by consciously leading one's soul to follow the path of God could one gain
inner peace and cleanliness. This inner control would then manifest itself
in the comportment and maintenance of the body. Thus, when missionary
Anna Knüsli described the conversion of a woman she had been working
with, she emphasized the notion that prior to her conversion, this woman—
called Gbadzawa—had always demonstrated a certain unsettled, nervous
quality. She would never answer a question directed to her in the class, but
when someone else in the class was asked a question, Gbadzawa often inter-
rupted the other student and answered "in jerks." After her acceptance of
Christianity and baptism, when she then became known as Frieda, Knüsli
pointed out the difference that this development made in her demeanor. She
noted that Frieda's "facial features gradually lost their hardness, their un-
settledness and gained a stiller, peaceful expression, a witness thereof [accord-
ing to Knüsli] that her soul had heard the Savior's voice."[42] For this Pietist
missionary and others who worked among the Anlo, it was possible for individuals to control their own soul, and as a Christian one was to do so by guiding it onto the path of righteousness. This act would manifest itself in how one
also controlled and comported the body. Anlo Christians were enjoined to
demonstrate the extent to which they had committed their souls to follow the
path of the Lord by leading a sober lifestyle in dress and behavior and to further mark their bodies by assuming Christian names.[43] According to the missionaries, proper control over the soul necessarily led to what they believed
was the proper type of control over the body.

The differences that existed between the Anlos and the Bremen missionaries in their understandings about the relationship between the body and the
soul resulted in additional divergences in belief about the ability of spiritual

Figure 14. An Anlo young woman's formal dress—a
state of undress, according to the Bremen Mission.
Photo entitled "Jungfrauenvereien," from *So Sahen Wir
Africa* (Bremen: Staatsarchiv Bremen, 1984) p. 41.

forces to influence the body for good or ill. The Anlo believed that the spiritual content of one's self could be fortified in ways that gave the body enhanced spiritual power. Such individuals could use this power for the welfare
of the larger society, as the *awǫamefia* was expected to do, but they could also
use these powers to harm, as witches did. Critical to both these notions was
the belief that the spiritual powers of the body, whether enhanced or natural,
could affect the bodies of self and others and did so in their negative form,
most often by causing illness. Not all illnesses were attributed by the Anlo to
sacred intervention, but most were, whether caused by the spiritual aspect
of the self, various deities, other spiritually powerful individuals, or the souls
of the dead. The Bremen missionaries rejected these notions, but not completely. They did not believe that the souls of individuals, whether alive or
dead, could affect self or others. They did not believe in the existence of the
Anlo's many deities. They did believe, however, in God and the Devil and their
ability to influence the body, even as they also accepted the rapidly chang-

Figure 15. The "proper" dress for young Christian Anlo women, according
to the Bremen Mission.
From *So Sahen Wir Africa* (Bremen: Staatsarchiv Bremen, 1984), p. 30.

ing late-nineteenth- and early-twentieth-century European scientific ideas
about the causes of disease.[44] In their minds, God had the power (indirect as
it might be) to heal by enhancing the efficacy of those medicines and techniques that were designed to combat the diseases caused by miasma and, later,
parasites and germs.[45] In the absence of trained medical personnel, the missionaries treated those who they could. Invariably, however, they recognized
their own limitations and requested medical practitioners from Bremen to
treat the physical ailments that afflicted those whom they served.[46] At the
same time, they reserved for themselves (and for those medical doctors specifically trained as missionaries) the treatment of so-called spiritual illnesses:
lust, gluttony, greed, and other anti-social and egotistical excesses. Such diseases, they believed, were caused by the Devil, an external spiritual force that
could lead one into a life of filth, debauchery, and sin.[47] In their view, only by
bringing the Anlo to God could they learn to distinguish between physical
ailments and spiritual ones and thus be able to successfully apply the appropriate techniques to combat disease. Physical ailments required purely physical treatment, whether in the form of herbal remedies or treatments designed
by scientists. Spiritual illnesses required cleansing the soul.[48] But in both cases,
recognition of the power of God and the Devil was important. It was the
Devil who encouraged many to engage in the sinful activities that often led
to the body being afflicted by certain illnesses, and it was God that gave medicine and men the power to heal. By consciously bringing one's soul to God,

one could obtain spiritual and bodily health, for control over the soul necessarily brought control over the body in ways that enhanced both physical and
spiritual health.

To encourage the Anlo to accept this perspective, the missionaries not
only propagated their views in sermons and in everyday conversations, they
also launched a multi-pronged attack against the Anlo notion that the body
was a spiritual site. They banned the use of Anlo names in favor of European
Christian names to combat the notion that by giving a child an ugly name, the
body had the power to deceive those spirits that might attempt to return the
child to the spirit world. They forbade Anlo Christians from participating in
all traditional religious ceremonies, including those that involved the enact-
ment of rituals on the body. They emphasized the extent to which illnesses
diagnosed by the Anlo as spiritually induced were most often, instead, the result of either natural causes or poisoning by local priests.

> In Anyako, the fetish has proven itself powerful again. A woman became a
> Christian and then wanted to regain custody of her daughter in order to
> raise her as a Christian even though the daughter had been promised to and
> was already serving a fetish. The fetish refused. But when the mother dog-
> gedly demanded the surrender of her daughter, the priest finally consented
> while quietly contemplating how to take revenge. One day the girl was lured
> aside by an intimate of the fetish priest and was forced to take poison. The
> effect of the poison became evident soon thereafter. The girl fell into an
> unconscious and speechless state in which she has remained today. How
> should one punish the priest's diabolical malice since English law only pun-
> ishes crimes attested by witnesses? The truth is obvious to everyone and on
> everyone's lips, but the mother has no witness and the poor child is speech-
> less.[49]

In publicizing this particular case, Bremen missionary Flothmeier hoped to
discredit the prevailing notion that local spiritual forces existed and could induce illness directly (rather than, as he believed, indirectly—if truly attributed
to spiritual forces—by the Devil who encouraged people to live a sinful and
unhealthy lifestyle). But he also gave vent to his own frustrations with the
British colonial government because of their inability to prosecute those who
supposedly poisoned the young girl. Yet it is clear from both missionary and
colonial records that the Bremen Mission found in the British government
considerable support for those aspects of their efforts designed to encourage
the Anlo to adopt a "rational" approach to the body and the causes of illness.
Such support came primarily in the form of educational and administrative
legislation and enforcement having to do with public heath and safety.[50] For
example, the British administration imposed various measures on the Anlo
after 1875 to encourage sanitation in the various communities and to educate
the young so that they would pass on their new knowledge to others. These

efforts, and many more, were directed largely to combat the spread of disease in ways that were informed by the prevailing scientific ideas. Thus, in addition to broadening streets to combat congestion and enforcing burial ordinances to prevent the development of "noxious" odors, colonial administrators also erected latrines and enforced their use. They hired sanitation inspectors for Keta and later Anloga to discourage the maintenance of standing water in uncovered containers and established a sanitation committee in Keta to advise the government on sanitation policies. They prosecuted those who allowed their domestic animals to roam freely through the streets and built a hospital at Keta that by 1900 drew more than 2,000 patients a year, many of whom lived considerable distances from the town. They also embarked on a vaccination campaign to combat smallpox, which was widely resisted at first, but which by 1902 had won the support of at least a number of the local chiefs.[51] After 1905, when the colonial government required the teaching of sanitation, the Bremen Mission schools (and those established by the Catholic Church and the African Methodist Episcopal Zion Church) included lessons on the causes of various diseases, the value of the smallpox vaccination, and the appropriate ways to prevent a variety of maladies (malaria, cholera, typhoid fever, sleeping sickness, guinea worm, yaws, etc.) caused by germs and parasites.[52]

All these efforts reinforced the notion that any number of diseases once thought to be caused by spiritual forces should instead be understood as naturally induced and capable of being contained, if not cured, through purely medical means rather than with a combination of religious and local herbal efforts. The body was to be handled as if it were a machine that could be adversely affected if exposed to unsanitary and unhealthy conditions but that would remain healthy with proper cleansing, with the proper diet, and when appropriately clothed and housed. Thus, in his text on tropical hygiene that was adopted as the standard text for Gold Coast schools by 1913, Henry Strachan emphasized that "all parts of our bodies are doing work at one time or another . . . [and] . . . bits of us are always being used and worn out. . . . It is absolutely necessary, therefore that our food should . . . supply to each part of the body just the one kind of chemical it needs—carbon, nitrogen, oxygen, lime, phosphorus, iron, sodium and so on—to restore it and make it able to work again."[53] This emphasis on the body as machine was further reinforced in 1920 with the requirement that all government and government-assisted Gold Coast schools (including the Bremen, Catholic, and African Methodist Episcopal Zion schools in Anlo) include a course of physical education in the curriculum. At that time, organized games—like the sanitation curriculum—were believed to help eliminate "disease, dirt and physical defects."[54]

In emphasizing the purely physical aspects of the body and completely omitting any reference to the soul, British colonizers distinguished their approach to the body from that taken by the Bremen Mission. Yet neither the colonial administration nor the missionaries who operated in Anlo found their respective approaches to be incompatible. The scientific developments that had been occurring in Europe since the seventeenth century were so influential a force that those who continued to be concerned primarily with the spiritual aspects of the body were forced to adjust their notions about the relationship between the body and the soul to accommodate the new scientific discoveries. But what of Anlo adjustments to these new ideas?

ALTERED BELIEFS

What impact did the efforts by both colonial officers and missionaries to alter Anlo understandings about the role spiritual forces play in causing disease have? Did traditional beliefs about the body change under the influence of colonialism and Christian missionizing? And if yes, how? Did there develop significant differences in belief between Anlo Christians and those who continued to believe in the ability of spiritual forces (whether located within or outside the body) to influence the health of self and others? The scattered evidence that exists suggests that changes did indeed occur among both "traditional" believers and Christians, but these changes were very gradual and involved both an alteration in some beliefs and wholesale abandonment of others.

We know, for example, that between 1920 and 1950, Anlo children and adults were increasingly exposed to European understandings about the body. By 1926, the Bremen Mission (renamed the Ewe Mission in 1923 after the 1916 deportation of the German missionaries), the Roman Catholic Church, and the African Methodist Episcopal Zion Church had established more than thirty schools in Anlo. This number increased by 1950 to more than 100 schools that served almost 10 percent of the population and then expanded in number again at an even greater rate after Ghana's independence in 1957.[55] All these schools taught the required curriculum, which emphasized the importance of understanding the body in scientific terms, where diseases of the body were caused not by spiritual forces but rather by germs, parasites, and viruses. Government action to enforce sanitary regulations and the provision of health services and the holding of Health Weeks and regular lectures on the cause of disease all contributed to a growing awareness within Anlo of alternative notions about the body. Yet previous understandings persisted, as evident in a report about the investigation of a "fetish" that was said to have been quite popular in the Keta district in the mid-1940s.[56] I quote extensively from this report because it illustrates so well the ways in which the human body (in this case, dismembered for ritual use) was still understood by many to be inherently powerful, composed of material and spiritual elements (as seen in the shadow of a person and manifest in a person's breath when speaking).

Murder of Ama Kakraba at Elmina
Rex -v-Kweku Equsie and others

It has been established that the Juju is of Ewe origin . . . [and] appears to be the same fetish as that we have been trying to suppress in the Keta District. . . . [It] is known in that language as "NYAFA" the literal translation of which is "case to cool down," the origin of the juju is unknown but it is practiced in the belief that it has the power to cause the person using it to succeed in any kind of lawsuit including cases before Magistrates and Judges.

The normal paraphernalia of this JUJU consists of human bones, particularly shin bones; human jaws; pieces of cloth, etc. known to have been handled or used by the opponents in the litigation; the blood of fowls and goats, palm oil, dogs skulls and feathers of various birds. It is believed, however, that if human blood or parts of a human body are used, the Juju will be rendered more efficacious.

The juju is usually made with a tree popularly known to the Ewe people as "nyati" or "case tree." The tree is cut into pieces about 14 inches long and 1 and /2 inches in diameter, which are split in two. Shinbones are sometimes used in place of pieces of the tree. The two pieces of wood or the two shinbones are tied at one end with a rope. This rope is besmeared with blood, either human or animal and between the pieces of stick or bone are inserted any articles which are known to have been handled or used by the opposite party. In serious cases, the parts of a human being such as lips, eyelids, etc., are inserted . . .

Whilst this process is being carried out the person tying the rope must be careful that his shadow does not fall in front of him or on the sticks, otherwise he is considered to have "tied" himself as well and presumably the result will not be to his advantage.

After binding the sticks with rope, alcoholic liquor is poured on the Juju and the person making it recites words to the effect that he wishes his opponents to behave as if demented when the case is tried. The Juju is then buried deep in the ground or placed under a heavy weight, preferably a heavy stone. The significance of this procedure is that it is believed that thus the case is buried forever, or is dead and if it is weighted down, it will mean that the opposite party is rendered incapable of carrying on with the case.

The significance of the various parts of the human body which were removed in such brutal fashion is as follows:

The lips are believed to deprive the members of the opposite party of the means of expressing themselves clearly in court;

Removal of both eyes are supposed to affect the Judge so that he is unable to clearly see documents and exhibits tendered in evidence, or to write his records.

The removal of the private parts and the anus is symbolical [*sic*] of preventing the witnesses from producing material evidence;

The removal of blood vessels is supposed to affect the financial position of the opponents so that they are unable to obtain legal assistance;

Sometimes the tongue is cut out or cut in two with the idea that this will cause the witnesses for the other side to become dumb when called to give evidence.[57]

According to the superintendent of the criminal investigative division that completed this investigation, it was rare for human parts to be used (with the exception of shinbones obtained through grave robbery). Nevertheless, indigenous beliefs about the body appear to have been familiar to large sectors of the population even if the number of actions taken on the basis of these beliefs were few. Investigators were able to obtain detailed information about the spiritual significance of the individual body parts without much difficulty; people told them that Anlo residents used to resist the use of cemeteries for their honored dead because of their fear of grave-robbers.

Traditional beliefs did not remain unaffected by the changing times, however, as evident in the religious order known as Brekete. This group, which entered Anlo in the 1920s and became very popular as an *atike-vodu,* or medicinal deity, initially reinforced belief in the body as a spiritual site that could inflict illness on oneself and others. It did so by offering much-demanded protection against witchcraft in which witches were defined as they were in the nineteenth century: individuals who consciously used their amended body's power to spiritually influence others, whether through verbal expressions of envy or jealousy or by separating their spiritual self from the body and then in this disembodied form inflicting harm on others. By 1950, however, Brekete had begun to reject these previously held beliefs about the body. Forced to adjust by the increasing prevalence of Christian and Western notions about the body and efforts to ban it from operating,[58] Brekete forbade its members from accusing others of being witches. In addition, it stated that those who felt they were affected by witchcraft should understand their illness to be caused not by witchcraft but by their having violated certain rules enforced by Brekete. In making this adjustment, Brekete disavowed its previously held belief that the body as a spiritual site could inflict illness on self and others. It focused its beliefs instead on the non-corporeal power of the Brekete god.[59]

This shift appears to have characterized a more general decline in nineteenth-century beliefs about the body. In the 1980s and 1990s, when I interviewed a number of indigenous religious adherents about the extent to which older beliefs about the body continued to inform cultural practices in Anlo, I heard numerous complaints from diviners (*bokonowo*) that their services were no longer in demand, as they once had been in the past. It had become uncommon for families to consult a diviner to determine which ancestor had reincarnated in the body of a newborn child. People just did not believe in reincarnation as they had in the past. Only the very elderly could remember being enjoined throughout their lives to recognize that they should conduct their lives in specific ways because they were themselves a deceased ancestor who had returned to life.[60] Only the famous from the distant past were associated with the power to leave their bodies and to transform themselves into various animals. And while illnesses were still defined as naturally induced (*dotsoafe*) or spiritually caused (*gbogbomedo*), where the former can be reassessed as a spiritually caused malady if it is resistant to accepted cures, the majority of traditional believers understood only certain illnesses (infertility, impotence, insanity, and convulsions, for example) to be caused by spiritual forces.[61] This is not to say, however, that indigenous Anlo belief in the power of the body to cause illness (or well-being for that matter) has disappeared. In her 1998 study of Anlo ways of knowing through the senses, Kathryn Geurts documents the fact that some still do believe in the power of the body (through the utterance of words) to affect others. She notes, for example, that it is not unusual for traditional birth attendants when supervising a birth to "brush the woman's abdomen with a twelve-inch whisk in an effort to discard the causes of *enu,* a very bad sickness which usually seized children but could also attack pregnant women." According to Geurts, "the cause of this illness . . . was bad will or enmity among household members or between people within the same family . . . enmity and bad will that flowed though openings [such as the mouth]."[62] Continued belief in the power of the body through the use of speech is also demonstrated in the rituals associated with the annual Hogbetsotso Festival (the history of which I discussed in Chapter 2). Integral to this event is a physical and spiritual cleansing of the community, Dodede, that includes the deliberate collection of refuse from the market. The purpose is to rid the community of those materials that might contain the ill will that has been brought into the market by Anlo and non-Anlo citizens alike when engaged in the sometimes rancorous business of trade. Such actions—those of the traditional birth attendants and the collection of refuse in the Dodede ritual—conform quite nicely with notions prevalent in nineteenth-century Anlo that the body (through the mouth) had the power to influence the health of others. But they also contain traces of the "modern." In the past, when illnesses and death could be traced time and again to specific individuals, such individuals were tried as witches. Today, however, witchcraft accusations are virtually nonexistent, replaced by efforts to reconcile those at odds with one another. In addition, the power of the body to spiritually induce illness is almost always understood to affect others rather than the self.[63] This marks a significant change. In the nineteenth century, the body was believed to affect not just others but also the self. Individuals conducted rituals on the physical self to acknowledge the power of the spiritual self to inflict illness on the self. None of this seems to have survived into the present, however. Instead, the body is understood by those who continue to adhere to indigenous religions as an entity that has the power to induce illness, but only in others. It experiences illness, but such illnesses when diagnosed as spiritually induced come only from outside the self, never from within. Indigenous beliefs about the body have thus been altered in significant ways. The body, for some, still has power (and this power can affect others with or without one intending to do so, as seen in the Dodede ritual), but this power is evident in only a much more limited number of circumstances (in cases of infertility, impotence, and convulsions, for example) and rarely, if ever, is its power to cause illness evident within the self.

But what of beliefs about the body held by Anlo Christians? Did they adopt completely missionary teachings which emphasized the notion that body should be handled with proper scientific care so that it could function properly as the machine it was? Did they come to believe in a single soul (as opposed to the Anlo's two souls) that if allowed to go astray would cause certain "spiritual illnesses" (envy, greed) but not physical illness in the body? How did Anlo Christians reconcile their Christian beliefs about the body with the indigenous beliefs that surrounded them at every turn, beliefs held by family members, friends, and neighbors? Did these Christians really believe that the body had no power to influence the health of self or others, that witches did not exist, and that witchcraft was to be explained as the use of poisons?[64] How, in fact, did Anlo Christians come to see the body? Evidence from the late nineteenth and early twentieth centuries suggests that many found it difficult to choose between these competing conceptions of the body. In 1903, for example, Missionary Flothmeier recounted the story of a young Anlo man who was considered a "seasoned" Christian within the Bremen Mission community in Keta. Yet, in his words, he still succumbed to "the power of heathendom." This occurred, according to Flothmeier, when the young man, to overcome his fear of the person who supervised his work as a clerk, paid a Hausa merchant in Keta for the use of a leaf that was supposed to strengthen his entire self, giving him courage and making him more popular with his boss.[65] In 1927, some twenty-four years after this incident, local ministers still despaired at the fact that Anlo Christians found it difficult to maintain their Christian faith when faced with particularly difficult circumstances. They noted, for example, that it was not unusual for Christian women —in trying to save a grandson—to have the child (who had already been baptized as a Christian) participate in the ritual that recognized the influence of a deceased ancestor over the child's health. These same ministers also frequently observed Christians actively and openly joining in indigenous funeral rites that recognized the power of the dead to influence the living.

These examples suggest that many Christians were simply unwilling to sever themselves completely from indigenous beliefs about the body. That this was indeed the case is evident from the fact that by the 1950s, virtually all the oldest Christian denominations in Anlo (the former Bremen Mission, known by that time as the Ewe Evangelical Church, the Roman Catholic Church, and the African Methodist Episcopal Zion Church)[66] had begun to overlook, if not accept, a blending of Christian and indigenous beliefs and practices.[67] Drawing on the beliefs first introduced by the European Christian missionaries, for example, virtually all Anlo Christians associated with the traditional missionary churches have accepted the notion (as many traditional believers also now have) that the body is to be understood as not only distinct but as separate from its spiritual component. It is to be cared for according to the scientific principles that inform good hygienic and medicinal care. Proper care of the soul involves maintaining one's faith in God and eschewing belief in the notion that the soul of a living person (whether single or two in number) has the power to physically harm the self or others. Words produced by the body cannot cause physical maladies. Deceased relatives do not reincarnate into the bodies of newborns. Ancestral spirits do not cause disease, and how one disposes of the bodies of the dead has no significance for the physical health of the living.[68] But these Anlo Christians also believe in the ability of spirits (disembodied, however, and largely unconnected to a material reality) to affect the body. Thus, many Christian men and women who suffer the death of a spouse bathe at the ocean to rid themselves of the spirits of their deceased spouse. Christians living elsewhere in Ghana are known to return to Anlo in order "to pour libation to their dead relatives to ask for their blessings for quicker promotions or prosperity in their various fields."[69] Belief in the Devil (understood to be a disembodied spirit operating with purely evil intentions) remains strong, as does belief in the power of individuals to use magical means (as opposed to simple poison) to harm others.

What distinguishes Christians from indigenous believers in their common understanding about the power of external spiritual forces to both harm and help the body is that most mainline Christians rely on God to protect them when harm is the concern. When they participate in rituals at the seashore to separate themselves spiritually from the power of their deceased spouses, they make use of seawater as traditional believers do, but they also bathe thereafter in water specifically blessed by a church official. When burying their dead, they refuse to include money, as followers of the indigenous religions still do, and they do not bury accident victims at the edge of the cemetery to discourage their spirits from reincarnating into the bodies of newborns.[70] Instead, they bury them often with the same pomp and celebration accorded those who died at an elderly age, and they include a Bible, a hymn book, and the baptismal and confirmation certificates of the deceased to ensure the acceptance of the deceased's soul into heaven.[71] Such beliefs and practices suggest that Anlo Christians associated with the descendants of the missionary churches—despite all their diversity—do understand the body in very specific ways. It is both spiritual and material, where the spiritual content of the self has power to affect others only after death. Diseases of the body are the result of viruses, parasites, and germs. In 1981, roughly 60 percent of Catholics believed this, as did 67 percent of Presbyterians (the denominational affiliation of the former Bremen Mission) and 66 percent of Methodists. Only a much small number within these same groups (roughly 30 percent) believed that certain diseases such as infertility and impotence and other bodily concerns—success in business and school, feelings of envy and jealousy, fear and all-consuming love—could be caused and remedied by external spiritual forces.[72]

In blending the old with the new, Anlo missionary-based Christian understandings of the body draw on a double inheritance, one that comes not only from the colonial period but also from their own nineteenth-century past. Even as most Anlo Christians make use of hospitals and clinics and emphasize the importance of handling the body with scientific care, they also continue to believe in the ability of spiritual forces external to the body and largely unconnected to the material to physically affect the self. These forces are often defined as manifestations of the Devil,[73] but they also include other spiritual forces (whether defined as the spirits of the dead or other unspecified powers). All are believed to have the power to affect the body. In this way, Anlo Christians associated with the former missionary churches, like their traditional believer counterparts, have constructed new beliefs about the body by building on memories of the old and incorporating new beliefs and meanings introduced by colonialism and the missionary encounter.

NOTIONS OF THE BODY RECONFIGURED

That Anlo concepts of the body (whether held by Anlo Christians associated with the mainline churches or indigenous believers) have been amended since the nineteenth century is clear. The body is no longer considered by most to be the sacred site it once was. It has spirituality, but this aspect of the *living* body is believed by most to have the inherent power to influence self and affects others only under a very limited set of circumstances. Far more power and concern are associated with the dead or other spiritual forces external to the body. And even then, the diseases inflicted by such forces are far more limited in number than was the case in the past, as many more Anlos have come to accept the causes of most illnesses as having a material basis. Diviners and traditional spiritual healers are no longer necessarily the first individuals that most Anlos consult after home remedies fail. Most consult Western-trained doctors. Children and adults, when sick, are sent to the hospital. Those who suffer untimely deaths are taken to the morgue for postmortem examinations. Diviners find their services less and less in demand, and traditional healers are increasingly consulted only when individuals do not have the funds to pay for the Western-trained medical services, when the latter fail to heal, or when the disease is associated from the beginning with spiritual causes. The increasing prevalence of schooling within the population and the obvious advances made by Western medicine in treating many past chronic and fatal maladies[74] has meant that the body is seen increasingly by all as primarily a material entity. And because of this, far more emphasis is placed on understanding the body as an object to protect from external harm (whether this harm is located in the material world of germs, parasites, and viruses or in the spiritual world of ghosts, magic, and the bodily power of others) than on understanding the body as a spiritual site capable of influencing both self and others.

5

Contested Terrain

OVER THE LAST 100 YEARS, the Anlo have invented and displaced, retained and forgotten, abridged and amended the many meanings and memories they once associated with a number of sacred sites. All this began in the precolonial period but accelerated tremendously with the advent of colonial rule and missionary influence. By the early nineteenth century, for example, the Anlo had abbreviated their memories about the historical significance of Notsie as other centers of spiritual power captured the attention of the Anlo. But during the colonial and post-colonial periods, these same memories were creatively expanded upon as various interests within and outside Anlo sought to harness the site to support both new and older identities and economic development concerns. The spiritual meanings that the Anlo once attributed to various water bodies, to the placing and spacing of the dead, and to the human body itself have also undergone significant changes. Most Anlos no longer understand these locations, once viewed as sites of great spiritual power, as their ancestors did in the past. Although many still believe that the souls of the dead are capable of influencing the living, many others no longer think it possible for the living to influence the dead by taking action on individual corpses. Most would also now say no if they were asked whether one's own soul (*gbɔgbɔ*) could induce illness in the physical self even as they remain convinced that while one's soul can't harm the self, it can still affect others. Very few currently believe that the water levels in the lagoon are controlled by the deity Tovuntsikpo, if they ever were, and the ocean as sacred site is increasingly challenged by fishermen and -women who disregard belief in the power of women to render the ocean barren. Old meanings and memories have not been completely forgotten, however. Much remains, retained in bits and pieces by some, forming the very foundation upon which the new is made sensible.

The development of such diverse beliefs within the Anlo population—generated most recently by British colonialism and European missionary societies but evident as well in the pre-colonial period—has frequently been accompanied by a great deal of tension and conflict. When the British colonial government attempted to alter Anlo understandings about the body by requiring the teaching of health in the schools, by organizing Health Days, and by embarking on a vaccination campaign throughout Anlo, resistance was widespread. Many refused to send their children to school, others avoided European medical care unless near death, and still others held on to their belief that it was the deity Sakpana that caused smallpox.[1] Others resisted, sometimes violently, colonial efforts to vaccinate them and their families, while still others vilified and threatened to destool those Anlo chiefs who supported the government's campaigns. Anlos who had accepted Christianity frequently found themselves publicly ridiculed by their neighbors, friends, and family.[2] Disputes over how to bury the dead (when family members were of different religious faiths) were not uncommon.[3]

And while these tensions in recent years have eased considerably as both traditional religious orders such as Brekete and the mission-based Christian denominations have incorporated elements of the other into their belief systems and/or practices, tensions and conflicts remain. In May of 1987, for example, members of the charismatic-style Church of Pentecost in the town of Anloga[4] found themselves under attack. Within a period of twenty days, a number of town residents who were supporters of Anlo traditional religious practices broke into one of two Pentecostal chapels in the town and seized the drums that church members used in their worship and prayer services. The vandalized building was then set ablaze and burned to the ground. Several days after this first fire, flames engulfed and destroyed the second chapel. Church members were swift in identifying the culprits. Earlier in the year, priests associated with the most powerful gods worshipped by traditional religious believers in Anloga had declared a ban on drumming for the period between April 26th and May 26th. The ban was imposed as part of the customary rites that community leaders had held for over 100 years to renew the town's association with those deities that were believed to have the greatest influence over the well-being of the community and all its citizens. The Church of Pentecost, which was introduced into the town in 1948, had never recognized or acknowledged the importance of this ritual; in fact, from the first days of their existence in Anloga they defied the ban by refusing to silence their drums during the proscribed period. Why such practices, after thirty-five years, suddenly become so offensive is discussed elsewhere.[5] What is of concern here is that even with the attack on their premises, the Church of Pentecost (joined later by other Christian denominations) continued to defy the annual ban on drumming. Nine years later, in 1996, tensions that had continued to simmer under the surface since 1987 erupted again when supporters of the ban attacked two Christian groups that were using the classrooms of the Avete Primary School as a temporary worship site.

These attacks illustrate the continued tensions that exist between older and newer beliefs about the material and spiritual world in which the Anlo live, but perhaps even more important is the fact that these clashes and many of the more violent confrontations that have taken place in the past have all occurred or begun in Anloga. Why there? Although this community was once the spiritual center of the Anlo polity, that is no longer the case. Nyigbla— which once had its shrine in Anloga and was considered by most in the late eighteenth, nineteenth, and early twentieth centuries to be the Anlo's national war god—is a shadow of its former self. The membership of the Nyigbla order consists largely of older women. It no longer dominates the religious culture of Anlo or Anloga, as it did in the past. And while the much more popular Yewe religious order, once banned by Nyigbla from operating in Anloga, recently outdoored its new initiates in the town, even Yewe's strongest centers of worship are not in Anloga. Rather, they are found in the towns of Woe (immediately east of Anloga) and Nogokpo (north of the Keta Lagoon). Yet Anloga continues to be the site, as it was in the past, of the most persistent tensions and conflicts between Christians and traditional believers. Why?

In this chapter, I explore Anloga's history as a sacred site, one whose meaning and memory has been continuously contested since the nineteenth century. I chart its development as the political and religious center in Anlo. I then discuss the various tensions and conflicts that arose during the nineteenth and twentieth centuries as different religious groups entered Anlo and attempted to reshape its meaning by establishing a commanding presence in the town. I argue that even with Anloga's decline as a major center of traditional religious beliefs after the first decade of the twentieth century, it is the memory of the town's former meaning as the center for Anlo traditional religious culture that keeps Anloga at the center of tensions between older beliefs and the new beliefs that were introduced by European missionaries and British colonizers. At the center of this memory is the notion that control over the meaning of this site is critical for influencing how all Anlos understand themselves and their cultural history. In the past, this town was considered "a second Notsie,"[6] where adherence to traditional beliefs and belief in particular gods was an integral part of the town's very identity. With the arrival of European missionaries and their Anlo converts, however, this identity was challenged in ways never seen in the past. Tensions developed throughout Anlo, but it was in Anloga that tensions developed into sustained and sometimes violent conflict. And it is these tensions that continue to erupt periodically, again primarily in Anloga, as different constituencies engage in a public struggle over the meanings they encourage others to associate with Anloga and the polity as a whole.

ANLOGA AS PRECOLONIAL SACRED SITE

The history of Anloga's association with powerful spiritual forces dates from the seventeenth century, when Ewe-speaking immigrants first entered the area. According to Anlo oral traditions, the town of Anloga was first founded by Togbui Wenya, ancestor of the Lafe clan, but soon thereafter others followed, attracted by easy access to fresh water and the availability of both good hunting grounds and fertile agricultural lands. Among those who moved into the town were Sri I (a nephew of Wenya) and his family and a relative of Sri named Gli. Shortly after Gli's arrival, a battle is said to have ensued between him and Sri over who had ultimate authority over the town. According to the traditions, it was Sri who eventually prevailed. He is said to have succeeded, in part, because he was able to obtain from Notsie—then a major spiritual center in the region—a spiritually powerful object known as a *tsikpe*. Reputed to have the power to alleviate the droughts that were so common in the area at the time, Sri used this object to win followers, to gain ascendancy over Gli, and to become the *awǫamefia* of Anlo, the political and religious leader of the growing and expanding polity of Anlo. He later reinforced his authority by joining with Gli and another spiritually powerful family headed by Gblea Akoli (who had custody of the gods associated with blacksmithing) to form the ruling clan known as the Adzovia in the early decades of the eighteenth century. By maintaining their residence in Anloga and by providing services associated with the spiritual production of rain, the enhancement of fertility, and the making of the tools necessary for both farming and war, the town soon became a religious center for the residents in the area. Connections to Notsie, from which the Adzovia gained their spiritual authority to rule, were reinforced through periodic visits, but over time these pilgrimages diminished in number and Anloga became a center of spiritual authority in its own right. By the 1730s, it ritually installed its own political and military leaders, making recourse to Notsie only when a new *awǫamefia* came into office or died. It operated as the final court of appeal for the Anlo district, and between 1730 and 1750, Nditsi,[7] the *awǫamefia* at the time, also instituted on his own authority a new form of punishment to deal with the increasing incidents of lawlessness that are said to have plagued the polity. All decisions to implement these new institutional forms were taken in Anloga, and thereafter all the activities association with these institutions—installations of chiefs, hearings, judgments, and executions of legal decisions—also took place in Anloga. Of particular interest is the fact that the Anlo integrated their religious beliefs into these new institutional forms. This is perhaps most evident in accounts of the Nyiko custom, introduced by Nditsi.

> Some . . . years ago, virtue was the ideal of all boys and girls born in Anlo land. In order to preserve it, there existed two . . . customs for the punishment of wrong-doers: (a) Banishment by slavery and (b) the Nyiko custom. The chief evils of those days were (in order of gravity):
>
> • Taking away any one's life through witchcraft or the practice of the native black-magic art.
> • Stealing.

- Meddling with another's wife.
- Incurring debts.
- Disobedience to parents.
- Untruthfulness.

Of these evils, the first was always punished at the offense by the Nyiko custom (now to be explained), the second and third by the said custom, but only at the third offense; and the fourth, fifth and sixth were punished either by banishment in slavery or by the Nyiko custom, and that also at the third offense.

A young man, say, twenty-five had, for instance seduced another's wife for the third time. This meant that he had passed the limit considered proper, for his conduct in that line had, on each of two previous occasions, cost the family thirty-six shillings[,] which debt had, perhaps, been paid by depriving two younger members of the family of necessaries. . . . To shelter him further is to incur supernatural displeasure for the whole lineage. . . . This is more than is bearable in Anlo land. "This son of ours will be the ruin of the family," muttered the elders who, forthwith, in secret consultation among themselves decided upon the punishment mentioned above.

One of the elders who had sat in the council was then dispatched next day to Anloga, the capital, to acquaint the elders of the relations there that Mr. So-and-So had been doomed by them for death by Nyiko. These latter in their turn would inform the Field Marshall [or the military commander of the Anlo army, the *awadada*]. . . . He would then appoint a day for the execution. The elder sent to Anloga then returned to his people with a message respecting the appointed day. Meanwhile, all was made ready in Anloga for the execution; to wit: the executioners were informed, and forthwith restored the two Nyiko drums . . . a male and female (*trowo*) . . . the beating of which announced the fact that someone had just been subjected to punishment by Nyiko.

Now all this preliminary business of consultation, et cetera, as just described was transacted with the most astonishing secrecy that the victim could not suspect the least evil.

In the early morning of the appointed day, however, the maternal uncle—if any—of the doomed person, or one of the elders, would say to the criminal, "I want you to go to our kinsman, Mr. So-and-So at Anloga to fetch me [something]. . . . The young man obeyed and at once set out. On arriving at Anloga at about 9 a.m. he was received by the head of his relatives, who would presently indulge in a flood of expressions, communicative partly of his pleasure to do his kinsman such a good turn, and partly of his regret that the required thing was not just ready at hand, and finally round off with the request that the messenger would kindly stay overnight to enable him to get back the required thing from Mr. So-and-So, who lived some miles off. . . .

At about 10 p.m., that is after the house had retired, the head or elder of the family would wake the doomed messenger from his sleep, and request him and another elderly person (also of the house) kindly to lead him with a lamp to the latrines, which were usually outside the town. The young man, having waked, would sleepily obey, and, with the lantern in his hand, join in the solemn procession of three, led by the first elder, and the rear of which was brought up by the second elder. This order was strictly kept, for the man in the middle was, according to a pre-conceived plan, the person to be assailed. Thus the three persons would wend their way through the lanes of the town and then through a winding path through the thick bush outside the town; and once come to a place called Agbakute ... (*ne egbea aku,* if you refuse to conform, you die).... About half a mile from the town, the front man would pretend going to attend to his minor needs in the bush, while the rear man stopped. All at once there came out of the bush, a band of three or four persons who, armed with iron bars, beat the victim on the head and neck till he died. His body was then carried and buried in a shallow grave so that the hyenas could dig it up and eat it. His clothes and dresses, which had been sent secretly to Anloga a day previous by his maternal uncle or other responsible person ... were spread on shrubs or cactus plants about the place. A messenger then ran to inform the drummers that the deed was done, upon which the drum at the south end would play: *Miede za, miegbo za; Miede za, miegbo za* (We went at night and came back at night).... The second drum responded: *Gbewoe nye nye gbe,* I concur.

Next day a messenger left Anloga to inform the uncles and elders that the deed was done.... No one spoke any more of him in the house. His absences was never remarked upon. But should any one be so incautious as openly to ask where he was, the intimation: *Eyi toko atolia* (he is gone to the fifth river side ... which is the euphemism for *wofe nyiko de dezi,* he has been tabooed) was enough to satisfy him of his fate.[8]

Emphasized throughout this account is the extent to which the family was involved in each stage of the judgement and punishment. But equally important is the fact that all such executions always involved the spiritually powerful, who were all based in Anloga. The "field marshal" or *awadada,* had to consent to the wishes of the family, but his authority was reinforced by his own association with those gods that gave him the power to lead others to victory in war. The Nyiko drums, which were beaten over the victim, were believed by many to be the home of deities, who lent their own spiritual authority to the proceedings. That such rituals and customs were conducted in Anloga reinforced the significance of the town as a spiritually powerful site. It was here that the gods in the custody of the *awoamefia* and the *awadada* who oversaw the welfare of the entire polity existed. It was here that the many unhappy spirits of those executed could roam about, along with others who had died an untimely death, without harming the population because of the power of the deities that protected the town and the polity.

This image of Anloga as the spiritual center of the Anlo polity was further reinforced by events that occurred in 1769, the origins of which date to the beginning of that century when the Anlo faced a series of military disasters. In 1702, the polity was conquered by the Akwamu and forcibly incorporated in the latter's empire until 1730. In 1741, it was defeated again by Anexo and administered by the same until 1750. During the latter period, Anlo was forced by Anexo to accept a Danish monopoly over trade in the area, which established a ceiling for the rates at which the Anlo were able to sell slaves to the Danes. In 1750, after gaining its independence from Anexo, Anlo engaged in a conflict known as the Nonobe War, in which an initial victory over the Agave (then located immediately north of the Anlo littoral in the marshlands west of the Keta Lagoon) was reversed when the Agave and their Ada allies received assistance from the Danes in the form of firearms and the paid cooperation of the Krobo and a Larte contingent from Akuapem. With these additions to their forces, the Agaves and their allies were able to cross the Volta, rout the Anlo from their towns on the littoral, and capture at least sixty-four people, whom they sold to the Danes.[9]

This stream of defeats had a devastating impact on the Anlo population's confidence in their leaders' abilities to militarily and spiritually deliver the battlefield victories that were necessary for their survival. Faced with the possibility of losing control over the trade routes and fish production areas that were so important for their economic prosperity, the Anlo sought new approaches and tactics by the end of the first half of the eighteenth century. As a result, in 1769, when the Anlos successfully defeated the Adas and gained control over the lower Volta, they attributed the victory not to the gods of those who held the most important political, religious, and military roles in the society but rather to a stranger god called Nyigbla. Their support for this new god so threatened the political and religious establishment in Anlo that the latter attempted to force the god and its priest out of Anlo, but the popularity of the deity among the general population prevented this. Eventually the political and religious leadership in Anlo accepted the Nyigbla priest as a member of the governing council, and they allocated to him land in Anloga on which he could erect a shrine to Nyigbla. By the beginning of the nineteenth century, Nyigbla was the undisputed national war god of the entire Anlo polity, as the following 1853 account indicates:

Nyigbla is . . . a personified revelation of Mawu [the supreme deity]. He is the most intimate servant of Mawu, charged with the most important mission. He procures the fertile rain for the earth, the blessing of fertility for the country. He especially rules over the fate of human beings, the wars on earth and supervises them. . . . They imagine him riding on a horse. . . . The horse appears as a symbol of war. If the "shooting-star" appears, it is Nyigbla who has sat down on a horse in order to carry out important business or to amuse himself in the vast universe. If it is raining, they say . . . "Nyigbla is walking about." . . . If there is a continuous lack of rain, which is a frequent plague of all African regions, they have to regain Nyigbla's goodwill. If he refuses rain for too long a time, they believe they must have committed a

great sin and his disgust must be resting upon them. Then, his priests and
the King of Anlo send messengers to Notsie to get advice from the "god's
place." . . . Medicinal herbs are brought and put in water, with which the
whole people have to bathe so as to rid themselves of their sins in order to
appease Nyigbla. . . . This is the oldest, greatest and formerly the only inter-
mediary god of the Anlo. He is still their principal god and only he is worshipped as a national god. The Anlo insist that they have seen him commanding them, and they insist that no enemy can stand in front of him. . . .
Once a year, they celebrate him with a feast. Everyone in the entire Anlo
nation smears themselves with a certain pollen, and the general procession
marches through and around the towns and villages of the whole country
singing, dancing and drumming.[10]

More important, the fact that the shrine to Nyigbla was located in Anloga
enhanced the image of this town as the most spiritually significant site in the
entire polity. Once the Nyigbla order gained the authority to implement new
laws for the entire polity, it strengthened even further the spiritual connection
that linked the Anlo population to the town. It required every Anlo family
living outside Anloga to bury their dead in the town and to inter the placentas
of all twins born in the polity in Anloga. Every clan (*hlǫ*) was strongly urged
to establish its clan shrine in the town, to which every child born into a *hlǫ*
was to be brought to be ritually connected to both the clan and Anloga. Thus,
by the beginning of the nineteenth century, Anlo had become a center to
which every Anlo citizen was ritually, spiritually, and politically connected, a
place whose meanings were soon to be challenged with the arrival of European missionaries.

ANLOGA AND ITS ENCOUNTER WITH CHRISTIANITY

When the Bremen Mission first established itself in Anlo, its missionaries opened two stations: the first in Keta in 1853 and the second in Anyako
in 1857, each with its own school. Attracting converts and students for the
school proved initially quite difficult. Gradually, however, a number of Anlos
accepted the faith, and attendance in the schools expanded as both Christians
and non-Christians began sending their children for education with the mission so that they could take advantage of the opportunities that accompanied
Western schooling. Many used this new knowledge primarily to benefit their
family business concerns and to work more effectively with the British colonial government. But others—all men[11]—strengthened their attachment to
the mission not only by attending primary and middle school but also by en-
rolling in the seminary (relocated from the interior to the Anlo towns of Anyako in 1869 and then Keta in 1875), where they were trained as "native assistants." In that capacity, they taught the European missionaries the Ewe

Figure 16. Native assistant Besa and his wife at the Bremen School in Woe.
Photo entitled "die Schule in We mit den Gehuelfen Besa und Frau," in G. Mueller,
Geschichte der Ewe Mission (Bremen: Bremen Mission, 1904), p. 221.

language, assisted with the production of Ewe-language hymns and the Ewe
Bible, helped spread the gospel by serving as interpreters, and eventually returned to their home villages to preach and open schools.[12] Their services
were absolutely essential: the average European missionary had only a scant
knowledge of the Ewe language, and many died from the unfamiliar disease
environment.[13] Thus, of the eight towns in which the Bremen Mission operated schools in 1903, six of these towns were able to offer Western education
to their residents only because of initiatives taken by local Anlo Christians.

As the efforts to recruit Christians gained increasing success by the beginning of the twentieth century, the indifference and amusement[14] with which
the average Anlo initially greeted the mission's religious goals developed into
hostility. Direct attacks on the European missionaries were discouraged by
the heavy fines imposed by Anlo political authorities and the fear of arrest
and imprisonment by the British colonial government. But local Anlos who
had converted to Christianity and who also carried the Christian message to
towns and villages throughout Anlo gained no such automatic protection. In
some of the more mild incidents, Christians only had to suffer public humilia-
tion, as one missionary recounted:

> [Some in Anyako] mocked [the Christians] with the words, "You are hungry,
> that is why you wish to sell your children to the missionaries." . . . [In addi-
> tion], the priests knew the beliefs of the young and old and told them of the

horrible things that would happen if they went to a church service or to the
school: "You are enraging the gods."[15]

But more serious assaults were also known to occur. One of the most well
known involved the Yewe religious order, a powerful and popular traditional
religious group that saw its very existence threatened as members who left the
order to become Christians began to reveal some of its most hidden practices
and beliefs in order to undermine its status within the polity. One such convert, Stephano Kwadzo Afelevo, was attacked and severely beaten in 1881, and
when this failed to intimidate him, efforts were made to take away his land
and to destroy his ability to work by burning his canoe and his seine fishing
net. This incident was probably the most frightening experience that the mission and its supporters had suffered up to that point. Even though they sought
protection from the British colonial government, the mission was still forced
to transfer Afelevo from Woe to the town of Wuti for his own safety. Yet for
the missionaries and the local Christians in Anlo, it was Anloga that loomed
far larger. As one of the most populous towns in the area, it was the "bastion
of heathendom" in the district. It still had no school, no church, and no resident Christian community fifty years after the Bremen Mission established its
first station. And when citizens of the town did eventually seek to bring the
new religion and a school to the town, the mission saw the most sustained and
violent opposition to its activities.

Initial efforts to bring Christianity and education to Anloga began around
1900 with Anloga resident Tay Agbota. Sent to attend the Bremen Mission
school in Keta, he returned home and began to give free private lessons in
reading and writing to seventeen other young men from the town. These
classes were short-lived, however, because Agbota's maternal uncle objected to
him engaging in an activity that not only brought no direct economic benefit
to the family but took away from the time Tay could have been engaged in
work that produced an income. Only in 1903, therefore, did the young students
find another teacher, Adade Setudo, who had been enrolled at the school in
Keta but who had to bring an abrupt end to his studies when his father refused
to spend any more money on his schooling. Determined to continue their education, but fearful that they would lose a second teacher, the students contracted with Adade to teach them for a shilling each a month, a fee even
higher than the one Adade had requested.[16] Unlike Tay, however, Adade did
not confine his teaching to reading and writing. Instead, he emphasized learn-
ing the Christian scriptures. This immediately provoked the ire of the political
and religious authorities in Anloga, as Adade indicated in a letter he sent to
the Bremen Mission:

> The king and the village elders do not like my attempt to start a school.
> They caused much unrest for my father and my brothers, so that they would,

in turn, forbid me to work at the school. But I did not pay any attention to them. I answered their every word with speeches and responses. At times, the elders sent drunken, evil people to take away the students' books to burn them. They accused me of luring the missionaries into the town against the will of the great god Nyigbla. They also sometimes hired young people to befriend me so that they could then put something [poison] into my schnapps when there was an opportunity to do so.[17]

It was this opposition that forced Adade to relocate his school to the outskirts of town, where he believed he would be beyond the reach of the authorities in Anloga. This was not to be the case, however. The individual who had offered Adade a portion of his farmland on which to relocate the school was Dezo Akpoxolo, the highest-ranking member and therefore the head (*dzogbana*) of the Afa divination religious order in Anloga.[18] Akpoxolo was prepared to do this, according to Anlo oral traditions, because of the bitter disappointment he felt after the death of his daughter. As remembered by a number of elders in Anloga, he tried everything in his power when his daughter fell ill. He appealed to the gods; he invited those associated with other deities to try; he invited a renowned herbalist from Atito to come heal his daughter. Every effort failed. It was at this point—when his daughter died—that Akpoxolo is said to have lost faith in the belief system that he had followed his entire life. Nothing had worked; all the sacrifices, all the consultations had been for naught. Akpoxolo decided to become a Christian. And it was this that renewed the deep anxiety Anloga leaders had first felt when Adade had opened his school within the town. If Akpoxolo, as the most knowledgeable person associated with the divination system that every Anlo citizen used to identify the reincarnated and to communicate with those spiritual forces that could determine one's daily fate, abandoned his belief and became a Christian, many others would follow. The very foundation upon which political and religious authority rested would be greatly undermined.[19] Relocation, therefore, did not bring an end to the harassment. Rather, the efforts to destroy the school only escalated. The elders of the town passed a law stipulating that anyone who visited the school would have to pay to the *awọamefia* a cow, a nanny goat, a sheep, and 37.50 marks.[20] Others attempted to poison students by dumping dead frogs in the wells from which they drew their drinking water. Still others set fire to the walls of the school, which were made of woven coconut-palm fronds.[21] Under this kind of pressure, Adade was forced to discontinue the school. Thereafter, he held only Bible-reading and prayer sessions on Wednesday and Sunday evenings, but even these sessions were threatened when the elders ordered the arrest of those who attended the sessions. The accusation: the continued holding of even Bible-reading and prayer sessions had so angered the god Nyigbla that he had destroyed with fire 180 houses in Anloga, fully one-third of the town. No school was to be held, and anyone who continued to attend sessions was to be arrested. Thus, after five years of struggle, from 1900 to 1905, Anloga still remained without a school, without a church, without a resident Christian community. The leadership of Anlo and the vast majority of the residents of the town understood Anloga to be the one place where Christianity could not be allowed to take hold. It was the religious center of the Anlo social and political system, and it was the home of Nyigbla. And if the very belief systems that had stood at the heart of Anlo culture since the seventeenth century were to be undermined, what future was there for the polity as they knew it?

Christianity and Western education did arrive, however, within a decade of Tay Agbota's efforts. One of the critical factors that contributed to this change was the death of the *awǫamefia,* Amedo Kpegla. Remembered as an inveterate opponent of European influence in the region, he was able to rally enough support among those elders who were of the same opinion to keep at bay others who were much more supportive of the efforts of missionaries and the British colonial government to bring "civilization" to Anlo. His death in 1906 ushered in a period of openness to change. Immediately after Kpegla's funeral, the elders and chiefs from all over the Anlo district who had gathered for the event announced that they would allow the establishment of a church and a school in Anloga. This decision and the subsequent installation in 1907 of Fia Sri II, a product of the Bremen Mission school in Keta, signaled a major effort on the part of the Anlo leadership to alter the image of Anloga. The town was no longer to be seen as the center of opposition to Christian missionary and British colonial influence. Rather, it was to lead the way—under the direction of Fia Sri II—to a more enlightened Anlo. Thus, it was Sri II who refused—with the support of others on his advisory council—to undergo all the installation rituals that were designed to infuse his body with such spiritual power that his physical presence could harm others who gazed at him. And it was Sri who also refused to remain secluded in his home in Anloga as had been required of previous *awǫamefiawo.* Instead he traveled freely, undermining belief in the spiritual authority of the office and its occupant. He challenged those spiritual practices associated with the Keta Lagoon that he felt stood in the way of the economic development of the district. He insisted that Anloga be rebuilt according to "modern" city-planning principles when the entire town burned to the ground in 1911. He did this all with the support of a majority of the Anlo chiefs who served as his advisors.

Yet even this level of support among the political elite in Anlo did not destroy the sense among many that as the traditional spiritual center of the polity, Anloga should not go the way of other towns. For these individuals, the *awǫamefia* was supposed to rule in concert with the priest of Nyigbla, as had been the case since the late eighteenth century, and if Togbui Nyigbla objected to certain developments, the health and safety of the entire polity would be

Figure 17. Fia Amedor Kpegla, seated behind the boy.
Photo entitled "Oberhauptling und der oberpriestes
Kpegla, Anloga," Staatsarchiv Bremen, 7, 1025/107.

threatened if such objections were not heeded. Thus, when Anloga citizens began erecting a school, they found that their building had been set on fire by
persons or powers unknown, even though the project had been approved by
the political leadership of the polity. And when the Bremen Mission at Keta
sent iron roofing sheets to be used in the construction of a new building, the
Nyigbla priest protested that when Nyigbla walked to the sea, the reflection
from the sheets would bother his eyes. Those working on the building continued their construction until the night of April 15th, 1907, when a section of
the swish walls that had just been made ready to support the roofing sheets
inexplicably collapsed. On June 15th, during heavy rains, the remaining walls
fell as well.[22] The Nyigbla priest claimed it was the work of Togbui Nyigbla;
others said it was the work of mortal men. Undeterred and perhaps determined to prove the greater power of their Christian god, Anloga's Christians
changed the location of the site on which they hoped to erect the school. Instead of rebuilding on the outskirts of town, where they had retreated in 1903,
they relocated to the area much closer to the town that others believed was

haunted by the spirits of those who had died "bad" deaths. Completion of their school in 1907 and their obvious success in warding off the power of Nyigbla and the hostile spirits that they had disturbed did not end the harassment, however. As Robert Afetogbo, whose mother in 1909 was among the first to be baptized in Anloga, recounted, individuals still suffered tremendous ostracism. "Before the baptism, my mother would carry a large pot to collect water and the other women would help her lift it onto her head. After the baptism, no one would help her and she was forced to use a much smaller pot. After the baptism, they paraded through the town and people threw stones at them. One hit my mother leaving a large scar thereafter on her forehead."[23]

Opposition to the advance of Christianity cooled after 1909, when the first Anloga citizens became Christians and when Togbui Sri II not only joined the worshippers but openly opposed many of the ritual injunctions that the priest of Nyigbla attempted to impose on the entire polity.[24] Efforts by traditional religious leaders and followers to maintain some influence within the polity and to gain respect from those who had converted to Christianity never disappeared completely, however. Some traditional believers modified the approach they took to their religion by incorporating elements from Christianity into their beliefs and practices. Others made public efforts to show respect for Christian practices to encourage a similar approach to their own beliefs. But tensions remained. And it was these tensions—centered once again in Anloga—that erupted into violence when different understandings about the relationship between religion and politics impinged upon Anloga's status within the polity.

ANLOGA AND ITS ENCOUNTER WITH BRITISH COLONIALISM

Traditionally, Anloga served not only as the religious center of the Anlo polity, it was also the political capital. Anloga was the town in which most meetings that concerned the entire district took place, where sub-chiefs were installed, where the *awǫamefia* resided, where the Nyigbla priest had his headquarters. With the establishment of colonial rule in Anlo, however, Anloga became increasingly marginalized despite the protests of its citizens. Togbui Sri II shifted his primary residence and office to Keta in the mid-1930s and limited his visits to Anloga. The majority of the local council meetings, chaired by Sri II, took place in Keta. This latter town was also the local headquarters of the British colonial government. It was in Keta that decisions were made by Fia Sri II and the "native council," the tribunal of chiefs that came from both the Anlo polity and from the various divisions that comprised Greater Anlo. It was this tribunal, after being authorized to do so by the colonial government's 1936 Native Treasuries Ordinance, that determined the kinds of taxes that were to be imposed on the local population. These moneys were supposed to be used for the development of the entire district, but many in Anloga felt that the town had been greatly neglected in terms of public works projects. Much of the revenues collected, it was thought, had gone into the pockets of particular individuals and/or were spent only on projects in Keta. Anloga's perception that it was being marginalized was not unfounded. More important, however, are the reasons for this development. According to minutes of the Anlo State Council (an advisory body to Fia Sri II composed of chiefs from both the Anlo polity and the surrounding districts, which the British colonial government had administratively constituted as Greater Anlo), many, including the *awǫamefia,* felt that Anloga—as the traditional religious center in the district—was "unprogressive" when it came to supporting the "modern" development of the district. As a result, chiefs from the other divisions within Greater Anlo who supported taxation schemes to improve roads, water supplies, and sanitation, for example, often refused to attend council meetings if they were held in the traditional political and religious center of the polity.[25] Anloga residents saw the situation differently, however. They stated that their opposition to the tax had nothing to do with a desire to live in the past. Rather, they simply distrusted those in Keta to distribute the tax revenues fairly, an opinion they voiced quite often and vociferously, as noted by British colonial District Commissioner T. A. Mead in 1945:

> Native society here has completely broken down. The people in many places are on terms of open enmity with their chiefs and *nowhere* is the relationship between the chiefs and people what it should be. At public meetings, young men of influence . . . address themselves to the elders with complete contempt, threaten them with destoolment and even with physical violence if they do not yield to their wishes.

> The people of Anloga are intensely irritated by the failure of the Awoame Fia to live in their town as he should, and as a result, his influence there may be described as negligible. . . .

> The reason originally given to the people of Anloga for the Awoame Fia's residence in Keta was, I am told, that it was desirable that the District Commissioner and the Paramount Chief should live in the same town so that they could keep in touch without inconvenience. Since this has been going on here for some years, it should occasion us no wonder that the Chiefs are regarded as government agents and that the people should have no confidence in them.[26]

These verbal forms of discontent had no impact, however, and tensions finally boiled over into a deadly riot in 1953. To fully understand why this occurred, it is important to review the events leading up to the violence.

In 1949, a commission appointed by the colonial government chaired by Sir J. H. Coussey recommended that the governance structures that then operated in the Gold Coast Colony be reorganized to encourage greater local self-governance. Attempts to implement the recommendations in Anlo immediately brought into the open a number of internal conflicts and divisions within the area, but of concern here are those that involve the question of Anloga's status in the polity. Anloga residents decided to resist efforts by the local governance structure in Keta to levy a head tax of two shillings on all Anlos.

Opposition is said to have come from all quarters, "literates and illiterates" alike,[27] and to have become so strong by 1951 that the citizens of Anloga resorted to the use of the Nyiko drums.[28] To those who opposed the tax, the beating of the Nyiko drums meant that the new proposed tax was banned. No one was to discuss the issue again unless they were prepared to court the power of the particular gods that were believed to manifest themselves in the drums.[29] Immediately thereafter, the taxation issue no longer figured in the deliberations of the Anlo Council. But it wasn't long before it reemerged again in a way that illustrates the extent to which the citizens of Anloga refused to separate the religious from the political and instead continued to identify their town as the sacred governmental center of the polity.

In December 1952, the colonial government subdivided the Anlo District into local councils, as recommended by the Coussey Commission. These included the Keta Urban Council and the South Anlo Council. The latter was established as a separate body from the Keta Council in response to the citizens of Anloga who had insisted that the town be designated as the headquarters of its own local authority district so that it could avoid being dictated to and taxed by officials based in Keta. The elected members of this council included many of the literate individuals among the population who had worked together with others in the town to ban the 2-shilling head tax. But once they assumed office, they quickly came to realize that they were unable to pursue the particular projects they deemed important for the district, the same projects that had been ignored under the former Native Authority Council. As Sophia Amable indicated in her study of this particular period in Anlo history:

> Each local council had to cater for itself, including paying its staff and financing its projects. The new councilors realized that the council could no longer depend on market tolls, court fines and fees as sources of revenue. [But] the councilors' attempts to renew the suggestion of payment of a direct tax or levy [caused] unrest and a split within the Anlo Youth Association [the group that had spearheaded the Anloga opposition to the head tax]. . . . Payment of the levy was to some an attempt at exploitation and economic coercion. To others it was a civic duty which patriotic citizens were obliged to render. Those who accepted payment of the levy were branded as Dzoemiduawo: "collect-and-let-us-squander."[30]

The taxation issue came to a head on January 1953, when the town exploded in a riot. Two men were killed, and two others were kidnapped and hidden in the Nyiko grove, the forest that held the shrine to Nyigbla, the Anlo's war god, the forest where the drums were beaten banning all discussion about and payment of the tax in the entire polity. Rioters also destroyed the recently founded Zion Secondary School and razed with fire fifty-five houses, all belonging to supporters of the tax, all in Anloga.[31] Of significance here is the fact that many who opposed the tax from the villages and hamlets outside the town rushed to the Anlo capital to demonstrate their opposition. All came to Anloga. It was in Anloga that the riot occurred. It was in Anloga that the rioters killed the two tax supporters. That all occurred in this single town was no accident. In the minds of almost everyone in the district, Anloga stood as the center of the polity. Even though the Nyigbla as the national war god no longer commanded the respect it had in the past, and even though colonial government sanitation policies, educational efforts, and the spread of Christianity was bringing to an end the practice of taking to Anloga all newborns, the placentas of twins, and the bodies of the Anlo dead, every Anlo nevertheless understood and remembered the historical significance of Anloga as a sacred center. Thus, it was in Anloga that protests and then finally riots broke out as residents and non-residents alike protested the town's marginalization and the fact that their own chiefs had ignored the ritual ban (issued from Anloga) on discussing and paying the tax.

These events forced the British colonial government and many Anlo supporters of the tax to recognize the extent to which decisions about the political and economic affairs in Anlo could not ignore the spiritually based political significance of Anloga. Fia Sri responded by encouraging his fellow chiefs on the Anlo District Council to continue to hold meetings in Anloga despite the riot. But the British colonial government took a very different approach.[32] Expressing no interest in being conciliatory, it decided to effect a major redefinition of the town by disconnecting it from its image as a sacred site. The government brought men incarcerated in the Keta prison into the town, who then proceeded to destroy every tree, every bush, and every man-made structure in the grove that had once been on the site where the Nyiko custom and the Nyigbla shrine were located. In essence, they obliterated all that had once physically symbolized some of the most potent spiritual forces that existed in the town. In the grove's place, they erected a police station: a symbol of the triumph of their rational colonial order over the superstition-ridden and lawless town of Anloga.

These actions were not without consequences. In the wake of the grove's destruction, much changed in Anloga. The annual rites for the god Nyigbla—which at one time involved residents from every town and village in the polity—could no longer be performed in the old location. Instead, both the rites and

Figure 18. The Nyiko grove in Anloga, 1928. Notice the
man standing at the entrance.
Photo entitled "Eingang zum Fetish-hain in Anloga,"
Staatsarchiv Bremen, 7, 1025/105.

the shrine to Nyigbla had to be moved farther out of town to another grove,
but even this stand of trees was razed in the early 1960s with the establishment
of the Anlo Secondary School. During this same period, Togbui Adeladza II,
the successor to Fia Sri II, opted to confine his participation in the rituals for
Nyigbla (the one god that had once united all Anlos from the town of Anloga)
to those that took place during the national festival, Hogbeza. As the town
grew and expanded, it became by the 1990s the home not only of a public library, several primary schools, and two secondary schools but also of a number of churches that were new to the town, such as the Church of the Lord
Brotherhood, the African Methodist Episcopal Zion Church, the Calvary Ministry, the Salvation Army, and the New Apostolic Church. Thus, efforts by the
colonial government officials, missionary groups, and local residents in the
town and the district to alter Anloga's image as a traditional sacred site seem
to have had a tremendous influence on the town. No longer defined solely by
its former status as the religious and traditional political capital of Anlo, resi-

Figure 19. The police station erected on the grounds of the former Nyiko grove.
Photo by author.

dents understand the town to be a fairly cosmopolitan place in terms of religious activity. Why then did violence erupt yet again in Anloga in 1987 and 1996, precipitated by the refusal of the Church of Pentecost to abide by a prohibition on drumming declared by the adherents of Nyigbla, when this church had been doing the same since 1948? And why did the violence erupt in Anloga when Church of Pentecost chapels existed elsewhere in Anlo? To answer these questions, it is important first to review a number of developments that occurred after the 1953 riot.

POST-COLONIAL ANLOGA

Immediately after the 1953 riot, tensions ran very high in Anloga. Those who had been supporters of the tax remained bitter for years about the property losses they suffered, while opponents of the tax harbored feelings of being betrayed by the supporters and remained fearful of government retribution for the damage done. Each group also refused to attend the funerals of the other, a serious indication of the hard feelings that remained.[33] Yet efforts were made to reconcile the groups and to construct a common understanding about the significance of Anlo that was acceptable to all, Christian and non-Christian, educated and non-educated alike. For example, District Commissioner Aiden, who was appointed by the newly elected Nkrumah government of Ghana in 1954, made conscious efforts and was largely successful in healing the rift between the supporters and the opponents of the tax. In 1962, when the Hogbetsotso Festival was first organized, these reconciliation efforts continued with the holding of a Nugbidodo ritual[34] to heal on a polity-wide level any rifts between individuals, families, and clans that might hinder the existence of good relations within the polity. Also included were both traditional religious and Christian ceremonies, where participation was open to all regardless of religious faith. And when tensions did arise, significant efforts were made to effect reconciliation between the contending parties or to encourage tolerance. Central to this effort was T. S. A. Togbo, a businessman, an advocate of modern development, and an advisor first to Fia Sri II and then to his successor, Fia Adeladza II. Togobo was a strong supporter in the late 1940s of the effort to move the Anlo State Council meetings from Keta to Anloga. He consciously respected the customs and rites associated with the traditional religious orders in Anloga even as he remained a prominent member of the Evangelical Presbyterian Church. According to some, for example, it was Togobo who used his influence with the paramount chief's council to urge others to tolerate the activities of the Church of Pentecost despite their willful defiance of every request made by the Nyigbla religious order that all in the town refrain from drumming during a particular period in the year. In 1984, however, Togobo fell gravely ill and died. Tensions and conflicts resurfaced shortly thereafter when the Church of Pentecost again ignored the ban on drumming imposed by the traditional religious authorities. This time, however, on the order of the paramount chief and his council, the drums were seized and then released to the church with a warning not to repeat their actions again. The following year, in 1985, Pentecost members again defied the ban. This time their drums were seized and retained and Pentecost members were prohibited from worshipping outside their homes. By 1987, the church had collected enough funds to purchase another set of drums, and they again defied the ban. It was at this time that a number of individuals within the community—without the approval or knowledge of the paramount chief and his council—took it upon themselves to torch the Church of Pentecost chapels in Anloga. By 1996, when yet another confrontation occurred, it involved not only the Church of Pentecost but a number of other Protestant and Catholic churches as well. What was going on?

Discussion with the different parties often yields conflicting answers. In 1987, for example, Togbui Awadzi indicated that during Fia Sri II's reign (1907–1959), an agreement had been reached between the Nyigbla religious order and the Anlo Christians to end the conflicts that had gone on for so long between the two groups. This agreement stated that any ban on drumming (and any other loud noise-making) ordered by the Nyigbla order would apply to the older sections of town, while the Bremen Mission and the Church of

Figure 20. T. S. A. Togobo.
From the author's collection.

Pentecost (both initially located in the newer sections of town that had been opened for residential development by Sri after a 1911 fire destroyed virtually the entire town) could ring their church bell and play their drums, respectively, in the new township.[35] In other words, according to Awadzi, the town was divided into Christian and Nyigbla religious jurisdictions, and the current problems arose only because the Nyigbla order "attempted to re-impose the ban throughout the town."[36]

Others, however, speculated that it was with the death of Togobo that problems began. According to this view, those on the paramount chief's council who were hard-line supporters of the traditional religious orders were able to gain ascendancy in the council with Togobo's demise. Once this ascendancy was achieved, they were able to persuade their fellow council members that it was time to be less tolerant of those who showed disrespect for traditional beliefs. Still others, leading elders of the town, de-emphasized the politico-religious politics on the council and stressed instead the notion that those who attacked the Christians at Gbakute did so (without their permission or approval) because of what they saw as the need to maintain the cultural heritage

of Anlo in the face of an increasingly insistent evangelical Christian movement. From their perspective, if Nyigbla adherents could not demand respect
for their rites in Anloga, then where could they do so? As linguist and elder
of the Adzovia clan Klobotua Efia Nunyanu stated:

> Within every society there are rules and regulations that bind all together
> for a future purpose. . . . It is customary in this town that at certain seasons,
> particular actions are not permitted. . . . When we [the traditional authori-
> ties] started our celebrations, they refused to stop their drumming. . . . The
> church was ridiculing [the Nyigbla] customs and ridiculing [the Nyigbla ad-
> herents] because they were fetish people. . . . Our celebrations will make the
> town good even for themselves, but they refused, so we said they should take
> their religion out of town.[37]

This concern about respect being shown for traditional cultural and religious
practices, especially by those who live, work, and worship in Anloga, is also
evident in the recent efforts to keep the Church of Pentecost from rebuilding
their chapel at another location in town. After the first chapel was destroyed
by fire, a member of the affected church, D. D. Deku, donated some of his own
land in the center of Anloga to the church. By the end of 1996, however, they
had yet to complete the building because the Traditional Council had indicated that they wished to use the site for a new post office.[38] From the perspective of the Church of Pentecost, of course, the Traditional Council's interest in
the land as a possible site for a post office was just another effort to drive
them out of town.

These explanations about the precipitating events and the ultimate cause
of the conflict between the supporters of the traditional believers and the
Church of Pentecost differ markedly. Yet one theme emerges quite clearly. For
all, Anloga remains a site of tremendous significance despite the changes that
have been wrought in the town by Christian missionary influence and British
colonialism. It is still remembered as the home of Nyigbla, a religious order
that continues to be given respect despite its decline in popularity and power,
because for many the town of Anloga, through its association with Nyigbla,
represents a past that is still a present reality, a past that needs to be remembered and respected because it remains central to Anlo's cultural identity. It
is for this same reason that Anloga remains important to the Christian denominations that worship in the town. Because they battled to enter this community, because it constituted the very heart of Anlo political and religious
culture, they feel that maintaining a presence in Anloga is of paramount importance. The Bremen Mission first achieved this foothold, which allowed
other denominations to enter the town. And for a while, significant efforts
were made to reconstitute the meaning of Anloga so that it was seen as a town
that was not only the center of Anlo traditional culture but was also the home
of many Christian denominations. This peaceful co-existence was disrupted

first in 1953, when a largely Christian and educated group of chiefs and community leaders attempted to ignore the traditional religious ban placed on the effort to collect a 2-shilling tax. It was disrupted again in 1987 and 1996, when the Church of Pentecost incurred the wrath of the supporters of Anlo's traditional religious believers when they refused to show respect (after being requested to do so) for the beliefs that had governed Anlo ritual practices since the late eighteenth century. For the members of this church, however, to observe the ban was tantamount to recognizing the existence and influence of Togbui Nyigbla. For the supporters of the ban, the church's refusal to cease drumming, clapping, and making loud noises during a designated part of the year was reminiscent of the kind of disrespect that the first European missionaries had shown to the culture and traditions of the Anlo. For both, Anloga must necessarily be the site where they express their discontent with the actions of the other. It is this town which is so infused with memories and spiritual meanings that are central to the very identities of those who live in the district. To many it remains the home of Nyigbla and the residence of the *awoamefia,* the political and traditional spiritual leader of the entire polity. It stands at the very heart of Anlo cultural identity. It is here that the Hogbetsotso Festival is held; it is here that traditional religious rituals are held on behalf of the entire polity. For others, however, it continues to be "a bastion of heathendom," where the "worship of idols, shrines, voodoo, etc." generates a wealth of devilish thoughts and actions that must be opposed at every opportunity.[39] Thus, it is when these divergent meanings dominate the memories of those in Anlo and Anloga, when newer meanings that were forged in the effort to bring reconciliation within the polity are forgotten, that the town becomes once again contested terrain.

Conclusion
Explaining Cultural Adaptation and Epistemological Abandonment

IN 1985, DAVID WILLIAM COHEN challenged historians of Africa to do more than chart the history of Africa in terms of its responses to large world processes. They should also concentrate at least equally on exploring those intimate areas of social life within African communities that shifted and changed in response to local forces, changes which then intersected with the large structural forces to create social histories particular to the communities studied.[1] Many responded to Cohen's challenge. Countless studies have documented the ways in which local concerns have so entangled global processes that only by focusing on this entanglement can one truly understand the power and the limits of both the global and the local. Those historians who have taken this approach, however, have tended to emphasize the local alone. They have demonstrated the extent to which local communities created their own modernities. They have documented how these communities have drawn upon selective aspects of the West and their own past beliefs, redefining them according to largely local concerns and interests and then using them to structure everyday life. This approach has helped counter the notion that the West so dominated African societies that previous ways of knowing and operating were rendered irrelevant and useless for modern times. But insofar as these studies also tend to acknowledge only implicitly the power of the colonizing West to profoundly influence significant aspects of African societies, they fail to address certain questions critical to our understanding of why individuals and communities managed "the modern" as they did.

This study has addressed this questions by not only documenting the full range of ways that colonized Africans managed their colonial encounter with the West, from creatively adapting the old to selectively embracing Western epistemologies; it has also sought to explain why certain modernities developed among the Anlo as they did. It has shown, for example, that despite all the exhortations and initiatives launched by missionary groups and British colonial officers, most in Anlo (Christian and non-Christian, illiterate, semi-literate, and some among the highly literate) have continued to believe in the notion that many different spiritual forces exist in the world (forces other than those defined as God) and that these forces act and can be influenced in ways that affect the lives of the living. The majority of Anlo resident in the area still offer libations to their ancestors. They still pray to those spiritual forces that they believe can influence their destiny. Those with limited formal education, whether Christian or traditional believers, continue to believe in the power of a deceased individual's spirit to harm that person's living spouse. And while most have stopped erecting separate men's and women's bath-houses because they no longer accept the notion that men and sacred objects are disempowered when exposed even visually to the menses produced by women's bodies, I discovered in 1996 that this belief, in modified form, still influences how some handle certain situations. In that year, I was told about a recent incident in which a thief—caught in the act of stealing—was appre-hended by a crowd and forced to drink water recovered from the rinsing of menstrual cloths. Why this response? Those who caught the man decided that the only way to prevent any further stealing on his part was to render him harmless spiritually so that he would be unable to pursue his criminal activi-ties. By forcing him to drink the water containing menstrual blood rather than simply viewing a menstrual cloth, members of the community acted on their belief that the spiritual content of the body was vulnerable to external intervention. These beliefs and practices are not simply retentions, however. They are indeed adaptations. Libations offered to ancestors are no longer of-fered on so regular a basis as they were in the past. They now tend to be confined to special occasions. Where one buries the dead (for those who still believe in reincarnation) is influenced not only by this belief but also by a con-cern to inter the deceased in a location that will not contaminate the water supply. Menstrual blood affects men only when ingested; it no longer affects them when they merely see it.

Equally significant is the fact that while some older beliefs and practices have been modified or abbreviated, others have undergone more profound change. Among many in Anlo, for example, the body is still understood to be subject to external spiritual intervention through sorcery. But belief in the ability of the spiritual aspects of the body to affect the self and others has virtually disappeared. Witchcraft accusations are virtually nonexistent in con-temporary Anlo. Faith in the reality of reincarnation (where the spiritual con-tent of the living body is understood in certain instances to be that which had previously occupied the body of a deceased relative) has become so un-common that diviners complain bitterly about the lack of interest in their services. It is no longer routine for Anlo families to take infants to these prac-titioners in order to determine whose spirit has returned to the family. And the beads once worn to identify such individuals are now defined by most as just one form of traditional costume jewelry worn by anyone whenever they so desire. The notion that the body is an entity subject to chronic illnesses that are largely caused by spiritual forces no longer dominates Anlo understand-ings about the causes of most maladies.

The Anlo have also significantly altered their belief in the ubiquitous character of the spiritual world. Water bodies, once intimately associated with powerful spiritual forces, are now understood by most according to their material characteristics alone. Only the ocean retains an aura of the sacred, and even this understanding (insofar as it refers to a real, as opposed to a symbolic notion of spiritual power) is being challenged by mixed-sex fishing companies that reject the notion that the bodies of their female members will prompt the deities associated with the sea to deny them a bountiful harvest if women actually engage in the act of fishing. Notions about the spiritual characteristics of time no longer inform the actions of many in Anlo. The vast majority of women and children no longer refrain from walking about at night in the streets and lanes of villages and towns. The availability of electricity has meant that nights are no longer so dark, but more important is the fact that the Anlo no longer fear encountering the spirits of the dead, deities, and other spiritual forces that were once said to roam about in such places at that hour. Few are even cognizant of the fact that at one time it was believed that time in this realm existed in reverse for those in the spiritual world. Our night and day was thought to operate simultaneously as the day and night for deities and the spirits of the deceased. Towns such as Notsie and Anloga that once had great spiritual significance and were the site of religious pilgrimages continue to serve as sources of identity, but they are now understood in quite different terms. No longer visited to restore spiritually the political connections that existed between individuals and groups and the deities that were associated with these towns, they serve largely a symbolic function, heralded as important places because they represent a heritage worth remembering or contesting.

These creative adaptations and more profound epistemological shifts are not unique, of course, to the history of the Anlo-Ewe or other colonized African communities. Historians of other world areas have documented the ways in which certain older approaches to knowing and understanding the self and the environment have been retained in modified form while others have been largely supplanted by new forms. The more intriguing question is why people adapted certain aspects of older belief systems and abandoned others. In his influential study *Religion and the Decline of Magic*, Keith Thomas focused on the causes of abandonment. He argued that in Europe—even though "the [contemporary] presence of horoscopes in the newspapers and of lucky mascots in cars is consistent with a recent investigator's conclusion that about a quarter of the population . . . holds a view of the universe which can most properly be designated as magical"—there has nevertheless been a massive decline in such beliefs since the seventeenth century. Thomas documents how the seventeenth-century revolution in European scientific and philosophical thought (with its emphasis on mechanical understandings of the world and its insistence that truths be demonstrated) eventually "percolated down to influence the thought and behaviour of the people at large." He emphasizes the extent to which expanded educational opportunities, the publication of manuals and encyclopaedias, and the development of new technologies, insurance schemes, statistical laws, and the predictive social sciences allowed Europeans to think they could exercise control over what was once seemingly uncontrollable. But for Thomas, the most important factor was the rise of a new emphasis on self-help, a mental shift, as he describes it, that "saw the emergence of a new faith in the potentialities of human initiative," one that looked to human solutions rather than to divine intervention. He discusses, for example, efforts in Tudor England to control poverty and to end vagabondage. Agricultural writers launched campaigns against "the pattern of ancient ignorance," while politicians refused to be led by precedent based on questionable reasoning. According to Thomas, this desire to control without recourse to spiritual intervention became a dominant mode of thinking in early modern Europe. In fact, says Thomas, it became so even before the development of the actual means to control.[2]

While Thomas's proposition—that it was a particular convergence of events that led to a new faith in the power of human initiative—is helpful in understanding certain epistemological shifts, I find his second proposition less useful. If this new faith did indeed gain in popularity, certainly this occurred because the faith itself was reinforced by at least the perception of success. Only after having gained some sense that human initiative alone was capable of achieving a particular goal would most individuals then have an interest in or the confidence to expand into other areas, to broaden their efforts to control their lives without resorting to the spiritual world. This was certainly the case in Anlo. Nineteenth-century Anlo medical practices included an understanding of disease in which causation was attributed to both natural conditions and spiritual forces. Families were expected to control common diseases by administering certain natural remedies, and even those diseases attributed to spiritual forces—for example smallpox—were handled in ways that sought not only to influence the deity that caused the disease but also to control its spread by engaging in age-old public health campaigns to rid towns and villages of the physical dirt that was thought to be as much a source of disease as spiritual causes.

This desire to control was then given new impetus when the Anlo embraced new technologies and beliefs that they believed could (and in many instances did indeed) improve their lives. Constructing wells in homes and on farms (and ignoring those deities that they had once defined as central to the availability of drinking water in the area) made potable water more readily and easily available. Clearing naturally occurring dams (that some argued were created by the gods and which should therefore not be removed) facilitated the movement of goods and people in the area and increased prosperity within the polity because it opened the waterways traders used to link the area to commercial districts to the west. The fact that no divine retribution followed after they began ignoring the deities associated with the potable water ponds of Anlo, that no disaster befell those who cleared the dams, gave further impetus to Anlo efforts to control the material world without always making recourse to the spiritual world when faced with seemingly inexplicable or intractable problems. Thus, it was this embrace of new possibilities; this openness to the notion that perhaps one could indeed control place, space, and the body in ways not previously known; and the perceived successes achieved from taking this approach that eventually had profound consequences in Anlo for previously held notions about the material and spiritual worlds.

The fact that these new ways of understanding and interacting with the self and the world entered Anlo in the context of colonialism is equally important. Faced with a frontal assault launched by Christian missionaries and the British colonial government, the Anlo resisted and appropriated, but they also adjusted, creatively adapting not only their beliefs and practices to the "modern" but also the very terms by which they defined social status. Western education and belief in Christianity (two attributes that most often went hand in hand) became prestigious social markers. Those who had attended missionary schools and who had also obviously mastered "the trappings of civilization" were the ones whom families and communities most often elevated to positions of public responsibility. Knowledge of English and experience with colonial institutions began to outweigh other formerly central concerns, such as one's social standing within one's family, when elders had to select a candidate for a chieftaincy position. "The educated [and necessarily Christian] class in Anlo [became] the leaders of fashion."[3] By the 1960s, families no longer rubbed a bride with the spiritually and symbolically significant powder known as *eto* to mark her body as now being under the legal control of the groom. All, whether Christian or traditional believer, had begun to use the wedding ring, stripped of any spiritual significance, to symbolize the legality of the marriage.[4] Today, clan taboos are regularly ignored as superstitious, just as the clan itself, a social group held together by both material and spiritual linkages, has declined significantly in importance to everyday life.[5] Colonialism forced a selective abandonment of old epistemologies, but in doing so it also generated in Anlo a refusal to abandon all beliefs and practices that were vehemently condemned by missionaries and colonizers alike.

Many authors who focus on the continued existence of older religious beliefs (even if in modified form) emphasize the extent to which these beliefs have been retained not only as a form of resistance to power imposed but because they have also offered a way of understanding the new. In his study *The*

Modernity of Witchcraft, Peter Geschiere states that witchcraft and sorcery remain so important in many modern contexts in present-day Africa because they have helped explain the shocking inequalities that have developed in more recent times. He notes, for example, that the changes wrought by colonialism and post-colonial political and economic developments created a gap "between the familiar realities of the domestic community on the one hand and . . . unprecedented possibilities for enrichment [and new forms of impersonal] dependency . . . on the other." Belief in witchcraft has served "to personalize these shocking inequalities."[6] Birgit Meyer takes a similar approach in her analyses of Ewe notions about the Devil. She argues that ideas about the Devil were initially obtained by the Ewe from the Bremen Mission but that the Ewe quickly modified these ideas and made them their own because they "[provided] people with the possibility to reflect upon and fantasize about the problems and opportunities of their integration into a global modern political economy."[7] The same can be said for Anlo reconfigurations of certain nineteenth-century beliefs about sacred sites. Modified to conform with more contemporary understandings about self and the world, these newer versions of older beliefs gave meaning to the mysteries of everyday life. Thus, in addition to their openness to different approaches to interacting with the self and the world around them, in addition to the power of the colonial and post-colonial state to force a rethinking about the material and the spiritual, the Anlo have also been influenced by their own desire to make sense of themselves and the world in which they live. It is this desire, this felt need to fill the cracks, fissures, and chasms that had developed (as had never happened to this extent before) in their own understandings of self and the world that prompted the Anlo to create their own modernities. These modernities include both adaptations of the old and more profound epistemological shifts. They are modernities that have been constructed by individuals, groups, and entire communities for their own particular needs. They are modernities that have arisen as part of both a new consensus and ongoing contestations about meaning and memory.

Notes

Introduction: Managing the Modern

1. On colonialism's challenge to previous ways of understanding race, nationality, class, sexuality, and gender among colonizer cultures, see, for example, David Trotter, "Colonial Subjects," *Critical Quarterly* 32, no. 3 (1990): 3–37; Ann Laura Stoler, "Carnal Knowledge and Imperial Power: Gender, Race and Morality in Colonial Asia," in *Gender at the Crossroads of Knowledge,* ed. Michaela di Leonardo (Berkeley: University of California Press, 1991), 51–101; Lora Widenthal, "Race, Gender and Citizenship in the German Colonial Empire," in *Tensions of Empire: Colonial Cultures in a Bourgeois World,* ed. Frederick Cooper and Ann Laura Stoler (Berkeley: University of California Press, 1997), 263–283; Ann Laura Stoler, "Sexual Affronts and Racial Frontiers: European Identities and the Cultural Politics of Exclusion in Colonial South East Asia," in *Tensions of Empire,* 198–237; Warwick Anderson, "The Trespass Speaks: White Masculinity and the Colonial Breakdown," *American Historical Review* 102, no. 5 (1997): 1343–1370; and Anne McClintock, *Imperial Leather: Race, Gender, and Sexuality in the Colonial Context* (New York: Routledge, 1995). On the questioning of dominant Western medical practices within the West generated, in part, by the colonial encounter, see Ashis Nandy and Shiv Visvanathan, "Modern Medicine and Its Non-Modern Critics: A Study in Discourse," in *Dominating Knowledge: Development, Culture, and Resistance,* ed. Frédérique Apffel Marglin and Stephen A. Marglin (Oxford: Clarendon, 1990), 145–184. On the reevaluation of their religious beliefs, see Webb Keane, "Materialism, Missionaries and Modern Subjects in Colonial Indonesia," in *Conversion to Modernities: The Globalization of Christianity,* ed. Peter van der Veer (New York: Routledge, 1996), 137–170.

2. Jean Comaroff and John Comaroff, "Introduction," in *Modernity and Its Malcontents: Ritual and Power in Postcolonial Africa,* ed. Jean Comaroff and John Comaroff (Chicago: University of Chicago Press, 1993), xi–xii.

3. Dilip Parameshwar Gaonkar, "On Alternative Modernities," *Public Culture* II, no. 1 (1999): 2.

4. See, for example, Goankar, "On Alternative Modernities"; and Kwame Gyekye, *Tradition and Modernity: Philosophical Reflections on the African Experience* (New York: Oxford University Press, 1997), 263–271; Charles Piot, *Remotely Global: Village Modernity in West Africa* (Chicago: University of Chicago Press, 1999), Chapter 8; John L. and Jean Comaroff, *Of Revelation and Revolution: The Dialectics of Modernity on a South African Frontier,* vol. 2 (Chicago: University of

Chicago Press, 1997); Arjun Apparadurai, *Modernity at Large: Cultural Dimensions of Globalization* (Minneapolis: University of Minnesota Press, 1996); Gyan Prakash, "Introduction," in *After Colonialism,* ed. Gyan Prakash (Princeton: Princeton University Press, 1995), 3-17; Peter Geschiere, *The Modernity of Witchcraft* (Charlottesville: University of Virginia Press, 1997); and Birgit Meyer, *Translating the Devil: Religion and Modernity among the Ewe of Ghana* (Edinburgh: Edinburgh University Press, 1999).

5. Goankar, "On Alternative Modernities," 16.

6. Johannes Fabian, *Remembering the Past: Painting and Popular History in Zaire* (Berkeley: University of California Press, 1996), 270, 273, 276-277; and Bogumil Jewsiewicki, "Collective Memory and the Stakes of Power: A Reading of Popular Zairian Historical Discourses," *History in Africa* 13 (1986): 195-223. See also Jewsiewicki and Mudimbe, who identify Western epistemological influences in the works of Cheikh Anta Diop, Ki-Zerbo, Ade Ajayi, and Edward Blyden. Bogumil Jewsiewicki and V. Y. Mudimbe, "Africans' Memories and Contemporary History of Africa," *History and Theory* 32, no. 4 (1993): 8-10. See also V. Y. Mudime on Blyden's conception of the African past, *The Invention of Africa: Gnosis, Philosophy, and the Order of Knowledge* (Bloomington: Indiana University Press, 1988), 113-114; and Adam Jones, "Reindorf the Historian," in *The Recovery of the West African Past: African Pastors and African History in the Nineteenth Century— C. C. Reindorf and Samuel Johnson,* ed. Paul Jenkins (Basel: Basler Afrika Bibliographien, 1998), 115-133.

7. Fabian and Jewsiewicki have both discussed this issue with regard to Tsibumba Matulu's work. See Fabian, *Remembering,* 270. See also Gary Minkley and Ciraj Rassoul, "Orality, Memory and Social History in South Africa," in *Negotiating the Past: The Making of Memory in South Africa,* ed. Sarah Nuttail and Carli Coetzee (Cape Town: Oxford University Press, 1998), 89-99, which examines the connection between individual remembrances found in autobiography and collective memory in South Africa.

8. Maurice Halbwachs, *The Collective Memory* (New York, Harper & Row, 1980); and Paul Connerton, *How Societies Remember* (New York: Cambridge University Press, 1989), 1-5, 36-40.

9. In African history, collective memory has been discussed primarily in terms of oral traditions, the invention of traditions (in which emphasis is placed on the political), and the impact of historic events on contemporary memories in which the memory is discussed largely in ahistorical terms.

Studies of oral traditions are extremely numerous, but classic texts on the subject include Jan Vansina, *Oral Tradition* (Harmondsworth, England: Penguin Books, 1965); Joseph Miller, ed., *The African Past Speaks: Essays on Oral Tradition and History* (Folkstone, Kent: Dawson, 1980); and Bogumil Jewsiewicki and David Newbury, eds., *African Historiographies: What History for Which Africa?* (Beverly Hills: Sage, 1986). On the invention of tradition, see another classic, Terence Ranger, "The Invention of Tradition in Colonial Africa," in Eric Hobsbawm and Terence Ranger, *The Invention of Tradition* (Cambridge: Cambridge University Press, 1983), 211-262. An excellent example of the scholarship on the impact of traumatic events in Africa on contemporary memory is Liisa Malkki's *Purity and Exile: Violence, Memory and National Cosmology among Hutu Refugees in Tanzania* (Chicago: University of Chicago Press, 1995). Studies on memories of the slave trade include Pier M. Larson's *History and Memory in the Age of Enslavement: Becoming Marina in Highland Madagascar, 1770–1822* (Portsmouth, N.H.: Heinemann, 2000), and the papers delivered at a conference "The Atlantic Slave Trade in African and African-American Memory," organized by Ralph Austin in the Department of History at the University of Chicago, 1997.

10. This approach to collective memory has also been articulated by Alon Confino in his article "Collective Memory and Cultural History: Problems of Method," *American Historical Review* 5, no. 102 (1997): 1386–1403. The emphasis on the symbolic is my own.

11. Richard Terdiman, *Present Past: Modernity and the Memory Crisis* (Ithaca: Cornell University Press, 1993), 28.

12. Yi-Fu Tuan was among the first geographers in recent times to articulate the need for the field of geography to include the study of meaning in their analyses of place and space. See "Space and Place: A Humanistic Perspective," *Progress in Geography: International Reviews and Current Research* 6 (1974). See also his book *Space and Place: The Perspective of Experience* (Minneapolis: University of Minnesota Press, 1977); and Denis E. Cosgrove, *Social Formation and Symbolic Landscape* (Madison: University of Wisconsin Press, 1984).

Studies that have focused specifically on the geography of religion include David E. Sopher, "Geography and Religions," *Progress in Human Geography* 5, no. 4 (1981): 510–524; and Chris C. Park, *Sacred World: An Introduction to Geography and Religion* (London: Routledge, 1994). See also Richard P. Werbner, ed., *Regional Cults* (London: Academic Press, 1977); his *Ritual Passage, Sacred Journey: The Process and Organization of Religious Movement* (Washington, D.C.: Smithsonian Institution Press, 1989); and David L. Carmichael, Jane Huberd, Brian Reeves, and Adhilde Schanche, *Sacred Sites, Sacred Places* (London: Routledge, 1994).

13. For a discussion of how central figures in the field of anthropology such as Morgan, Maine, Durkeim, Levi-Strauss, Radcliffe-Brown, Eliade, and Mauss discuss place and space and the impact of their discussions on subsequent anthropological studies, see Hilda Kuper, "The Language of Sites in the Politics of Space," *American Anthropologist* 74 (1972): 411–425; Robert J. Thornton, *Space, Time, and Culture among the Iraqw of Tanzania* (New York: Academic Press, 1980), 8–16; and David Parkin, *Sacred Void: Spatial Images of Work and Ritual among the Giriama of Kenya* (Cambridge: Cambridge University Press, 1991), 3–6.

Those anthropologists who have focused in particular on the religious meanings assigned to particular places and spaces in Africa include Parkin, *Sacred Void;* Wyatt MacGaffey, *Religion and Society in Central Africa: The BaKongo of Lower Zaire* (Chicago: University of Chicago Press, 1986); Thornton, *Space, Time, and Culture;* Benjamin C. Ray, *Myth, Ritual, and Kingship in Buganda* (New York: Oxford University Press, 1991); Alma Gottlieb, *Under the Kapok Tree: Identity and Difference in Beng Thought* (Chicago: University of Chicago Press, 1992); Eugenia W. Herbert, *Iron, Gender, and Power: Rituals of Transformation in African Societies* (Bloomington: Indiana University Press, 1993); Henrietta L. Moore, *Space, Text, and Gender: An Anthropological Study of the Marakwet of Kenya* (London: Guilford Press, 1996); Ikemefuna Stanley Okoye, "History, Aesthetics and the Political in Igbo Spatial Heterotopias," *Paideuma* 43 (1997): 75–91; and Jean Comaroff, *Body of Place, Spirit of Resistance: The Culture and History of a South African People* (Chicago: University of Chicago Press, 1985), 54–60.

Anthropological studies on the body include the numerous studies that focus on initiation rituals, health and healing, dress, and body marks as well as religious aspects of the body. On the latter, see, for example, Michael Jackson and Ivan Karp, *Personhood and Agency: The Experience of Self and Others in African Cultures* (Washington, D.C.: Smithsonian Institution Press, 1990).

Both David William Cohen and E. S. Atieno Odhiambo and Nadia Lovell define the landscape to include the body. Cohen and Odhiambo, *Siaya: The Historical Anthropology of an African Landscape* (London: James Currey, 1989); and Lovell, "Introduction: Belonging in Need of Emplacement?" in *Locality and Belonging,* ed. Nadia Lovell (London: Routledge, 1998), 1–24.

14. Among the geographers who have emphasized this point are John A. Agnew and James S. Duncan, eds., *The Power of Place: Bringing Together Geographical and Sociological Imaginations* (Boston: Unwin, 1989); and Dolores Hayden, *The Power of Place: Urban Landscapes as Public History* (Cambridge, Massachusetts: MIT Press, 1995). See also Stephen Daniels, "Arguments for a Humanistic Geography," in *The Future of Geography,* ed. R. J. Johnson (London: Methuen, 1985), 141–158; Daphne Spain, *Gendered Spaces* (Chapel Hill: University of North Carolina Press, 1992); Peter Jackson and Jan Penrose, eds., *Constructions of Race, Place, and Nation* (Minneapolis: University of Minnesota, 1993); Kent C. Ryden, *Mapping the Invisible Landscape: Folklore, Writing, and the Sense of Place* (Iowa City: University of Iowa Press, 1993); and J. Nicholas Entrikin, *The Betweenness of Place: Towards a Geography of Modernity* (Baltimore: Johns Hopkins University Press, 1991).

15. Notable exceptions include Denis Cosgrove's *Social Formation* and Henrietta Moore's *Space, Text, and Gender.*

16. Thomas McCaskie, *State and Society in Pre-Colonial Asante* (Cambridge: Cambridge University Press, 1995), 223–224; J. Matthew Schoffeleers, *River of Blood: The Genesis of a Martyr Cult in Southern Malawi, c. A.D. 1600* (Madison: University of Wisconsin Press, 1992); and Patrick Harries, "Under Alpine Eyes: Constructing Landscape and Society in Late Pre-colonial South-East Africa," *Paideuma* 43 (1997): 171–191.

17. Terence Ranger, *Voices from the Rocks: History in the Matopos Hills of Zimbabwe* (Oxford: James Currey, 1999).

18. These distinctions are often central to discussions of sacred sites in East Africa and southern Africa. See, for example, Ranger's study on the Matopos, *Voices from the Rocks;* Michele Wagner, "Environment, Community and History: 'Nature in the Mind' in Nineteenth and Early Twentieth Century Buha, Tanzania," in *Custodians of the Land: Ecology and Culture in the History of Tanzania,* ed. Gregory Maddox, James L. Biuglin, and Isaria N. Kimambo (London: James Currey, 1996), 175–199; and Elizabeth Colson, "Places of Power and Shrines of the Land," *Paideuma* 43 (1997): 47–57. The Ewe, in contrast, appear to make a number of distinctions among their gods that often are not mirrored in the terms used to refer to them. For example, some deities called *trɔwo* are ancestral gods; others are stranger deities but are still called *trɔwo.* Spiritual powers that can be purchased

and yet have the same power as *trǫwo* are known as *voduwo.* Other spiritual powers, known as *edzo,* can also be purchased but are used primarily for physical protection.

1. Notsie Narratives

1. D. E. K. Amenumey, *The Ewe in Precolonial Times* (Accra: Sedco Press, 1986), vi, 2–11.

2. R. W. Wyllie, "Kponoe and the Tado Stool: A Problem in the Interpretation of the Anlo Migration Tradition (Ghana/Togo)," *Anthropos* 72, no. 1/2 (1977): 119–128.

3. Vernay Mitchell, "Choice and Resistance in Ethnic Relations among the Ewe in a Developing Togolese Town" (Ph.D. diss., Columbia University, 1998), 35; N. L. Gayibor, "Le Remodelage des Traditions Historiques: La Légend d'Agokoli, Roi de Notsé," in *Sources orales de l'histoire de l'Afrique,* ed. Claude-Hélène Perrot (CNRS: Paris, 1989), 211.

4. Similar sites—which have been invested over long periods of time with a wide variety of meanings and memories—exist elsewhere in Africa. See, for example, Ranger, *Voices from the Rocks.*

5. For a history of Notsie's economic situation, see Mitchell, "Choice and Resistance."

6. Dola A. Aguigah, "Le Site de Notse: Contribution à L'Archeologie du Togo" (These, Doctorat de Troisième Cycle, Université de Paris, 1986), 399. In this thesis, Aguigah notes differences in opinion about the function of the wall. She takes no position but states that noted archaeologist Merrick Posnansky believes the walls primarily served a prestige function. The notion that the walls served a defensive purpose is argued by Nii Otokunor Quarcoopome in "Notse's Ancient Kingship: Some Archaeological and Art-Historical Considerations," *African Archaeological Review* 11 (1993): 114–115. Even the lack of direct contact with the coast did not prevent the Europeans who were trading there from knowing about the town's existence; its location was noted in 1575 on the Atlas of Muenster, a map described in Roberto Pazzi, *Introduction à l'histoire de l'aire culturelle aja tado-lome,* Series A: Études et Documents de Science Humaines (Lome: Université de Benin, Institut National des Science de L'Education, 1979), 172.

7. See Aguigah, "Le Site de Notse," 373–383.

8. Significantly, this is said to have occurred when Mawu was introduced into the polity and is said to have supported the efforts of the Dahomean king Tegbesu (1740–1774) to entrench his authority as king.

9. William Bosman, *A New and Accurate Description of the Guinea Coast* (London: J. Knapton, 1705), 368.

10. Robin Law, *The Slave Coast of West Africa, 1550–1570* (Oxford: Oxford University Press, 1991), 111.

11. Sandra E. Greene, "Cultural Zones in the Era of the Atlantic Slave Trade: Exploring the Yoruba Connection with the Anlo-Ewe," in *Identity in the Shadow of Slavery,* ed. Paul E. Lovejoy (New York: Continuum, 2000), 86–101.

12. Jakob Spieth, *Die Religion der Eweer* (Gottingen: Vandenhoeck and Ruprecht, 1911), 4, 5, 46.

13. Spieth, *Die Religion der Eweer*, 22.

14. To the east of the Ewe-speaking communities, the interior polity of Dahomey, the coastal polity of Whydah, and the inland Yoruba kingdom of Oyo also exerted economic and religious if not political influence, and they too impacted the religious culture of the region. See Greene, "Cultural Zones"; and Edna Bay, *Wives of the Leopard: Gender, Politics, and Culture in the Kingdom of Dahomey* (Charlottesville, Virginia: University of Virginia Press, 1998), 186–192, 218, 255.

15. Sandra E. Greene, *Gender, Ethnicity, and Social Change on the Upper Slave Coast* (Portsmouth, N.H.: Heinemann, 1996), 52–55.

16. Bernhard J. Schlegel, "Beitrag zur Geschichte, Welt-und Religionsanschauung des Westafrikaners, namentlich des Eweers," *Monatsblatt der Norddeutschen Missionsgesellschaft* 8 (1858): 398. In the 1860s, Anlo did send a delegation to Notsie to receive military support for their operations in Aguoe. They received assistance in the form of the god Koliko. Spieth, *Die Ewe Stämme* (Berlin: Dietrich Reimer, 1906), 122–123. For more on the Agoue wars, see Kue Agbota Gaba, "The History of Anecho, Ancient and Modern," deposited at Balme Library, University of Ghana, Legon (1965); and Greene, *Gender, Ethnicity, and Social Change*, 133, fn. 62.

17. Greene, "Cultural Zones."

18. G. A. Robertson, *Notes on Africa* (London: Sherwood, Neely and Jones, 1819), 238.

19. A. B. Ellis, *The Ewe-Speaking Peoples of the Slave Coast of West Africa* (1890; reprint, Chicago: Benin Press, 1965), 32–33.

20. For a detailed discussion of the beliefs and early efforts of the Norddeutsche Missionsgesellschaft and subsequent efforts in Peki in particular, see Birgit Meyer, "Translating the Devil: An African Appropriation of Pietist Protestantism —The Cast of the Peki Ewe in Southeastern Ghana, 1847–1992" (Ph.D. diss., University of Amsterdam, 1995), Part I.

21. Hans W. Debrunner, *A Church between Colonial Powers: A Study of the Church in Togo* (London: Lutterworth Press, 1965), 109.

22. Birgit Meyer, "Christianity and the Arise of the Ewe Nation: On the Encounter between German Pietist Missionaries and Ewe Mission Workers," paper presented at the international conference "Religion and Nationalism in Europe and Asia" at the Research Center on Religion and Society, University of Amsterdam (1995), 5.

23. Ibid.

24. "Die Unruhen in Anglo-Gebeit," *Monatsblatt der Norddeutschen Missionsgesellschaft* (1885): 36.

25. Birgit Meyer, "Christianity and the Arise of the Ewe Nation," 4–5.

26. Ibid.; Debrunner, *A Church between Colonial Powers*, 4.

27. As an example of this effort, see the Ewe reader *Ewegbalexexle apka enelia* (Bremen: Norddeutsche Missiongesellschaft, 1936), 60–63.

28. Christian Hornberger, "Etwas aus der Geschichte der Anloer," *Quartalblatt der Norddeutschen Missionsgesellschaft* 82 (1877): 437–439.

29. Nicoué Lodjou Gayibor, *Recueil des Sources Orales du Pays Aja-Ewe* (Lome, Togo: Departement d'Histoire, University du Benin, 1977), 63.

30. The first European observer to comment on this transformation in the

meaning of the god Mawu was A. B. Ellis. This new understanding of Mawu was then later taken up by Christian theologians, who sought to challenge European statements about the inferiority of African religions by emphasizing the extent to which Africans had a concept of a supreme being that was just like the Christian god long before Christianity reached the area. See Ellis, *The Ewe-Speaking Peoples,* 32–33; and Okot p'Bitek, *African Religions in Western Scholarship* (Nairobi: Kenya Literature Bureau, 1971).

31. D. E. K. Amenumey, *The Ewe Unification Movement: A Political History* (Accra: Ghana Universities Press, 1989), Chapter 4.

32. Gayibor, "Le Remodelage des Traditions Historiques."

33. Ibid., 212; Sandra E. Greene, Field Note No. 240B, Interview with Tobui Kofi Ahosu et. al., Notsie, Togo, 1 September 1996.

34. Paul Nugent, *Myths of Origin and the Origin of Myth: Local Politics and the Uses of History in Ghana's Volta Region* (Berlin: Das Arabische Buch, 1997), 14–16.

35. Amenumey, *The Ewe Unification Movement;* and Paul Nugent, "Ewe Nationalism," *Journal of African History* 33, no. 3 (1992): 495–496.

36. For a discussion of the Ghanaian policy of national integration, especially as it focused on the arts, see Sandra E. Greene, "Developing the Arts for Development," *Africa Notes* (Feb. 1998): 1–5; and Janet Hess, "Exhibiting Ghana: Display, Documentary and 'National' Art in the Nkruman Era," *African Studies Review* 44, no. 1 (2001): 59–77.

37. *Anlowo Pe Hogbetsotso Nkeke* (Anloga, Ghana: Anlo Traditional Council, 1966), 20.

38. Adeladza II, "Foreword," in *Hogbeza* (Accra: Arakan Press, 1973), 3. For additional examples of development projects linked to the festival see *Hogbeza, 1978* (Accra: Arakan Press, 1978), 33–34, in which the establishment of the Awoamezi Foundation was announced. This foundation was to provide financial support for the Anlo Kotsiklolo Society, an organization that a number of Anlo citizens founded in 1973 to preserve the cultural heritage of the Anlo but which had become inactive due to a lack of funds. See also *Anlo Hogbetsotsoza* (Accra: Arakan Press, 1987), which was the 25th-anniversary souvenir brochure for the festival. At that year's festival, a special appeal was made for funds to support the festival itself. An appeal was also made for all to give serious thought to how local residents could work with the government to stem the coastal erosion which had by that time destroyed much of the commercial center of Keta. The theme for the festival that year was "Save Keta Now."

39. Similar observations have been made by others. See Vincent K. Gabegbeku, "The Socio-cultural Significance of Traditional Festivals: The Case of the Hogbetsotso of Anlo-Ewe of Ghana" (B.A. Honors Thesis, Department of Sociology, University of Cape Coast, Ghana, 1993).

40. Daniel D. Fianu, *The Hoawo and the Gligbaza Festival of the Asogli State of Eweland: A Historical Sketch* (Legon: Self-published, 1986).

41. J. M. Dotse, "Agricultural Geography of the Keta District" (Master's thesis, University of Ghana, Legon, 1969), 25–26.

42. Sandra E. Greene, Field Notes, No. 53, Interview with Togbui Afatsao Awadzi, 16 December 1987, Anloga; No. 54: Interview with Togbui Tse Gbeku,

16 December 1987, Anloga; No. 62: Interview with K. A. Mensah, 5 January 1988, Anloga.

43. Dietrich Westermann, *Die Glidyi-Ewe in Togo* (Berlin: Mitteilungen des Seminars für Orientalische Sprachen an der Universität Berlin, 1935), 146.

44. Charles M. K. Mamattah, *The Ewes of West Africa* (Keta, Ghana: Advent Press, 1979), 328.

45. Sandra E. Greene, Field Note No. 29, Interview with Miss Florence Adama, 24 September 1978, Agbosome.

46. See Mamattah, *The Ewes*, 119, where he draws parallels between the Ewe and the Jewish exodus. On page 89, he describes Notsie and the Biblical Babel, and on page 92, he draws parallels between Ewe ritual and law and that which prevailed in ancient Egypt during the time of Moses. Fianu, *The Hoawo*, 53, establishes a much closer link between Ewe history and the history of the Jews, as did Miss Adama in 1978. According to Fianu, "The Ewe . . . lay claim to being in bondage with the Israelites." See also Solomon M. K. Barawusu, *The Hogbetsotso Festival: A Comparison between the Liberation of the Ewes from Slavery in Notsie, Togo under the Wicked King Agorkoli and the Liberation of the Israelites from Slavery in Egypt under the Wicked King Pharoah* (Anloga, Ghana: Zion Secondary School, n.d.), cited and described in Kathryn Linn Geurts, "Sensory Perception and Embodiment in Anlo-Ewe Cultural Logic and Symbolic Life" (Ph.D. diss., University of Pennsylvania, 1998), 130.

47. See Sandra E. Greene, "The Past and Present of an Anlo-Ewe Oral Tradition," in *History in Africa* 12 (1985): 73-87, which discusses this imagery as it has impacted the way many in Anlo in particular remember their history.

48. See Emmanuel Akyeampong, *Between the Sea and the Lagoon: An Eco-Social History of the Anlo of Southeastern Ghana, c.1850 to Recent Times* (Athens: Ohio University Press; Oxford: James Currey, forthcoming), Chapter 7, where he provides an excellent discussion on post-colonial ethnic politics in Ghana.

49. See also note 37 and Amenumey, *The Ewe in Precolonial Times.*

50. Mitchell, "Choice and Resistance."

2. Of Water and Spirits

1. On the risks of engaging in ocean-fishing, see Charles W. Thomas, *Adventures and Observations on the West Coast of Africa and Its Islands* (1860; reprint, New York: Negro Universities Press, 1969), 246; G. K. Nukunya, "The Anlo-Ewe and Full-Time Maritime Fishing: Another View," *MAST* 2, no. 2 (1989): 158; and G. K. Nukunya, "Afa Divination in Anlo: A Preliminary Report," *Research Review* (Legon) 5/2 (1969): 12, fn. 1. For a thorough discussion of sea erosion of the town of Keta, see Akyemapong, *Between the Sea and the Lagoon.* See also many of the poems of Kofi Awoonor in which he discusses Anlo perceptions of the hardships that one can encounter in living in a world dominated by water. See, for example, "I Heard A Bird Cry," in *Night of My Blood* (New York: Anchor Books, 1971), 46; "A Dirge," in *Messages: Poems from Ghana,* ed. Kofi Awoonor and G. Adali-Mortty (London: Heinemann, 1971), 73; and "The Sea Eats the Land at Home," in *Modern Poetry from Africa,* ed. Gerald Moore and Ulli Beier (Baltimore: Penguin Books, 1968), 101. See also the numerous references to water, water bodies, and deities in

Christian R. Gaba, *Scriptures of an African People: Ritual Utterances of the Anlo* (New York: Nok Publishers, 1973).

2. Anlo farmers tend to maintain many plots scattered throughout the area in order to minimize the risk of flooding. See J. M. Dotse, *Shallot Farming in An-loga, Ghana,* Special Monograph by Curriculum and Teaching Department, University of Cape Coast (1980), 59.

3. For an excellent general discussion of the ritual use of water by the peoples of southern Ghana, see Emmanuel Akyeampong, *Drink, Power, and Cultural Change: A Social History of Alcohol in Ghana, c. 1800 to Recent Times* (Portsmouth: Heinemann, 1996), 9, 14, 28, 35, and 38. For a discussion of the ritual uses of water, specifically among the Anlo, see Spieth, *Die Religion der Eweer,* 41; Justice Mokpokpo Yao Amegashie, "The Concept of Renewal: A Study in Anlo Thought" (B.A. Honors Thesis, Department for the Study of Religions, University of Ghana, Legon, 1976), 15, 42, 45–46; Richard Tetteh Torgby, "The Origin and Organization of the Yewe Cult" (B.A. Honors Thesis, Department for the Study of Religions, University of Ghana, Legon, 1977), 5, 6, 28; Meyer, "Translating the Devil," 257; Kofi Anyidoho, "Oral Poetics and Traditions of Verbal Art in Africa" (Ph.D. diss., University of Texas at Austin, 1983), 82–83, 178–179; Tobias Wendl, "Preliminary Results of My Mama Wata Field Work among the Ewes of Togo and Ghana, 1985/86," in author's possession; Roseville Ediefiam Senaya, "Ancestral Worship in Anloland: An Artistic Expression" (B.A. Thesis, School of Art and Design, Winneba, Ghana, 1983), 11–12, 16–17, 41, 49–50, 52; Cletus Experience Kofi Kumado, "Customary Constitutional Rules and Procedures for Enstoolment and Destool-ment of a Chief among the Anlo-Ewe" (L.L.M. Degree Thesis, University of Ghana, 1974), 95; and Eustace Yaw Egblewogbe, "Ewe Personal Names: A Sociolinguistic Study" (Ph.D. thesis, University of Ghana, 1977), 178.

4. C. Spiess, "Verborgener Fetischdienst under den Eveern," *Globus* 98 (1910): 13.

5. Administrative Papers of the Secretary of Native Affairs (1912), 159, ADM 11/1/1661, National Archives, Accra, Ghana. All collections with ADM location numbers are housed in these archives.

6. Stephano H. Kwadzo Afelevo, "Ein Bericht über den Yewekultus der Ewe. Herausgegeben mit deutscher Übersetzung und Anmerkungen von D. Westermann," *Mitteilungen des Seminars für Orientalischen Sprachen* 33/3 (1894/1930).

7. D. A. Bates, "Geology," in *Agriculture and Land Use in Ghana,* ed. J. B. Willis (London: Oxford University Press, 1962), 75–76; A. S. Boughey, "Ecological Studies of Tropical Coastlines: The Gold Coast, West Africa," *Journal of Ecology* 45, no. 23 (1957): 665–687.

8. The significance of the high water table is also remembered as the origin of the Amlade taboo on killing and eating crocodiles. According to Amlade traditions, "When their ancestors came [to Anloga], they met people who ate [both crocodiles and antelope], but they didn't. The reason is that most of the terrain was arid, almost a desert and they were dying of thirst. Prior to this taboo, they ate crocodile, but when they were dying of thirst they found a crocodile and chased it. It went into a forest, but they continued after it. The crocodile started to dig into the ground to get away and water came out. So they stopped, watched and realized that the water table was quite high. They started to dig themselves and filled their

water containers with water. They then realized that if it hadn't been for the crocodile, they would have continued to die in the thousands so they saw it as some kind
of sacred animal and instituted the taboo." Greene, Field Notes, No. 14, Interview
with Togbui Trygod Yao Zodanu, 11 August 1978, Anloga.

9. Greene, Field Notes, No. 76, Interview with Togbui Aklorbortu Efia Nun-
yanu, 6 January 1988, Anloga; No. 134, Interview with Elvis Adika, 28 March 1996,
Anloga; No. 153, Interview with Togbui Tekpor Sedzorme, 20 March 1996, Anloga;
No. 191, Interview with Togbui Aklorbortu Efia Nunyanu and Zadzie, 2 May 1996,
Anloga; No. 202, Interview with Togbui Tudzi, 15 May 1996, Anloga.

10. *Anlowo Pe Hogbetsotso Nkeke* (Anloga: Anlo Traditional Council, 1966),
13.

11. The oldest residents interviewed about the ponds were between 92 and a
self-reported 127 years of age.

12. Greene, Field Notes, No. 153, Interview with Togbui Tekpor Sedzorme,
20 March 1996, Anloga; No. 176, Interview with Tekpor Sedozorme, 20 April 1996,
Anloga.

13. Paul Erdman Isert, *Voyages en Guinée et dans les îsles Caraïbes en Amerique. Tirés de sa correspondence aves ses amis. Traduits de l'allemand* (Paris: Maradan, 1973), 96; Robertson, *Notes on Africa,* 233–234.

14. See Robin Law, "Between the Sea and the Lagoon: The Interaction of
Maritime and Inland Navigation on the Precolonial Slave Coast," *Cahiers d'Études
Africaines* II4, XXIX-2 (1989): 213, which provides an extensive listing of European sources that suggest continuous navigation on the inland lagoons between
the Volta River and Lagos.

15. For a detailed discussion of the trade routes that linked Anlo with communities to its east and west as well as to the north during the late seventeenth,
eighteenth, and nineteenth centuries, see Ray A. Kea, "Akwamu-Anlo Relations,
c. 1750–1813," *Transactions of the Historical Society of Ghana* 10 (1969): 29–63;
Sandra E. Greene, "Social Change in 18th Century Anlo: The Role of Technology,
Markets and Military Conflict," *Africa: The Journal of the International African
Institute* 58, no. 1 (1988): 70–86; I. B. Sutton, "The Volta River Salt Trade: The Survival of an Indigenous Industry," *Journal of African History* 22 (1981): 47; and
R. A. Kea, "The Salt Industries of the Gold Coast, 1650–1800" (unpublished manu-
script, Institute of African Studies, University of Ghana, Legon, 1966).

16. For an excellent discussion of the production activities conducted on the
Keta Lagoon, see J. M. Grove, "Some Aspects of the Economy of the Volta Delta
(Ghana)," *Bulletin de L'Institut Fondamental d'Afrique Noire* XXVIII, no. 1–2
(1996): 382–432; and Albert de Surgy, *La Pêche Traditionnelle sur le Littoral Evhe
et Mina—De l'embouchure de la Volta au Dahomey* (Paris: Groupe de Chercheurs
Africanistes, 1966), 20–27.

17. Greene, Field Notes, No. 170, Interview with Togbui Tekpor Sedzome,
14 April 1996, Anloga; No. 180, Interview with Togbui Akpate I, 23 April 1996,
Srogboe.

18. Leftover food was forbidden because it was considered vulnerable to the
actions of witches attempting to harm the person who ate the food. Introduction
of harmful substances might not only physically hurt the person who ate such food
but might also render them spiritually contaminated. In such a state they could

not expect to gain the benefits of a relationship with a deity. See Anonymous, "Vom Hexenglauben der Eweer," unpublished manuscript, c. 1932, (Norddeutsche Missions-Gesellschaft 7, 1025; Keta, 14/1), 13, Staatsarchiv, Bremen.

19. Ibid.; Greene, Field Notes, No. 171, Interview with Togbui Awuku Dzrekey, 18 April 1996, Whuti; C. Spiess, "Fünfzig Jahre Missionsarbeit in Anyako," *Monatsblatt der Norddeutschen Missionsgesellschaft* (January 1908): 3.

20. H. S. Newlands, District Commissioner, Quittah, to Chief Ocloo, Quittah, Chief Anthonio II, We, Chief Preku, Tegbi, Chief Adri, Atiave, Chief Pomenya, Anyako, Chief Tamakloe, Hute, Chief of Alakple, Chief of Abolove, Chief Kagalo, Aferingba, 23 July 1914, Item Number 21—Fetish Customs (30/1909-15/6/28), National Archives of Ghana, Ho.

21. Birgit Meyer, "Translating the Devil," 44–45.

22. This term comes from a Bremen publication by E. Salkowski, "Anloga: Eine Hochburg des Heidentums," *Bremer Missionschriften* 20 (1907): 25.

23. Missionary Forster, "Die Tause der Erstlinge von Anloga," *Monatsblatt der Norddeutschen Missionsgesellschaft* 70 (1909): 84–85.

24. C. Spiess, "Sturz eines heidnischen Gottes," *Monatsblatt der Norddeutschen Missionsgesellschaft* 88 (1927): 109–110.

25. For detailed biographical information on Sri II, see Mamattah, *The Ewes of West Africa,* 207–210; Togbi Sri II, Awoame Fia of Anlo, 40th Anniversary Celebration of . . . , A. M. Frank, Assistant D.C., to Commissioner, Eastern Province, Koforidua, 2 December 1947, ADM 39/1/602, No. 0083/s.f.1/23.

26. These two chiefs are frequently cited as those who were particularly influential in the selection of Kwawukume. See Mamattah, *The Ewes,* 207; and Greene, Field Notes, No. 57, Interview with Robert G. Kofi Afetogbo, 22 December 1988, Anloga.

27. Acolatse, for example, would buy the liquor that the British government granted to government-affiliated chiefs at very low cost. He would then sell this liquor to retailers and provide them with the information they needed to avoid being caught if they wished to sell the liquor or smuggle the liquor out of the territory without paying any tariffs. See Francis A. Lamb, District Commissioner, Kwitta, to the Honorable, the Colonial Secretary, Victoriaborg, 24 September 1889, ADM 11/1/1113, Part 2.

28. Greene, Field Notes, No. 72, Interview with Christian Nani Tamaklo, 13 January 1988, Keta.

29. Greene, Field Notes, No. 74, Interview with A. W. Kuetuade-Tamaklo, 19 January 1988, Tegbi.

30. Greene, Field Notes, No. 81, Interview with Togbui Joachim Acolatse IV, 26 January 1988, Keta.

31. Greene, Field Notes, No. 91, Interview with Togbui Joachim Acolatse IV, 5 February 1988, Tema; No. 97, Interview with J. G. Kodzo Vordoagu, 24 February 1988, Tegbi.

32. Notes of Evidence, Commission of Enquiry, 1912, Awuna, Addah, and Akwamu, 97, ADM11/1/1661.

33. Greene, Field Notes, No. 69, Interview with Togbui Dzobi Adzinku, 7 January 1988, Anloga.

34. James M. Dotse, "The Geography of Transportation in the Anlo District"

(B.A. honors thesis, University of Ghana, Legon, 1966), 3. It is unclear why this ban was imposed at this particular time. Sails had been in use by British colonial officers traveling on the Keta Lagoon since the 1870s, when they were involved in efforts to stop the smuggling of goods from German Togoland. A. B. Ellis, District Commissioner, Quittah, to the Colonial Secretary, Christiansborg, Accra, 24 October 1878, ADM 1/2/12. It is possible that the drought in 1904 which completely dried the lagoon (as had not happened since 1872/1873) prompted this response. See Report Descriptive of the Towns, Lagoon and Rivers lying between the Volta and Puda [sic] Rivers, W. G. Lawson, Assistant Colonial Surveyor, to the Acting Assistant Colonial Secretary, Lagos, 22 August 1879, ADM1/2/361; and Keta Lagoon, File 40/1906, ADM 39/1/173.

35. H. S. Newlands, District Commissioner, Quittah, to Chief Ocloo, Quittah, Chief Anthonio, We, Chief Preku, Tegbi, Chief Adri, Atiave, Chief Pomenya, Anyako, Chief Tamakloe, Hute, Chief of Alakple, Chief of Abolove, Chief Kajalo, Aferingba, 23 July 1914.

36. Greene, Field Notes, No. 154, Interview with Togbui Tekpor Sedzorme, 21 March 1996, Anloga. Note also that in 1910 Sri worked closely with the colonial government to encourage greater communication within the region by opening the clogged waterways that connected the Keta Lagoon to the more northerly Avu, Lota, Tamajega, Nkunr, Nkunotse, and Avida Lagoons. Quittah Lagoon—Proposed Connection with Certain Inland Lagoons, Commissioner of the Eastern Province to Acting Secretary of National Affairs, Victoriaburg, Accra, 5 May 1910, ADM 11/1/228; A. H. C. Richards, District Commissioner, Quittah, to Provincial Commission, Akuse, 8/4/10; Cornelius Kofi Kwawukume, Sri II, Fia, Anloga, to A. H. L. Richter, Esq. District Commissioner, Quittah, 5 April 1910, both in ADM 11/1/228. In 1882, the colonial government widened and deepened the channel at Atoko that connected the Volta River and the lagoon. But this was solely a government initiative. See Brandford Griffith, Governor, Addah Foah, to the Right Honorable J. Holland Bart, Gold Coast, M. G., 21 February 1888, ADM 1/2/42.

37. W. Winniet, Governor, Cape Coast, to Colonial Secretary, 6 April 1850, ADM 1/2/5.

38. C. Spiess, "Ein Erinnerungsblatt an die Tage es Sklavenhandels in Westafrika," *Globus* (Braunschweig) 92 (1907): 205.

39. Greene, Field Notes, No. 56, Interview with William Tiodo Anum Adzololo, 22 December 1987, Anloga; No. 100, Interview with Togbui Awusu, II, 29 March 1988, Atoko.

40. H. S. Newlands, District Commissioner, Quittah, to Commissioner of the Eastern Province, Akuse, 15 November 1913, Item 21—Fetish Customs (30/1909-15/6/28), National Archives of Ghana, Ho.

41. Atakpa, Chief of Anyako, et. al, to His Excellency Alexander Rainsford Slater, Esq., Acting Governor and Commander-in-Chief of the Gold Coast Colony per the Honorable Torgbi Sri II, Awame-Fia-Awuna, Awunaga, 26 August 1920; K. G. Webster for Executive Engineer, Public Works Department, Koforidua, to the Honorable, the Commissioner of the Eastern Province, Koforidua, 3 November 1920; Sri II Awoame Fia of Anlo, Anloga, to the District Commissioner, Keta, 30 January 1932. All in ADM 39/1/173: Keta Lagoon. Other technological efforts —which were disastrous in terms of the loss of life and property—occurred in the

1890s and in the 1960s. In 1893, a German trader by the name of Meyer decided to relieve serious flooding in Keta caused by the lagoon by cutting a canal to connect Tagbamu with the ocean. In 1963, the British colonial government cut yet another canal for the same reason. See Akyeampong, *Between the Sea and the Lagoon*, Chapter 4; see also Grove, "Some Aspects of the Economy," 428.

42. Greene, Field Notes, No. 170, Interview with Togbui Tekpor Sedzorme, 14 April 1996, Anloga.

43. Greene, Field Notes, No. 22, Interview with Togbui Trygod Yao Zodanu, 1 September 1978, Anloga; No. 158, Mama Ami Nutsugah, 24 March 1996, Whuti; No. 180, Togbui Akpate I, 23 April 1996, Srogboe; No. 168, Togbui Sorkpor, 19 April 1996, Anloga.

44. Worship of Mama Blolui is handled by the Ame clan, which is said to have deposited the deity in the pond after their capture and resettlement in Anloga by the Bate clan ancestor, Adeladza. See Greene, Field Notes, No. 45, Interview with Togbui Dzobi Adzinku, 8 November 1978, Anloga.

45. Located between Anloga and Whuti (and like Blolui) at some distance from any settlement, the pond Tale is also remembered through its association with a deity whose worship required women on their menses to refrain from going near the pond. But far more prominent is Tale's association with the Taleto War, a dispute that erupted in 1885 between Anlo political leaders based on the littoral and those in Anloga and on the northern shore of the Keta Lagoon. It involved serious disagreement over how best to deal with British efforts to curb smuggling between the British-controlled Gold Coast Colony (of which Anlo was a part) and the German colony of Togo. For additional information on this conflict, see G. A. Sorkpor, "Geraldo De Lima and the Awunas, 1862–1904" (Master's thesis, Institute of African Studies, University of Ghana, 1966); and Notes of Evidence, 94–97, ADM 11/1/1661.

46. A large literature exists on the history of European theories about the origins of malaria. For a discussion of the specific application of these theories to the Gold Coast, see Raymond Dumett, "The Campaign against Malaria and the Expansion of Scientific Medical and Sanitary Services in British West Africa, 1898–1910," *African Historical Studies* 1, no. 2 (1968): 153–197. For European understandings of the Anlo environment influenced by miasmic theories, see George McDonald, *The Gold Coast Past and Present* (London: Longmans, Green and Co., 1898), 246.

47. Greene, Field Notes, No. 113, Interview with Togbui Aklorbortu Efia, 10 February 1996, Anloga.

48. These include the deities Agbui, also known as Awleketi (a deity associated with the Yewe pantheon of gods), and Mami Wata.

49. Law, *The Slave Coast*, 110–111.

50. "Copy of a Letter from the Governor and Council at Cape Coast Castle," 9 July 1785, T70/33, Treasury Papers, African Companies, Public Records Office, Kew, England. Also note that prior to this, during the seventeenth century, Anlo commerce on the ocean was dominated by foreign sailors, mostly from the Fante- and Ga-speaking areas of the Gold Coast. See Sandra E. Greene, "Cultural Zones."

51. C. Spiess, "Verborgener Fetischdienst," 12–13.

52. G. Härtter, "Der Fischfang im Evheland," *Zeitschrift für Ethnologie* 38, no. 1–2 (1906): 63.

53. Greene, Field Notes, No. 176, Interview with Tekpor Sedzorme, 20 April 1996, Anloga.

54. Greene, Field Notes, No. 177, Interview with Togbui Akpate I, 22 April 1996, Srogbe. See also No. 198, Interview with Mama Korfobu Diaba, 11 March 1996, Srogbe, which also mentions sea nymphs, *tsitsibli*.

55. Greene, Field Notes, No. 181, Interview with Hianvedzu Nyamadi, 23 April 1996, Anloga.

56. Akyeampong, *Between the Sea and the Lagoon*. See also W. S. Chapman, *The Keta Sea Erosion and Dredging for Development, and Some Landmarks for Anlo History* (Accra: Arakan Press, 1984).

57. This spiritual quality remains even though women have begun to fish in the ocean, a practice once forbidden by the Anlo in both the lagoon and the sea for religious reasons. On the increasing practice of women fishing in the lagoon whether on their menses or not, see Emily Angela Essie Lotsu, "Women in Fishing: A Study of the Significance of Women's Roles in the Fishing Industry at Anlo-Afiadenyigba" (B.A. Long Essay, Department of Sociology, University of Ghana, Legon, 1994); on women fishing in the ocean, see Greene, Field Notes, No. 185, Interview with Aklorbortu Efia and Zanyiedo Kwawukume, 27 April 1996, Anloga.

58. On the history of the overfishing of the Keta Lagoon, see Greene, *Gender, Ethnicity and Social Change,* 165.

59. Nukunya, "Full-Time Maritime Fishing," 158–159. For additional information on the Anlo fishing industry as a business, see Polly Hill, *Studies in Rural Capitalism in West Africa* (Cambridge: Cambridge University Press, 1986); P. Jorion, "Going Out or Staying Home: Migration Strategies among the Xwla and Anlo-Ewe Fishermen," *MAST* 1, no. 2 (1988): 129–155; Robert W. Wyllie, "Migrant Anlo Fishing Companies and Socio-political Change: A Comparative Study," *Africa* XXXIX, no. 4 (1969): 396–410; Polly Hill, *Talking with Ewe Seine Fisherman and Shallot Farmers* (Cambridge: African Studies Center, 1986).

60. This figure comes from S. K. Kufogbe, "The Natural Resources of the Southern Ewes," in *A Handbook of Eweland,* vol. 1, *The Ewes of Southeastern Ghana,* ed. Francis Agbodeka (Accra: Woeli Press, 1997), 297.

61. The last observation of these animals in any written account I have been able to locate was made in 1878 by A. B. Ellis between Anloga and Atoko. A. B. Ellis, *West African Sketches* (London: Samuel Tinsley and Co., 1881), 258, 260. For more on Ellis as an observer of West African life, see Ray Jenkins, "Confrontations with A. B. Ellis, A Participant in the Scramble for Gold Coast Africana, 1874–1894," *Paiduema* 33 (1987): 313–335.

62. Nukunya, "Full-Time Maritime Fishing," 159.

63. See Greene, Field Notes, No. 176, Interview with Tekpor Sedzorme, 20 April 1996, Anloga; and No. 199, Interview with Togbui Ayike, 12 May 1996, Srogbe. It is interesting to note that the connection between notions of masculinity and working on the ocean as fishermen has been recently challenged by a number of women who have begun to participate in maritime fishing and the men who have encouraged them. See note 57 above. Studies on other fishing cultures, those in industrialized societies, comment as well on the religious rituals used by fishermen as they deal with the uncontrollable and unpredictable power of the sea. See,

for example, John J. Poggie Jr. and Carl Gersuny, "Risk and Ritual: An Interpretation of Fishermen's Folklore in a New England Community," *Journal of American Folklore* 85, no. 335 (1972): 66–72. I thank Emmanuel Akyeampong for this reference.

64. G. K. Nukunya, *Kinship and Marriage among the Anlo Ewe* (New York: Humanities Press, 1969), 205–208; Greene, Field Notes, No. 118, Interview with Akorbortu Efia, 14 February 1996, Anloga; and No. 188, Mama Xaedo Worgbale, 29 April 1996, Anloga.

65. This tendency for the Anlo to attribute far more significance to water than the missionaries would have is evident in the accounts of conversion published by the missionaries themselves. See especially C. Spiess, "Aus dem Leben eines Stadtgötzen," *Quartalblatt der Norddeutschen Missionsgesellschaft* 2/6–8 (1930): 14–15. For evidence of the continued use of seawater in widowhood rituals by Christians, see Dzifaa Kobla de Souza, "The Religious Significance of Rites of Passage among the Anlo-Ewe" (B.A. Long Essay, Department for the Study of Religions, University of Ghana, Legon, 1979), 50.

66. This account comes from Spieth, *Die Religion der Eweer,* 176, but it is based on an account first published in 1894 by Afelevo, "Ein Bericht über den Yewekultus der Ewe."

67. Minutes of the Awuna Dua State Council of the Eastern Province of the Gold Coast Colony and Protectorate held at Awunaga on the 17th day of April 1935, 73; Entry for 5 November 1938, Keta, 295; Entry for 23/2/40, Keta, 367; Entry for 26/2/40, Keta, 380. All in Anlo Council Minute Book (29 June 1934–5/7 November 1946), Anloga.

68. Wendl, "Preliminary Results of My Mama Wata Field Work." See also Akyeampong, *Between the Sea and the Lagoon,* Chapter 4. For more information on Mami Wata worship in West Africa, see Henry John Drewal, "Performing the Other: Mami Wata Worship in Africa," *The Drama Review* 32, no. 2 (1988): 160–185.

69. Torgby, "The Origin and Organization," 31.

70. Greene, Field Notes, No. 169A, Interview with Togbui Sorkpor, 19 April 1996, Anloga.

3. Placing and Spacing the Dead

1. I define the built environment as those areas with which the majority population interacted on a regular basis: houses, streets, farms, sacred groves, and burial sites. I also distinguish within this built environment—the central area of human habitation and the transition zone that separated homes and houses from the "bush"—that area where spiritual forces roamed freely and where only those who were sufficiently spiritually fortified felt comfortable operating.

2. Missionar Schiek, "Keta," *Monatsblatt der Norddeutschen Missionsgesellschaft* 22/263 (1872): 1193.

3. C. Spiess, "We, Anglo and Atoko," *Monatsblatt der Norddeutschen Missionsgesellschaft* 10 (1898): 34.

4. Salkowski, "Anloga," 11. See also A. Connal, Acting District Commissioner, Quittah, to Acting Commissioner of the Eastern Province, Akuse, 1 August 1911, ADM 41/1/16.

5. J. Spieth, "Ein Gökenhain," *Monatsblatt der Norddeutschen Missionsgesell-schaft* 5 (1893): 46.

6. See, for example, Anna Toepfer, "Ein Frauenbrief aus Keta," *Monatsblatt der Norddeutschen Missionsgesellschaft* 2/10 (1885): 24.

7. At times, the missionaries and their Christian converts did more than take comfort. They also took it upon themselves to obtain government support if they were unsuccessful in persuading the locals to do as they wished. See Martin Schlunk, *Die Norddeutsche Mission in Togo: Meine Reise durchs Eweland* (Bremen: Verlag der NDMG, 1910), 30, which describes the missionaries resorting in 1909 to the British colonial government when they faced difficulty getting the chiefs of Anyako to order a general cleanup of the town.

8. This period of physical and ritual cleansing, known as Dodede, was most often declared with the outbreak of an infectious disease. For descriptions of this nineteenth-century activity, see Missionary Flothmeier, "Bilder aus unserer Arbeit," *Monatsblatt der Norddeutschen Missionsgesellschaft* 9 (1903): 86; and Anonymous, "Wie man zu Anyako die Pocken vertreibt," *Quartalblatt der Norddeutschen Missionsgesellschaft* 68 (1873): 321–324. For a more recent discussion, see Amegashie, "The Concept of Renewal."

9. Christian Hornberger, "Wie es in Keta aussieht," *Monatsblatt der Norddeutschen Missionsgesellschaft* 25/295 (1875): 1380. Examples of Anlos being fined for littering or "committing a nuisance" can be found in Civil and Criminal Record Book, Keta, ADM 41/4/30; Inspection Book, ADM 41/5/2.

10. The 1910 laws supplemented a number of ordinances that had previously been directed solely at the towns of the Gold Coast. These earlier ordinances included the Towns Police and Health Ordinances of 1878 and 1892 and the Towns Amendment Ordinance of 1901. See Dumett, "The Campaign against Malaria," 159, 170. For information on the enforcement of the 1878 and 1892 ordinances in Anlo, see Inspection Books (27/8/1897–24/9/1903), Report of 27/1/1900, ADM 41/5/2; see also all of ADM 41/1/16. In this file is a report by Harry S. Newlands, District Commissioner, Quittah, to All Chiefs and Headmen, 13 June 1911. Here he reports to all Anlo chiefs and headmen that they are to enforce the Sanitary Bye-Laws of 1910—which were enacted as an amendment to the 1883 Native Jurisdiction Ordinance. These guidelines included stipulations that:

1. Latrines and rubbish pits must be established not less than 100 yards outside the town and those who refuse to use them can be fined 2 shillings, 6 pence by the chief.

2. Chiefs have the authority to order anyone to clean the ground around their house, to fill in all holes, to clear bush and dig latrines on pain of a fine of 10 shillings.

3. Chiefs must establish a cemetery not less than 100 yards outside the town. All dead bodies are to be buried there on pain of a fine of 20 shillings.

4. Chiefs must report all cases of infectious disease to the government and all residents must report cases of infectious diseases on pain of a fine of 20 shillings

5. No person should erect a building without the permission of the chief and all such buildings to be erected must be 12 feet from the nearest house, 30 feet from the front or back of any other building; it cannot be built on a roadway and provisions must be made for proper drainage.

6. Chiefs have the authority to have pulled down any house built without permission and the owner will be charged the cost of the demolition.

Copies of these Sanitary Bye-Laws can be found in ADM 11/1/450. For examples of prosecution of unlawful burials, see A. E. Griffith, District Commissioner, to the Honorable Colonial Secretary, Victoriaborg, Accra, 25 June 1894, ADM 41/1/8; and H. S. Newlands, District Commissioner, Quittah, to the Honorable Colonial Secretary, Accra, 11 March 1912, ADM 41/1/17.

11. Greene, Field Notes, No. 169A, Interview with Togbui Sorkpor, 19 April 1996, Anloga; see also the text of the prayer recorded by Christian Gaba which emphasizes the notion that "the red substance" is always present in a woman's bathroom in *Scriptures of an African People,* 59; C. Spiess, "Der Eintritt der Menstruation und die damit verbundenen Zeremonien bei den Evhenegern in Süd-Togo," *Anthropophyteia* (Leipzig) 8 (1911): 277; and C. Spiess, "Heidenische Gebräuche der Evhe Neger," *Archiv für Religionswissenschaft* 15 (1912): 168.

12. Schlegel, "Beitrag zur Geschichte," 407–408; Spieth, *Die Religion der Eweer,* 226–233; G. Binetsch, "Beantwortung mehrerer Fragen unser Ewe-Volk und seine Anschauungen," *Zeitschrift für Ethnologie* 38 (1906): 34–36; and J. Spieth, "Die Religiösen Vorstellungen der Eweer," *Monatsblatt der Norddeutschen Missionsgesellschaft* 3 (1906): 22.

13. Spieth, *Die Religion der Eweer,* 233.

14. Schlegel, "Beitrag zur Geschichte," 398.

15. Spieth, *Die Religion der Eweer,* 236.

16. Binetsch, "Beantwortung mehrerer Fragen," 47.

17. Ibid., 48.

18. In addition to these interviews—some of which are cited below—extensive discussions about Anlo burials and the beliefs that inform these practices exist in academic studies on the subject. See, for example, G. K. Nukunya, "Some Underlying Beliefs in Ancestor Worship and Mortuary Rites among the Ewe," in *La Notion de Personne en Afrique Noire,* ed. G. Dieterlen (Paris: Editions du Centre national de la recherche scientifique, 1973), 119–130; D. E. K. Fiawoo, "The Influence of Contemporary Social Changes on the Magico-Religious Concepts and Organization of the Southern Ewe-Speaking Peoples of Ghana" (Ph.D. diss., University of Edinburgh, 1959), 139; D. K. Fiawoo, "Ancestral Worship among the Ewe-Speaking People of Southern Ghana: A Study in Religious Change," *Ghana Journal of Sociology* 5, no. 2 (1969): 18–22; Kofi Anyidoho, "Death and Burial of the Dead: A Study of Ewe Funeral Folklore" (Master's thesis, Indiana University, 1983); Christian R. K. Bensah, "Anlo Belief in Life after Death" (B.A. Long Essay, Department for the Study of Religions, University of Ghana, 1979); D. K. Fiawoo, "Characteristic Features of Ewe Ancestor Worship," in *Ancestors,* ed. William H. Newell (The Hague: Mouton, 1976), 263–281; Dzifaa Kobla de Souza, "The Religious Significance of the Rites of Passage"; and D. K. Fiawoo, D. N. Nortey, E. H. Mends, J. M. Assimeng, and P. A. Twumasi, "Funeral Customs in Ghana: A Preliminary Report" (unpublished paper, Department of Sociology, University of Ghana, Legon, 1978).

19. Greene, Field Notes, No. 162, Interview with Togbui Awuku Dzrekey, 25 March 1996, Whuti.

20. Spieth, *Die Religion der Eweer,* 249. See also Jakob Spieth, *Die Ewe Stämme* (Berlin: Dietrich Reimer, 1906), 380.

21. Greene, Field Notes, No. 172, Interview with Mama Dzagba, 19 April 1996, Anloga. The emphasis on firstborn children being buried in the house seems

to be based on the belief that if this is not done, the mother will never successfully give birth again.

22. In using the term "transition zone," I emphasize a tripartite understanding of the environment—town/transition zone/bush—rather than a bipolar division (town/bush) because the Anlo environment had been so transformed by human occupation by the nineteenth century that the only real "bush" that existed in Anlo—areas that were far more the home of spiritual forces than human activity—was the ocean. All other areas were shaped in one form or another by the human hand: farms, burial sites, sacred groves, and the towns and villages where people maintained their primary residences. This notion of a transition zone is also based on Anlo descriptions of their own environment. Most elderly people in Anlo distinguished settled areas (home and village) from those areas where one was more likely to encounter spiritual forces (the transition zone) from those areas more fully dominated and controlled by such forces; for example, the ocean. John William Johnson discusses a similar division of space made by the Mande. See John William Johnson, *The Epic of Son-Jara: A West African Tradition* (Bloomington: Indiana University Press, 1986), 10–12.

23. Elaborate funeral rituals designed to facilitate the deceased spirit's entrance into the land of the dead (Tsiefe) were also denied such individuals in order to prevent their spirits from finding a way to return to the families through reincarnation. In Anloga, such burials took place in an uninhabited transition zone to the west of the town known as Kpota. Greene, Field Notes, No. 180, Interview with Togbui Akpate I, 23 April 1996, Srogbe; No. 141, Interview with Mama Daolo, 13 March 1996, Whuti.

Those who killed using supernatural means and some who died of disease were buried in yet another location outside of town at Avevoeme. Greene, Field Notes, No. 202, Interview with Togbui Tudzi, 15 May 1996, Anloga; No. 204, Interview with Togbui Sewornu, 5 June 1996, Anloga. At the same time, the burial places of priests and individuals associated with great spiritual power were kept secret altogether to ensure that their physical remains—which, according to Anlo belief, continued to have certain spiritual power—would not be unearthed by grave-robbers and used for nefarious purposes. Greene, Field Notes, No. 113, Interview with Togbui Akorbortu Efia, 10 February 1996, Anloga; No. 165, Interview with Tekpor Sedzorme, 27 March 1996, Anloga; No. 138, Interview with Togbui Kojo Lavoe, 3 March 1996, Srogbe. See also Acting Chief Commissioner, W. R. Gosling, Cape Coast, to the Honorable, the Commissioner of the Eastern Province, Koforidua, 29 August 1945, ADM 11/1/1679: Native Customs and Fetish.

Social concerns were not the only factors influencing the placing and spacing of the dead in nineteenth-century Anlo. Political concerns also influenced who was buried where. Between the late eighteenth and the early nineteenth centuries, the political leadership in Anlo began requiring that all residents outside Anloga, especially those who lived in villages founded by former Anloga residents, bury their dead in Anloga. This involved transporting them by boat and interring them on the outskirts of town. For a discussion of the historical origins of this practice, see Greene, *Gender, Ethnicity, and Social Change,* 81–88. See also Greene, Field Notes, No. 173, Interview with Tekpor Sedzorme, 15 April 1996, Anloga. For similar reasons, the Anlo government required that the placentas and umbilical cords of twins be buried in Anloga, the political and religious capital of the polity. The government seems to have required this in order to establish a firm link between these spiritually blessed individuals and the entire polity. For information on twins and twin burials, see Greene, Field Notes, No. 148, Interview with Mama Semefa, 17 March 1996, Anloga; No. 157, Interview with Sedzorme, 23 March 1996, Anloga; No. 209, Interview with Togbui Dedzo Megbemegbi, 13 June 1996, Anloga; and P. A. Witte, "Der Zwillingskult bei den Ewe-Negern in Westafrika," *Anthropos* SSIV, no. 5-6 (1929).

24. These graves were made intentionally shallow to expose the body to scavenging animals and birds, further reinforcing the rejection of the soul through rejection of the body. Debtors were refused burial altogether. Instead their corpses were placed on platforms on the outskirts of town and were either left to dry naturally or were smoked. They could be interred only if someone, their family or friend, was prepared to pay the debt. See Greene, *Gender, Ethnicity, and Social Change,* 103–104.

25. Greene, Field Notes, No. 234B, Interview with Togbui Tudzi, September 1996, Anloga; Elom Dovlo, "Sexual Morality among the Anlo Ewe" (B.A. Long Essay, Department for the Study of Religions, University of Ghana, Legon, 1976), 14.

26. Carl Spiess, "Der Legba-Kult in Seinen Verschiedenen formen an der Westafrikanischen Küste," *Bassler-Archiv* (Berlin) 6/4-6 (1922): 143-154; Michelle V. Gilbert, "Mystical Protection among the Anlo Ewe," *African Arts* XV, no. 4 (1982): 60-65, 90; Spieth, *Die Religion der Eweer,* 249; Senaya, "Ancestral Worship," 59-60.

27. Spieth, *Die Religion der Eweer,* 226; Greene, Field Notes, No. 116, Interview with Togbui Tretu, 13 February 1996, Anloga; No. 121, Interview with Togbui Awusu II, 18 February 1996, Atokor; Senaya, "Ancestral Worship," 35.

28. Greene, Field Notes, No. 205, Interview with Kofi Sorkpor, 8 June 1996, Anloga; No. 212, Interview with Kwasi Tome, 18 June 1996, Anloga; No. 218, Interview with Togbui Nyable and others elders of Tsiame, 13 July 1996, Tsiame; No. 230: Interview with Mama Nugblanuitor, 20 July 1996, Srogbe.

29. H. Seidel, "Krankheit, Tod und Begräbnis bei den Togonegern," *Globus* 10 (1897): 45; Anonymous, "Wie man zu Anyako"; Spieth, "Die Religiösen Vorstellungen," 23; Spieth, *Die Religion der Eweer,* 4. See also Greene, Field Notes, No. 175, Interview with Togbui Klomegah, 20 April 1996, Anloga.

30. Greene, Field Notes, No. 185, Interview with Aklorbortu Efia and Zanyiedor Kwawukume, 27 April 1996, Anloga; Spieth, *Die Religion der Eweer,* 4.

31. See Anthony Kwame Adanua, "Adevu: A Study of Ve Hunter's Music" (Music Diploma Thesis, Institute of African Studies, University of Ghana, 1990), 30-31 for a discussion of this ritual among the central Ewe. A similar ceremony was conducted by the Anlo as indicated in Greene, Field Notes, No. 152, Interview with Togbui Awuku Dzrekey, 19 March 1996, Whute. See also Kofi Awoonor's *This Earth My Brother* (London: Heinemann, 1972), 70.

32. Jakob Spieth, "Krankenbehandlung bei den Eweern in Togo," *Flugschriften des Bremer Vereins für ärtliche Mission* (Bremen: Bremen Mission, 1909), 8; Spieth, *Die Ewe-Stämme,* 280.

33. See Meyer, "Translating the Devil," Chapter 2, where she discusses the

Pietist belief in the Devil and how the souls of the dead—especially those of non-Christians—can become agents of Satan.

34. Spieth, "Ein Gökenhain," 46. See also Birgit Meyer, "Christian Mind and Worldly Matters," *Journal of Material Culture* 2, no. 3 (1997): 318, 319.

35. Meyer, "Translating the Devil," 28; Craig M. Koslofsky, *The Reformation of the Dead: Death and Ritual in Early Modern Germany, 1450–1700* (New York: St. Martin's Press, 1999), 46–48.

36. Toepfer, "Ein Frauenbrief aus Keta," 23.

37. The rules and regulations followed by the Bremen Mission were virtually the same as those used by the much larger Basel Mission. They included the requirement that one not participate in any "heathen" rituals or practices, that one desist from participating in the selling and buying of slaves, and that one attend services regularly, send children to school, and pay church taxes. The Basel regulations were published in revised form in 1902 under the title *Ordnung für die Evangelischen Gemeniden der Basler Mission auf der Goldküste* (Basel: Werner-Riehm, 1902). For a discussion of the intimate relations between the Basel and Bremen Missions, see Meyer, "Translating the Devil," 18–19.

38. The missionaries banned the carrying of the dead on the heads of mourners in order to combat the notion that if a person died prematurely and was thought to have been the victim of witchcraft, the spirit of the dead person would enter the bodies of those carrying the corpse and direct them to the person the spirit held responsible for his or her death.

39. Like other nineteenth-century European Protestants, the Bremen missionaries believed that "excessive attachment to the idea of burial in hallowed ground was . . . superstitious. God would resurrect the bodies of the dead where they lay, however complete their apparent destruction." See Ralph Houlbrooke, "Death, Church and Family in England between the Late Fifteenth and the Early Eighteenth Centuries," in *Death, Ritual and Bereavement,* ed. Ralph Houlbrooke (New York: Routledge, 1989), 38.

40. Sophie Spiess, "Heidnische und Christliche Totenfeiern und Begräbnisse," *Quartalblatt der Norddeutschen Missionsgesellschaft* 2 (1931): 7–8; Koslofsky, *The Reformation of the Dead,* 104.

41. Koslofsky, *The Reformation of the Dead,* 47; Houlbrooke, "Death, Church and Family," 100; Theophelus W. Adjorlolo, "The History of Education in Anlo with Special Reference to Keta, from 1850–1960" (B.A. Long Essay, History Department, University of Ghana, Legon, 1977), 10; A. E. Griffith, District Commissioner, Kwitta, to Registrar of Death, Accra, 12 March 1894, ADM 41/1/8.

42. For more on the history of burial practices in England, see Jim Morgan, "The Burial Question in Leeds in the Eighteenth and Nineteenth Centuries," in *Death, Ritual and Bereavement,* ed. Ralph Houlbrooke (New York: Routledge, 1989), 95–104. See also Perry Williams, "The Laws of Health: Women, Medicine and Sanitary Reform, 1850–1890," in *Science and Sensibility: Gender and Scientific Enquiry, 1780–1945,* ed. Marina Benjamin (Oxford: Blackwell, 1991), 64–65, 69–70, which discusses the history of the rise of public health concerns in Britain and the role of miasma theories of disease. See also Chapter 3 on public health and the Victorian state in Dorothy Porter, *Health, Civilization, and the State: A History of Public Health from Ancient to Modern Times* (New York: Routledge, 1999).

43. The missions were prosecuted for illegal burials just as local Anlo residents were by the colonial government. See Rex per E. H. Vanderpui -v-The Father Superior of the Catholic Mission, 30 March 1903, ADM 41/4/30: Civil and Criminal Record Book, Keta; and Harry S. Newlands, District Commissioner, Quittah, to the Commissioner of the Eastern Province, Akuse, 8 March 1912, ADM 41/1/17.

44. Morgan, "The Burial Question," 100.

45. Ibid., 101.

46. Dumett, "The Campaign against Malaria," 159. More specific guidelines for burials were developed in the Cemeteries Ordinance of 1891. See Harry S. Newlands, District Commissioner, Quittah, to Acting Commissioner of the Eastern Province, Akuse, 28 June 1911, ADM 41/1/16. For an excellent discussion of the history of colonial sanitation, see Stephen Kojo Addae, *The Evolution of Modern Medicine in a Developing Country Ghana, 1880–1960* (Edinburgh: Durham Academic Press, 1997), Chapter 6.

47. See Civil and Criminal Record Book, Keta, for accounts of the earliest recorded inspections before 1911 in such towns as Keta, Dzelukofe, Denu, and Woe, ADM 41/4/20 (1882–1883). The few instances in which individual Anlos were actually prosecuted for violation of the law or where the government received tips about improper burial can be found in Report by J. W. Stevens, 27 January 1900, Inspection Books (27/8/1897–24/9/1903), ADM 41/5/2; Harry S. Newlands, District Commissioner, Quittah, to Acting Commissioner of the Eastern Province, Akuse, 14 February 1912, ADM 41/1/17; Harry S. Newlands, District Commissioner, Quittah, to the Commissioner of the Eastern Province, Kpong, 1 December 1913, ADM 41/1/19; Minutes of the Sanitary Committee, 10 July 1922, ADM 39/1/206: Keta Sanitary Committee.

48. Greene, Field Notes, No. 138, Interview with Togbui Kojo Lavoe, 3 March 1996, Srogbe; No. 144, Interview with Mama Daolo, 15 March 1996, Whuti; Felix Arthur, Officer in Charge, Customs House, Jellah Coffee, to the Officer in Charge of Customs, Kwitta, 26 January 1900, ADM 11/1/1113. The traditional way of burying the dead in Anlo was to wrap the body in a mat. Coffins seem to have been introduced by Christian missionaries, although the history of this change—which falls outside the scope of this study—has yet to be written.

49. H. Seidel, "System der Fetischverbote in Togo," *Globus* LXXIII, no. 18 (1898): 342.

50. A. E. Griffith, District Commissioner, Kwitta, to the Honorable Colonial Secretary, Accra, 19 March 1894 and 29 June 1894, ADM 41/1/8.

51. Adjorlolo, "The History of Education in Anlo," 23.

52. "Annual Report of the Medical Department, (1907)" *Gold Coast Medical Annual Report, 1905–1909,* 10, available at the Korle Bu Teaching Hospital Library; *Report of the Educationist's Committee Appointed by His Excellency the Governor on 5th March 1920 on Educational Matters together with Minutes of the Committee* (Accra: Gold Coast Government Press, 1920), 24. This requirement for sanitary education in all classes was subsequently amended in 1909, when the teaching of hygiene was made obligatory for classes only after Standard III. That the Bremen Mission did indeed change its curriculum to conform with this new legislation was noted by Schlunk in his book *Die Norddeutsche Mission,* 19. For

a detailed history of educational efforts in Anlo more generally and the particular difficulties the officials of the Bremen Mission faced because of their desire to teach in the Ewe language rather than in English, see Adjorlolo, "The History of Education in Anlo"; H. O. A. McWilliam, *The Development of Education in Ghana* (London: Longmans, 1959), 20–21, 23–24, 30; Carl Osswald, *Fifty Years' Mission Work at Keta* (Bremen: Norddeutsche Missionsgesellschaft, 1903), 17–23–30; and Karl Schielingen, Missionary of the North German Mission Society, Mission House, Quittah, to the Secretary of the General Board of Education, 27 March 1883, ADM 11/1/1457: Report on the Education Department (1852–1897).

53. "Annual Report of the Medical Department (1907)," 10; *Medical and Sanitary Report for the Year 1911;* "Appendix No. 4: Report on the Teaching of Hygiene in the Schools of the Gold Coast Colony (1913)," 83; and "Appendix No. 2: Report on the Teaching of Hygiene in the Schools of the Gold Coast Colony (1914)," 101. All available at the Korle Bu Teaching Hospital Library.

54. Henry Strachan, *Lessons in Elementary Hygiene for the Use of Pupils in Tropical Schools* (London: Constable and Company, 1913), 70, 113–114.

55. *Medical and Sanitary Reports and Appendices,* Appendix No. 2: "Report on the Teaching of Hygiene" (1914), 101. Available at the Korle Bu Teaching Hospital Library.

56. A. H. L. Richter, District Commissioner, to [Missionary Leaders] Reverend Salkowski, Reverend Foster, Reverend Ahmling, Reverend Reymann, Reverend Stauffer, Reverend Frery et al., Quittah, 8/2/10, ADM 41/1/15. For additional information on health education efforts sponsored by the government, see Addae, *The Evolution of Modern Medicine.*

57. According to Addae, *The Evolution of Modern Medicine,* 143–144, the colonial government in Accra began supporting Health Weeks around 1925. The first evidence of this effort being implemented in Anlo is in 1927, but the event had to be cancelled. 1930 appears to be the first date by which Health Weeks were actually held in the Anlo town of Keta. See 8 January 1927 and 12 August 1930 in Keta Sanitary Committee, ADM 39/1/206.

58. These four chiefs demonstrated their support by serving on the Keta Sanitary Committee. See their many reports in ADM 39/1/206: Keta Sanitary Committee.

59. In 1922, for example, the medical officer assigned by the colonial government to Keta reported to the Keta Sanitary Committee that he had received reports indicating that burying corpses in houses was a common practice in Anloga. Minutes of the Keta Sanitary Committee, 10 July 1922, ADM 39/1/206. Kofi Awoonor suggests the late 1940s as the date by which almost all burials took place in cemeteries in his novel *This Earth, My Brother,* 73–74. He recounts an incident in which friends of an impoverished World War II veteran had difficulty finding a place to bury their friend. The Methodists refused him burial because he was not a member. The Presbyterians (with whom those associated with the Bremen Mission affiliated when the German missionaries left after the end of World War I) refused to accept his body because he had not been baptized. Finally, his friends found a spot in the "pagan" cemetery.

60. Dovlo, "Sexual Morality among the Anlo Ewe," 10. See also Bensah, "Anlo Belief in Life after Death," 22.

61. Greene, Field Notes, No. 151, Interview with Mama Nanevi, 19 March 1996, Anloga.

62. Greene, Field Notes, No. 117, Interview with Kwasi Tome, 14 February 1996, Anloga.

63. An adjustment in the meaning of home burials was just one of the many changes that began to occur as families responded to the changes wrought by colonialism and "modernity." The practice of burying the placenta and umbilical cords of newborns in the floor of the bath house seems to also have undergone a change as economic prosperity allowed families to cement bathing-room floors. Perhaps in response to this change, and perhaps to accommodate Christianity, the umbilical cord and the placenta no longer represent the spirit mother of the child. Rather, during the rites that introduce the child to the material world (known as an outdooring, *vi yeye dego*), a woman born on the same day as the child is selected to serve as the spirit mother. During the outdooring ceremony, the actual physical mother of the child has to "purchase" her newborn from the "spirit mother" by paying a certain token amount in money. F. R. K. Tagbor, "Marriage, Birth and Death Ceremonies in South Anlo" (Specialist Training College, Winnega, n.d.), 14; Senaya, "Ancestor Worship in Anloland," 10.

64. Government reports about the fire, the rebuilding of the town, and objections to government plans can be found in A. Connal, Acting District Commissioner, Quittah, to Acting Commissioner of the Eastern Province, Akuse, 17 August 1911 and 21 August 1911; J. Phillips, District Commissioner to the Commissioner of the Eastern Province, Akuse, 4 September 1911, 11 September 1911, 18 September 1911, and 22 September 1911, all in ADM 41/1/16; J. Phillips, District Commissioner, Quittah, to Commissioner of the Eastern Province, Akuse, 8 December 1911, ADM 41/1/17; and Judicial Council Court Record: Native Tribunal of Fia Sri II, Awunaga, 10 December 1918: Linguist Davordjie of Awunuaga -v- Agbemawonu of Anloga, 10 December 1918, District Court Grade II, Anloga. Eyewitness accounts exist in Greene, Field Notes, No. 173, Tekpor Sedzorme, 15 April 1996. See also No. 180, Interview with Togbui Akpate I, 23 April 1996, Srogbe; and No. 189, Togbui Tudzi, 20 April 1996, Anloga.

65. Elia Awuma, "Reste des Heidentums in der Christlichen Gemeinde," *Monatsblatt der Norddeutschen Missionsgesellschaft* 88 (1927): 11.

66. For more information on the use of beads for both protection and for other identification purposes, see Emily Selormey, "The Importance of Beads with Particular Reference to the Anlo Traditional Area" (Long Essay, Specialist Training College, Winneba, 1978). See also Greene, Field Notes, No. 234D, Interview with Akorbortu Efia, 15 September 1996, Anloga.

67. Adjorlolo, "The History of Education in Anlo," 20–24. A similar larger movement has emerged in the Evangelical Presbyterian Church in Ghana, the successor of the Bremen Mission. For a discussion of this larger movement—which has manifested itself in a split within the Evangelical Presbyterian Church—see Meyer, "Translating the Devil," 194–211. See also Julius Kwame Ahiable, "Physical Education in Anlo Schools from 1933 to the Present Time" (Long Essay, Specialist

Training College, Winneba, 1969), 12, which examines the role of Rev. E. W. Tamakloe in championing the inclusion of local forms of drumming and dancing in the schools under his authority as head of the Anlo district diocese. See also Harris W. Mobley, *The Ghanaian's Image of the Missionary* (Leiden: E. J. Brill, 1970), which discusses critiques by Ephraim Amu of the Bremen Mission efforts to disengage Ewes from their own culture and critiques by Ghanaians published by European missionaries between 1897 and 1965.

68. This caveat is necessary because practices vary so widely even among non-Christians. While I was told by residents in Anloga in 1996 that everyone is buried in cemeteries except perhaps chiefs and traditional priests, in other towns (especially those on the northern side of the Keta Lagoon), burials continue outside town for those who died in car accidents. In 1973, for example, I (unknowingly at the time) witnessed such a burial when attending the interment of a fellow University of Ghana student who had lived in the residential hall where I also stayed.

69. For more information on the history of modern cemeteries and burial practices in Anlo, see C. K. Dotse, "The Development of Death Sculpture in South Anlo Traditional Area" (Long Essay, School of Art, Home Science and Physical Education, Winneba Specialist Training College, 1976); and Michelle V. Gilbert, "Ewe Funerary Sculpture," *African Arts* XIV, no. 4 (1981): 45–46, 88.

4. Belief and the Body

1. See, for example, Greene, Field Notes, No. 173, Interview with Tekpor Sedzorme, 15 April 1996, Anloga; No. 192, Interview with Togbui Tudzi, 3 May 1996, Anloga; No. 203, Interview with Aklorbortu Efia and Zanyiedor Kwawukume, 16 May 1996, Anloga; No. 215, Interview with Mama Daolo, 21 June 1996, Whuti. A similar attitude is reported to have existed in other communities on the Gold Coast and in southern Nigeria. See Addae, *The Evolution of Modern Medicine,* 361; and Eva Gilles, "Causal Criteria in African Classifications of Disease," in *Social Anthropology and Medicine,* ed. J. B. Loudon (London: Academic Press, 1976), 364. Interestingly, the Bremen missionaries, who were among the first to discuss Anlo ideas about the causes of illness in writing, focused so exclusively on serious illnesses that they ignored completely the more common diseases and the fact that the Anlo did not associate these with spiritual causes. See, for example, Spieth, "Krankenbehandlung," 1–16 and *Die Ewe-Stämme,* 248–255; and G. Härtter, "Sitten und Gebräuche der Angloer (Ober-Guinea), *Zeitschrift für Ethnologie* 38 (1906): 48.

2. Greene Field Notes, No. 171, Interview with Togbui Awuku Dzrekey, 18 April 1996, Whuti; and Spieth, *Die Ewe-Stämme,* 250.

3. Anyidoho, "Oral Poetics," 100, 103. The relationship that is implied between the body's mouth and the *gbɔgbɔ* in this account is discussed in Ellis, *The Ewe-Speaking Peoples,* 107. Here he notes that when one died, the *gbɔgbɔ* exited from the mouth and that many precautions were taken to keep the mouth closed on certain occasions so that the spirit of another would not enter one's body through the mouth.

4. Ellis, *The Ewe-Speaking Peoples,* 98. See also Härtter, "Sitten und Gebräuche der Angloer," 41.

5. Spieth, *Die Religion der Eweer,* 229–230.

6. Ellis, *The Ewe-Speaking Peoples,* 102, 106–107.

7. Härtter, "Sitten und Gebräuche der Angloer," 42.

8. Ellis, *The Ewe-Speaking Peoples,* 105.

9. This quote, which so aptly describes the Anlo concept of the person as a physical and spiritual unity, comes from Fritz Kramer, *The Red Fez: Art and Spirit Possession in Africa* (London: Verso, 1993), 65.

10. W. H. Adams, District Commissioner, Kwitta, 4/12/96, ADM 41/1/9.

11. Schlegel, "Beitrag zur Geschichte," 407–408; Spieth, *Die Religion der Eweer,* 232–233.

12. Dovlo, "Sexual Morality among the Anlo Ewe," 10.

13. Spieth, *Die Ewe Stämme,* 252; Spiess, "Entritt der Menstruation," 183–184; Härtter, "Der Fischfang," 55; Spiess, "Heidenische Gebräuche," 169.

14. For more on the Amlade, see Greene, *Gender, Ethnicity, and Social Change,* 48–68.

15. Detailed descriptions of the Anlo investiture ritual for the *awoamefia* are not available in nineteenth-century accounts or in contemporary oral narratives. This account, therefore, is based on more limited information collected during oral interviews in Anloga and on the study of investiture among other Ewe-speaking communities in the area by Nii Otokunor Quarcoopome in his "Rituals and Regalia of Power: Art and Politics among the Dangme and Ewe, 1800 to Present" (Ph.D. diss., University of California, Los Angeles, 1993), 90–91, 96–97. Proper management of the *awoamefia*'s body included keeping him from seeing corpses and having him participate directly only in those rituals in which the body of a sacrificial animal was killed by strangulation or suffocation rather than through use of a knife.

16. According to Nukunya, more contemporary Anlo beliefs attribute witchcraft to inheritance from the mother, a trait that is passed on to all uterine kin. Nukunya, *Kinship and Marriage,* 46, 52.

17. Anonymous, "Vom Hexenglauben der Eweer." See also Binetsch, "Beantwortung mehrerer Fragen," 40.

18. See Anonymous, "Vom Hexenglauben der Eweer," 13; Schlegel, "Beitrag zur Geschichte," 408. Being held responsible by others or by oneself for one's own witchcraft among the Anlo is a practice that contrasts with practices among the Effutu. See, for example, R. W. Wyllie, "Introspective Witchcraft among the Effutu of Southern Ghana," *Man* 8, no. 1 (1973): 74–79.

19. For a discussion of the contemporary meanings of these spiritual objects, cords, and cowry shells, see Suzanne Preston Blier, *African Vodun: Art, Psychology, and Power* (Chicago: University of Chicago Press, 1995), 242–249, 254–258, 293–297.

20. See Anonymous, "Vom Hexenglauben der Eweer"; Spieth, "Krankenbehandlung," 1–16; and Spieth, *Die Ewe-Stämme,* 248–268.

21. See Ellis, *Ewe-Speaking Peoples,* 107, on nineteenth-century Ewe notions about spirit possession. See Judy Rosenthal, *Possession, Ecstasy, and Law in Ewe Voodoo* (Charlottesville; University Press of Virginia, 1998) on late-twentieth-century understandings of spirit possession among the Ewe.

22. Spieth, *Die Ewe-Stämme,* 250.

23. Spieth, "Krankenbehandlung."

24. Ibid., 1.

25. A. Knüsli, "Afrikanisches Frauenleben," *Monatsblatt der Norddeutschen Missionsgesellschaft* 68 (1906): 11.

26. This nineteenth-century understanding of illness and the body is perhaps most clearly discussed by Spieth in his "Krankenbehandlung."

27. The intimacy of this relationship was evident in the terms for a priest. Such individuals were called *troshi,* spouse of a god, and *tronua,* the mouth or spokesperson of a god. For information on nineteenth-century adornment practices and/or their symbolic significance, see Quarcoopome, "Rituals and Regalia of Power," Chapter 4; Charles Nani Ayayee, "Twins and Their Ceremonies among the Anlos" (B.A. Long Essay, Department for the Study of Religions, University of Ghana, Legon, 1975); Witte, "Der Zwillingskult," *Anthropos* XXIV, no. 5–6 (1929): 943–951; Dzifaa Kobla de Souza, "The Religious Significance of the Rites of Passage"; Maxine Kumekpor, "Some Sociological Aspects of Beads with Special Reference to Selected Beads found in Eweland," *Ghana Journal of Sociology* 6, no. 2/7, 1 (1971): 100–108; Greene, Field Note No. 234D, Interview with Togbui Aklorbortu Efia, 15 September 1996, Anloga; No. 239, Interview with Togbui Kwasi Tome, 9 September 1996, Anloga; District Commissioner, Quittah, to the Commissioner of the Eastern Province, Victoriaborg, Accra, 19 January 1916, Item 21—Fetish Customs (30/1909—15/6/28), National Archives of Ghana, Ho; and L. T. K Dogbe, "The Significance of Body Marks in Anlo" (Art Diploma, Specialist Training College, Winneba, 1971). See H. Seidel, "Der Yewe-Dienst im Togolande," *Zeitschrift für Afrikanische und oceanische Sprachen* 3 (1897): 164, where he discusses the ritual induction of initiates into the Yewe religious order. The induction culminates in the ingestion of "holy water" and is understood to be the way in which an initiate takes Yewe into her body. See also Hugo Zöller, *Das Togoland und die Scklavenküste* (Berlin: W. Spemann, 1885), 96–98; and Ebenezer Atieku, "Colour in Anlo Traditional Religion" (Department of Art, Specialist Training College, Winneba, 1978).

28. Roy Porter, *The Greatest Benefit to Mankind: A Medical History of Humanity* (New York: W. W. Norton and Co., 1998), 247.

29. Spieth, *Die Religion der Eweer,* 232.

30. For a discussion of the spiritual aspects of alcoholism in colonial and postcolonial Ghana, see Emmanuel Akyeampong, "Alcoholism in Ghana: A Sociocultural Exploration," *Culture, Medicine and Psychiatry* 19, no. 2 (1995): 261–280.

31. Meyer, "Translating the Devil," 26–30. See also Dennis F. Mahoney, "Human History as Natural History in *Die Lehrlinge zu Sais* and *Heinrich von Ofterdingen,*" in *Subversive Sublimities: Undercurrents of the German Enlightenment,* ed. Eitel Timm (Columbia, S.C.: Camden House, 1992), 2; and Arnd Bohm, "The Desublimated Body: Gottfred August Bürger," in *Subversive Sublimities,* 12. Both authors discuss the extent to which eighteenth-century German Enlightenment thinking encouraged individuals to understand the body as something that required "covering, disciplining and defining."

32. This emphasis on consciously choosing to become a Christian is emphasized by Missionary Forster in his account of the baptism of the first Christians in Anloga. See Forster, "Die Taufe der Erstlinge von Anloga," 85.

33. For a discussion of how the efforts by religious Europeans more generally and the Pietists in particular to define the soul's relationship to the body as seventeenth- and eighteenth-century scientific discoveries continually challenged European notions about the nature of God, the soul, and the body, see Suzanne E. Hatty and James Hatty, *The Disordered Body: Epidemic Disease and Cultural Transformation* (Albany: State University of New York Press, 1999), 3–21; Porter, *The Greatest Benefit,* Chapters 9 and 10; and Sabine Roehr, *A Primer on German Enlightenment* (Columbia: University of Missouri Press, 1995), 3–18, 70–72.

34. This lack of belief in witchcraft was a widespread phenomenon among Germans more generally and was not peculiar to the Pietists. See Mary Lindemann, *Health and Healing in Eighteenth-Century Germany* (Baltimore: Johns Hopkins University Press, 1996), 305–307.

35. A. Knuesli, "Afrikanisches Frauenleben: Lichtstrahlen vom Evangelium," *Monatsblatt der Norddeutschen Missionsgesellschaft* 68 (1907): 11.

36. Spieth, *Die Ewe-Stämme,* 230–235. For additional observations by Europeans on nineteenth-century Anlo body adornment, see Hans Zöller, *Das Togoland,* 92–97.

37. Knuesli, "Afrikanisches Frauenleben," 10.

38. Schlegel, "Beitrag zur Geschichte," 407.

39. "Heidnisches Leben," *Quartalblatt der Norddeutschen Missionsgesellschaft* 68 (1873): 320–321.

40. See, for example, Jakob Spieth, "Von den Evhefrauen," *Quartalblatt der Norddeutschen Missionsgesellschaft* IV (1889): 1–8; and Carl Spiess, "Brautsitten under den Evhe-Negern in Togo," *Anthropophyteia* (Leipzig) 8 (1911): 173–180, in which both authors, who had expressed very negative views on the topic elsewhere, discuss in quite positive terms the fact that non-Christian Anlo and other Ewe-speaking peoples in the region did have notions about modesty, bodily hygiene, and an abhorrence of lust.

41. *Ordnung für die Evangelischen Gemeniden der Basler Mission,* 36–37.

42. Knuesli, "Afrikanisches Frauenleben," 21.

43. Interestingly, the Bremen missionaries insisted that the Anlo take European Christian names even though they recognized that many Anlo names—those that referred to the power of god, Mawu or Se—were equivalent in meaning or sentiment to the European names. They banned the use of all Anlo names by local Christians so as not to be faced with the seeming inconsistency of allowing some names but not others. See Binetsch, "Beantwortung mehrerer Fragen," 41–42.

44. For a detailed discussion of Bremen missionary belief in the Devil, see Meyer, "Translating the Devil," 36–48.

45. "Neger-Doctoren," *Monatsblatt der Norddeutschen Missionsgesellschaft* 24, no. 283 (1874): 1313–1314.

46. Spieth, "Von den Evhefrauen," 5; Spieth, "Krankenbehandlung," 16. In taking this approach, the Bremen missionaries eschewed spiritual healing of naturally caused diseases, even though the early theologians associated with nineteenth-century Pietist thought at first had given credence to such approaches. For a history of Pietist thought on spiritual healing, see Frank D. Macchia, *Spiritual and Social Liberation: The Message of the Blumhards in the Light of Wuerttemberg Pietism* (Metuchen, N.J.: Scarecrow Press, 1993), 24–28, 61–75, 165–166.

47. See Carl Spiess, "Austribung eines böse Geistes," *Monatsblatt der Nord-deutschen Missionsgesellschaft* 88 (1927): 30–31; and Meyer, "Translating the Devil," 40. Based on her analysis of Jakob Spieth's autobiography, Meyer argues that the center of satanic action was the heart, since Spieth emphasized that the heart was the source of the feeling over which the Devil could gain control. Spieth, I believe, was very much influenced by Pietist and perhaps Romantic reactions to the German Enlightenment that argued for the importance of being in touch with one's feelings rather than relying solely on the power of reason. This emphasis on the heart, however, does not undermine the notion that for Spieth and the other German missionaries who operated in Anlo the only way to combat the Devil was through bringing the soul onto the path of righteousness; that is, to be as close to God within oneself as possible.

48. This cleansing did not involve exorcism, however, a practice that was condemned by the Reformed Pietist hierarchy and eventually abandoned by its most ardent supporter within the church, Johan Blumhardt, in the late nineteenth century. See Macchia, *Spiritual and Social Liberation.*

49. Flothmeier, "Bilder aus unserer Arbeit," 86–87.

50. Other areas of support came from refusing to abide by the ban on European clothing that the Nyigbla religious order maintained in Anlo and by simply being socially supportive despite occasional clashes. In 1856, Gold Coast Colony governor Sir Samuel Rowe was pelted with dirt when he rode through Anloga in European clothing and on a horse. The government responded quite vigorously to this, and therefore in 1884, the Anlo allowed Bremen missionary Binetsch to ride through the town fully clothed and on a horse without being assaulted. See H. Seidel, "System der Fetischverbote in Togo," 341. The Bremen missionaries also, at times, socialized with the colonial officers in Keta. See "Not und Hülfe im Diakonissenhause in Keta," *Monatsblatt der Norddeutschen Missionsgesellschaft* 3 (1907): 71–72.

51. For information on sanitation and public health efforts in Anlo and resistance thereto, especially with regard to smallpox vaccinations, see various entries in ADM 41/4/28 and 30; ADM 41/5/2; ADM 41/1/5, 8–9, 15–19 and 35; ADM 39/1/206; and ADM 11/1/450. The last recorded active resistance to the colonial smallpox vaccination campaign that I have been able to locate can be found in Commissioner of Police-v-Amega, Salo Agbeshie, and Awuti, ADM 41/4/35. Smallpox vaccination was made compulsory by the colonial government in 1920. See G. A. Ashitey, *Disease Control in Ghana* (Accra: Ghana Universities Press, 1994), 6. See also John Maxwell, ed., *The Gold Coast Handbook* (Westminster: Crown Agents for the Colonies, 1928), and this same title, published in 1937 by West Africa Publicity Ltd. London on health conditions in Anlo. See also entries on the Keta District in the annual journal *Medical and Sanitary Report on the Gold Coast Colony.*

52. See, for example, Strachan, *Lessons in Elementary Hygiene.*

53. Ibid., 87, 90.

54. McWilliam, *The Development of Education,* 54–55. See W. David Smith, *Stretching their Bodies: The History of Physical Education* (London: David and Charles, 1974); and Bruce Haley, *The Healthy Body and Victorian Culture* (Cambridge: Harvard University Press, 1978), Introduction and Chapter 1, which dis-

cuss the history of physical education in Britain. See also the *Report of the Educationist's Committee Appointed by His Excellency the Governor on 5th March 1920 to Advise the Government on Educational Matters* (Accra: Gold Coast Printing Press, 1920). For information on the curriculum content of the Bremen Mission schools prior to 1920, see Schlunk, *Die Norddeutsche Mission,* 18–23; see also Karl Schieling, Missionary of the North German Mission Society, Mission House, Quittah, to the Secretary of the General Board of Education, 27 March 1883, Report on the Education Department (1852–1897), ADM 121/1/1475. The Bremen Mission schools began receiving government support in the early 1880s and in so doing faced considerable pressure to increase their teaching of English despite their desire to emphasize teaching in Ewe. For those attending Bremen Mission schools in the 1920s, the inclusion of sports that focused on the entire body supplemented an earlier emphasis on "hand work" or vocational education (carpentry and weaving for boys; knitting, crocheting, and sewing for girls) and farm work. Games involving balls were played but were not supervised. Gymnastics and marching exercises took place in Anloga in 1902, but it seems likely that they were introduced by individual missionaries and they were not part of the usual curriculum. See G. Härtter, "Ein Schultag in Keta," *Monatsblatt der Norddeutschen Missionsgesellschaft* 1 (1890): 3–4; and Salkowski, "Anloga," 20. For information on the curriculum of the Catholic schools, see Report of the Acting Director of Education for the Year, 1892–93 (1893), 36–37, ADM 121/1/1475. Physically demanding games developed by the Anlo themselves had also been played by boys before the curriculum change. See G. Härtter, "Spiele der Evheer," *Quartalblatt der Norddeutschen Missionsgesellschaft* 38, no. 1 (1897): 1–8.

55. These are rather crude statistics based on a number of sources. See Philip Foster, *Education and Social Change in Ghana* (Chicago: University of Chicago Press, 1965), 117; D. J. Oman, *Report on the Direction of the Former Bremen Mission of the Government of the Gold Coast from June 1916 to March 1926* (Accra: Government Printer, 1927); and Adjorlolo, "The History of Education in Anlo." For more detailed statistical information on the history of schools in the greater Anlo area, see Francis Agbodeka, ed., *A Handbook of Eweland,* vol. 1, *The Ewes of Southeastern Ghana* (Accra: Woeli Pub., 1997), 326–393.

56. Many studies on witchcraft in colonial Ghana have emphasized the extent to which the colonial period saw a great upsurge in anti-witchcraft activity as individuals attempted to cope with the changes wrought by colonialism. Disagreements exist, however, about the cause of this increase and whether any increase occurred at all. Relevant studies on this topic include Barbara E. Ward, "Some Observations on Religious Cults in Ashanti," *Africa* XXVI, no. 1 (1956): 47–61; Jack Goody, "Anomie in Ashanti," *Africa* XXVII, no. 4 (1957): 356–363; Malcolm McLeod, "On the Spread of Anti-Witchcraft Cults in Modern Asante," in *Changing Social Structure in Ghana: Essays in the Comparative Sociology of a New State and an Old Tradition,* ed. Jack Goody (London: International African Institute, 1975), 107–117; and T. C. McCaskie, "Anti-Witchcraft Cults in Asante: An Essay in the Social History of an African People," *History in Africa* 8 (1981): 125–154. Evidence from Anlo suggests that witchcraft accusations existed long before colonial rule, but whether colonialism brought an increase in accusations is unclear.

57. Acting Chief Commissioner, W. R. Gosling, Cape Coast, to the Honorable, the Commissioner of the Eastern Province, Koforidua, 29 August 1945, ADM 11/1/1679. For a discussion of the political context that gave rise to this murder, see Roger Gocking, "A Chieftancy Dispute and Ritual Murder in Elmina, Ghana, 1945–6," *Journal of African History* 41, no. 2 (2000): 197–219.

58. On efforts to ban all *atike vodu* in Anlo, including Brekete (also known as Kunde), see Anlo State Council Minute Book (29 June 1934–5–7 November 1946), entries for 28/10/36 and 20 September 1934, 38–40, 179–180, Anlo State Council Office, Anloga.

59. Dzigbodi Kodzo Fiawoo, "The Influence of Contemporary Social Change on the Magico-Religious Concepts and Organization of the Southern Ewe-speaking Peoples of Ghana," Chapter 9; Rosenthal, *Possession, Ecstasy and Law,* 84–90; Kramer, *The Red Fez,* 46.

60. See Geurts, "Sensory Perception," 170–171.

61. See Logo Patrick Agbenyegah, "Perceptions of Childhood Disease in Mafi, Volo, Battor and Dorffor Traditional Arts in the Volta Region" (B.A. Long Essay, Department of Sociology, University of Ghana, Legon, 1993), 26. This study focuses on an area just north and west of Anlo located on the Volta River but illustrates the extent to which education has impacted the way local people in rural areas understand the causes of disease in much of southern Ghana (including the Anlo district). This point is made as well by Gabriel Fosu and Robert Wyllie. Gabriel Fosu, "Disease Classification in Rural Ghana: Framework and Implications for Health Behaviour," *Social Science and Medicine* 15B (1981): 471–482; and Robert W. Wyllie, "Ignorance and Etiological Anarchy," *Anthropos* 89, no. 1 (1994): 191–193.

62. Geurts, "Sensory Perception," 261.

63. A decline in the belief in witchcraft is seen in Ewe funeral poetry and practice, where the principal concern is with the evil use of occult powers rather than with witches per se. See Anyidoho, "Death and Burial," 34. Abandonment of those aspects of traditional religious orders that involved witch-finding is noted by Kramer, *The Red Fez,* 46.

64. Note that it was Christian chiefs and those educated Anlos who served in colonial administrative posts who spearheaded efforts to encourage the British colonial government to take action against many indigenous religious orders in Anlo in the 1920s and 1930s. See, for example, Francis Crowther, Secretary for Native Affairs, Accra, to the Commissioner of the Eastern Province, Akuse, 24 October 1912; Abraham Bor Klo, Acting Fia of Agbosome, to the District Commissioner, Keta, 2 November 1915; J. J. Phillips, D.C., Quittah, to the Commissioner of the Eastern Province, Victoriaborg, Accra, 4 December 1915; H. S. Newlands, District Commissioner, Quittah, to the Commissioner of the Eastern Province, Akuse, 15 November 1913; Mr. Tennyson Kue, Anecho, to the District Commissioner, 17 August 1923; Adamah II, Fia of Some (Keta) Fia's Office, Agbosome, Gold Coast, to the District Commissioner, Quittah, 28 June 1923. All in Item 21— Fetish Customs (30/1909–15/6/28), National Archives of Ghana, Ho.

65. Flothmeier, "Bilder aus unserer Arbeit," 87.

66. In focusing on those churches that are the descendants of the Mission churches, I am excluding the many Pentecostal or Apostolic churches that began to be established in the Anlo district after 1924. As indicated in Fosu's study, many

of the members of these churches believe as strongly in the spiritual causes of disease as do traditional believers. This probably has to do with educational level as well. See Fosu, "Disease Classification in Rural Ghana."

67. See Fiawoo, "The Influence," 292, 181–185, 210, 343. See also Harris W. Mobley, *The Ghanaian's Image of the Missionary: An Analysis of the Published Critiques of Christian Missionaries by Ghanaians, 1897–1965* (Leiden: E. J. Brill, 1970), which discusses the efforts of a number of Ghanaians (including Ephraim Amu, who was associated with the Bremen Mission) to counter the missionary orientation of opposing all indigenous cultural practices. See also Kofi Agawu, "The Amu Legacy," *Africa* 66, no. 2 (1996): 274–279.

68. Educational advances (evident primarily within the Christian community, since Western education has been and continues to be closely linked with the Christian faith) have furthered reinforced belief in the notion that the body and the mind are separate and distinct entities. In many a study conducted in recent years by Anlo university students, for example, discussions about Anlo belief in reincarnation are frequently followed by an analysis suggesting that genetic as well as psychological factors can easily explain the resemblances that traditional believers attribute to reincarnation. See, for example, Bensah, "Anlo Belief in Life after Death," 5. See also Geurts, "Sensory Perception," 285–286.

69. Bensah, "Anlo Belief in Life after Death," 5. See also Gustav Jahoda, "Social Aspirations, Magic and Witchcraft in Ghana: A Social Psychological Interpretation," in *The New Elites of Tropical Africa: Studies Presented and Discussed at the Sixth International African Seminar at the University of Ibadan, Nigeria, July 1964,* ed. P. C. Lloyd (London: Oxford University Press, 1966).

70. The inclusion of money was designed to ensure that the deceased had the means to pay the individual who ferried them across the river that separated the world of the living, Kodzogbe, from the world of the dead, Tsiefe.

71. Souza, "The Religious Significance of the Rites of Passage," 50; and D. K. Fiawoo, "Ancestral Worship," 20.

72. These statistics were calculated on the basis of a survey in Berekuso, a rural community twenty-five miles northwest of Accra, but they appear to be accurate for much of southern Ghana, including the Anlo district. Fosu, "Disease Classification in Rural Ghana." See also G. K. Nukunya, P. A. Twumasi, and N. O. Addo, "Attitudes towards Health and Disease in Ghanaian Society," *Conch* 7, no. 1–2 (1975): 113–136, which contains a brief study of attitudes toward health in the Anlo community of Dzelukofe.

73. For an excellent study of notions about the Devil among the Ewe-speaking peoples of Peki that is equally applicable to the Ewe-speaking Anlo, see Birgit Meyer, "Translating the Devil."

74. For a discussion of Ghana's efforts over the last 100 years to eradicate a number of diseases, including syphilis, gonorrhea, yaws, smallpox, guinea worm, and a number of respiratory illnesses that were common in the Anlo district, see Ashitey, *Disease Control;* and Addae, *Evolution of Modern Medicine.*

5. Contested Terrain

1. Some still do believe that smallpox is caused the by the deity Sakpana and that the only way to avoid its call is to be inoculated by knowledgeable elders.

See, for example, Greene, Field Notes, No. 203, Interview with Togbui Aklorbortu Efia and Zanyiedor Kwawukume, 16 May 1996, Anloga; No. 204, Togbui Sewornu, 5 June 1996, Anloga.

2. See C. Spiess, "Fünfzig Jahre," 4.

3. H. Seidel, "System der Fetischverbote," 342.

4. Charismatic-type churches are the relatively new Protestant denominations that have emerged in Ghana which distinguish themselves from both the former mission churches and the Pentecostal-style or independent African churches that developed in the 1930s. Features that differ from the older mission churches include an emphasis on healing and prosperity, using local instruments (now also embraced by many former mission churches), and possession by the Holy Spirit. Yet they forbid polygyny and allow women to cook for their male husbands and elders when on their menses, unlike some Pentecostal or independent churches such as the Apostles Revelation Society. Most are extremely hostile to traditional religious beliefs. See Greene, Field Notes, No. 195, Interview with Pastor L. K. Larbi and elders, 7 May 1996, Anloga; Rosalind I. J. Hackett, "Charismatic/Pentecostal Appropriation of Media Technologies in Nigeria and Ghana," *Journal of Religion in Africa* SSIV, no. 3 (1994): 241–265; Paul Gifford, "Ghana's Charismatic Churches," *Journal of Religion in Africa* XXVIII, no. 3 (1998): 258–277; "Church of Pentecost," unpublished manuscript, Institute of African Studies, University of Ghana, Legon; and Sandra E. Greene, "Sacred Terrain: Religion, Politics and Place in the History of Anloga (Ghana)," *International Journal of African Historical Studies* 30, no. 1 (1997): 1–22.

5. See Greene, "Sacred Terrain."

6. C. Spiess, "We, Anglo and Atoko," 35.

7. Sandra E. Greene, Field Notes, No. 37, Interview with Boko Seke Axovi, 4 October 1978, Anloga; D. Westermann, *The Study of the Ewe Language* (London: Oxford University Press, 1930), 243.

8. See Westermann, *Study of Ewe,* 242–245; and Fiawoo, "The Influence," 106–108. See also G. Härtter's description of Nyiko, which conforms quite closely with that of Werstermann and Schlegel. Härtter, "Sitten und Gebräuche der Angloer," 50; and F. K. Fiawoo, *The Fifth Landing Stage: A Play in Five Acts* (Accra: Sedco, 1983), originally published in 1943.

9. For additional information on these battles, see Sandra E. Greene, "The Anlo Ewe: Their Economy, Society and External Relations in the Eighteenth Century" (Ph.D. diss., Northwestern University, 1981).

10. Greene, Field Notes, No. 20, Interview with Togbui Alex Afatsao Awadzi, 30 August 1978, Anloga; No. 53, Interview with Togbui Alex Afatsao Awadzi, 16 December 1987, Anloga.

11. The Bremen Mission included girls in their primary education program from the beginning but opened a separate school for girls and women in 1883. See Osswald, *Fifty Years' Mission Work at Keta,* 17; and Adjorlolo, "The History of Education in Anlo," 7. Girls were not encouraged to seek higher educational levels beyond middle school, since they were supposed to become Christian wives and mothers.

12. For details on the development of the different mission schools in Anlo by the Bremen Mission, see *Report on the Direction of the Former Bremen Mission of the Government of the Gold Coast from June 1916 to March, 1926* (Accra: Gold

Coast Government Printer, 1927): 5. For more on the "native assistants" and the history of the first ordination of African ministers, see Debrunner, *A Church between Colonial Powers,* Chapters 7 and 9.

13. On the limited linguistic skills of the missionaries, the serious loss of life among their numbers, and the absolutely essential role that the "native assistants" played, see Debrunner, *A Church between Colonial Powers,* 76, 88, 134. See also E. Bürgi, "Der Alte Keta-Kirchhof," *Monatsblatt der Norddeutschen Missionsgesellschaft* 11 (1889): 100–103. The work carried out by the Bremen missionary women, known as deaconesses, was particularly hindered by illness and death. See "Not und Hülfe," 69–72, and "Einschräkung der Diakonissenarbeit in Keta," both in *Monatsblatt der Norddeutschen Missionsgesellschaft* 3 (1904): 22–24.

14. This indifference and amusement is widely discussed in the various reports of the early mission workers. See for example, Osswald, *Fifty Years' Mission Work at Keta,* 8–9; Spiess, "Fünfzig Jahre," 4; and Fredrick Plessing, "Briefe aus Keta," *Monatsblatt der Norddeutschen Missionsgesellschaft* 5/57 (1855): 244–248.

15. Spiess, "Fünfzig Jahre," 4.

16. Greene, Field Notes, No. 57, Interview with Robert G. Kofi Afetogbo, 22 December 1987, Anloga.

17. E. Salkowski, "Anloga," 7–8.

18. For more on the practice of Afa (known as Ifa among the Yoruba) in Anlo, see Albert de Surgy, *La Géomancie et le culte d'Afa chez les Evhé du littoral* (Paris: Publications Orientalistes de France, 1981); Jacob Spieth, *Die Religion der Eweer,* 15, 189–225; Peter Kwami Akli Akoussah, "Afa Divination as a Means of Social Control" (B.A. Long Essay, Department of Sociology, University of Ghana, Legon, 1978); Dan Atsu Agbeko, "Elements of Art in the Worship of the Afa-Cult among the People of Dzodze" (Long Essay, Department of Art Education, Specialist Training College, Winneba, n.d.); and Atieku, "Colour in Anlo Traditional Religion," 7–11.

19. Greene, Field Notes, No. 57, Interview with Robert G. Kofi Afetogbo, 22 December 1987, Anloga.

20. E. Salkowski, "Eine offene Tür in Anlo-Ga," *Monatsblatt der Norddeutschen Missionsgesellschaft* 4 (1906): 31.

21. "Offene Tür und widersacher in Anloga," *Monatsblatt der Norddeutschen Missionsgesellschaft* 68 (1907): 67; Greene, Field Notes, No. 56, Interview with William Tiodo Anum Adzololo, 22 December 1987, Anloga.

22. These dates are from the pamphlet *Anloga Evangelical Presbyterian Church 75 Years Jubilee Celebration, 1906–1981* (N.p., n.d.).

23. Greene, Field Notes, No. 57, Interview with Robert G. Kofi Afetogbo, 22 December 1987, Anloga.

24. Sri's efforts to undermine the authority of the Nyigbla priest and other religious authorities in Anlo is discussed most thoroughly in Chapters 2 and 3.

25. Fia Sri made this comment at a state council meeting in 1944. See Anlo State Council Minute Book, June 1934–November 1946, 659, Anlo State Council Office, Anloga. See also Memo on Anlo Native Authority by Mr. Kwesi Plange, Ministerial Secretary, 5 June 1951, ADM 39/1/1.

26. District Commissioner [T. A. Mead], Keta, to the Commissioner of the Eastern Province, Koforidua, 30 April 1945, ADM 39/1/120.

27. "Minutes of the Meeting of the Anlo Native Authority Council, Anloga,

21 March 1950—Address by the Acting District Commissioner, Mr. J. M. L. Peake at 11:00 am," Traditional Council Minute Book, March 1947–April 1952, 176.

28. Togbui Sri II's response to the Nyiko banning included an effort—which ultimately proved unsuccessful—to convince others on the council that the Nyiko ban could not apply to the tax because Anlo religious beliefs did not permit the tabooing of something that was financially beneficial to the state. He also argued that the ban did not mean that the tax issue was irrevocably dead. In his words: "Have you never heard that a person who had been tabooed 'in absentia' returned and later enjoyed life fully among ourselves?" See Traditional Council Minute Book, March 1947–April 1952, 178–179, Anlo State Council Office, Anloga.

29. Fiawoo, "The Influence," 106–108.

30. Sophia Amable, "The 1953 Riot in Anloga and Its Aftermath" (B.A. Long Essay, History Department, University of Ghana, Legon, 1977), 20.

31. Different figures exist on the amount of damage caused by the riot. The number of houses destroyed indicated here comes from Regional Officer (unsigned) to the Permanent Secretary, Ministry of Local Government and Housing, P. O. Box 1421, Accra, March 1953, ADM 39/1/161. See also an eyewitness account about the event by an opponent of the tax in Greene, Field Notes, No. 190, Interview with Akorbortu Efia and Zadzie, 30 April 1996, Anloga.

32. See Regional Officer (unsigned) to the Permanent Secretary, Ministry of Local Government and Housing. Most on the council supported the relocation of their meetings to Keta, as did the regional officer who penned this report.

33. See Greene, Field Notes, No. 190, Interview with Akorbortu Efia and Zadzie, 30 April 1996; and No. 243, Interview with Colonel Courage Togobo, October 1996, Accra.

34. For more on this ritual, see Amegashie, "The Concept of Renewal."

35. Note that the Anloga Bremen Mission congregation received its first church bell in 1909, while the Church of Pentecost did not begin holding services in Anloga until 1948. It is unclear, therefore, exactly when this agreement was reached, since we can presume that the Bremen Mission used the bell, first to announce the beginning of school and then later for church services, immediately after it was received. Nyigbla adherents complained that the bell hurt the ears of their god. *Anloga Evangelical Presbyterian Church 75 Year Jubilee Celebration, 1906–1981,* 4.

36. Greene, Field Note 53, Interview with Togbui Afatsao Awadzi, 16 December 1987, Anloga. It is interesting to note that according to the members of the Church of Pentecost, both the traditional believers and the orthodox churches in Anloga reacted with great hostility to the coming of the Church of Pentecost. The orthodox churches accused them of engaging in paganistic practices by using drums, clapping, and speaking in tongues in the worship service. The traditional believers objected to the fact that they ignored the ban on drumming that was issued every year. See Greene, Field Notes, No. 193, Interview with V. Y. Dotsey, 4 May 1996, Anloga; No. 194, Interview with Sister Mary, 6 May 1996, Anloga; and No. 195, Interview with D. D. Deku, 6 May 1996, Anloga.

37. Greene, Field Notes 64 and 67, Interviews with J. N. K Dogbatse, 5 January 1988, Anloga, and Togbui Klobotua Efia Nunyanu, 6 January 1988, Anloga.

38. Greene, Field Note 195, Interview with Mr. D. D. Deku, 6 May 1996, Anloga.

39. This image of Anloga as steeped in nefarious practices that have their origin in the practice of traditional religions was made clear to me when I first began making plans to live in Anloga in 1977. When I first revealed my intentions to those who were quite familiar with the area, I was gently encouraged to consider living in Keta, since—as one friend intimated to me—no one goes to Anloga, stays the night, and leaves the town alive to tell about it.

Conclusion: Explaining Cultural Adaptation and Epistemological Abandonment

1. Olivier Zunz, "Introduction," in *Reliving the Past: The Worlds of Social History,* ed. Oliver Zunz (Chapel Hill: University of North Carolina Press, 1985), 6–7.

2. Keith Thomas, *Religion and the Decline of Magic* (New York: Scribners, 1971), Chapter 22.

3. Nukunya, *Kinship and Marriage,* 93.

4. Ibid., 89, 91, 93.

5. For a discussion about the declining significance of clan affiliation, see Greene, *Gender, Ethnicity, and Social Change,* 177–179.

6. Geschiere, *Modernity,* 24–25, 199.

7. Birgit Meyer, "Modernity and Enchantment: The Image of the Devil in Popular African Christianity," in *Conversion to Modernities: The Globalization of Christianity,* ed. Peter van der Veer (New York: Routledge, 1996), 214–222.

Bibliography

BOOKS AND ARTICLES

Addae, Stephen Kojo. *The Evolution of Modern Medicine in a Developing Country: Ghana, 1880–1960.* Edinburgh: Durham Academic Press, 1997.

Adeladza II. "Foreword." In *Hogbeza.* Accra: Arakan Press, 1973.

Afelevo, Stephano H. Kwadzo. "Ein Bericht über den Yewekultus der Ewe. Herausgegeben mit deutscher Übersetzung und Anmerkungen von D. Westermann." *Mitteilungen des Seminars für Orientalischen Sprachen* 33/3 (1894/1930): 1–55.

Agawu, Kofi. "The Amu Legacy." *Africa* 66, no. 2 (1996): 274–279.

Agbodeka, Francis, ed. *A Handbook of Eweland.* Vol. 1, *The Ewes of Southeastern Ghana.* Accra: Woeli Publications, 1997.

Agnew, John A., and James S. Duncan. *The Power of Place: Bringing Together Geographical and Sociological Imaginations.* Boston: Unwin, 1989.

Akyeampong, Emmanuel. "Alcoholism in Ghana: A Socio-cultural Exploration." *Culture, Medicine and Psychiatry* 19, no. 2 (1995): 261–280.

————. *Between the Sea and the Lagoon: An Eco-Social History of the Anlo of Southeastern Ghana, c.1850 to Recent Times.* Athens: Ohio University Press; Oxford: James Currey, forthcoming.

————. *Drink, Power, and Cultural Change: A Social History of Alcohol in Ghana, c. 1800 to Recent Times.* Portsmouth, N.H.: Heinemann, 1996.

Amenumey, D. E. K. *The Ewe in Precolonial Times.* Accra: Sedco Press, 1986.

————. *The Ewe Unification Movement: A Political History.* Accra: Ghana Universities Press, 1989.

Anderson, Warwick. "The Trespass Speaks: White Masculinity and the Colonial Breakdown." *American Historical Review* 102, no. 5 (1997): 1343–1370.

Anlo Hogbetsotsoza. Accra: Arakan Press, 1987.

Anloga Evangelical Presbyterian Church 75 Years Jubilee Celebration, 1906–1981. N.p., n.d.

Anlowo Pe Hogbetsotso Nkeke Souvenir Brochure. Anloga, Ghana: Anlo Traditional Council, 1966.

Appadurai, Arjun. *Modernity at Large: Cultural Dimensions of Globalization.* Minneapolis: University of Minnesota Press, 1996.

Ashitey, G. A. *Disease Control in Ghana.* Accra: Ghana Universities Press, 1994.

Awoonor, Kofi. "A Dirge." In *Messages: Poems from Ghana,* ed. Kofi Awoonor and G. Adali-Mortty, 73. London: Heinemann, 1971.

————. *Night of My Blood.* New York: Anchor Books, 1971.

——. "The Sea Eats the Land at Home." In *Modern Poetry from Africa,* ed. Gerald Moore and Ulli Beier, 101. Baltimore: Penguin Books, 1968.

——. *This Earth My Brother.* London: Heinemann, 1972.

Awuma, Elia. "Reste Des Heidentums in der Christlichen Gemeinde." *Monatsblatt der Norddeutschen Missionsgesellschaft* 88 (1927): 11.

Barawusu, Solomon M. K. "The Hogbetsotso Festival: A Comparison between the Liberation of the Ewes from Slavery in Notsie, Togo under the Wicked King Agorkoli and the Liberation of the Israelites from Slavery in Egypt under the Wicked King Pharoah." Anloga, Ghana: Zion Secondary School, n.d.

Bates, D. A. "Geology." In *Agriculture and Land Use in Ghana,* ed. J. B. Willis. London: Oxford University Press, 1962.

Bay, Edna. *Wives of the Leopard: Gender, Politics, and Culture in the Kingdom of Dahomey.* Charlottesville: University of Virginia Press, 1998.

Binetsch, G. "Beantwortung mehrerer Fragen über unser Ewe-Volk und seine Anschauungen." *Zeitschrift für Ethnologie* 38 (1906): 34–40.

Blier, Suzanne Preston. *African Vodun: Art, Psychology, and Power.* Chicago: University of Chicago Press, 1995.

Boahen, A. Adu. *African Perspectives on Colonialism.* Baltimore: Johns Hopkins University Press, 1987.

Bohm, Arnd. "The Desublimated Body: Gottfred August Bürger." In *Subversive Sublimities: Undercurrents of the German Enlightenment,* ed. Eitel Timm, 12–26. Columbia, S.C.: Camden House, 1992.

Bosman, William. *A New and Accurate Description of the Guinea Coast.* London: J. Knapton, 1705.

Boughey, A. S. "Ecological Studies of Tropical Coastlines: The Gold Coast, West Africa." *Journal of Ecology* 45, no. 23 (1957): 665–687.

Bürgi, E. "Der Alte Keta-Kirchhof." *Monatsblatt der Norddeutschen Missions-Gesellschaft* 11 (1889): 100–103.

Carmichael, David L., Jane Huberd, Brian Reeves, and Adhilde Schanche. *Sacred Sites, Sacred Places.* London: Routledge, 1994.

Chapman, W. S. *The Keta Sea Erosion and Dredging for Development, and Some Landmarks for Anlo History.* Accra: Arakan Press, 1984.

Cohen, David William, and E. S. Atieno Odhiambo. *Siaya: The Historical Anthropology of an African Landscape.* London: James Currey, 1989.

Colson, Elizabeth. "Places of Power and Shrines of the Land." *Paideuma* 43 (1997): 47–57.

Comaroff, Jean. *Body of Place, Spirit of Resistance: The Culture and History of a South African People.* Chicago: University of Chicago Press, 1992.

Comaroff, John, and Jean Comaroff. "Introduction." In *Modernity and Its Malcontents: Ritual and Power in Postcolonial Africa,* ed. Jean Comaroff and John Comaroff. Chicago: University of Chicago Press, 1993.

——. *Of Revelation and Revolution: The Dialectics of Modernity on a South African Frontier.* Chicago: University of Chicago Press, 1997.

Confino, Alon. "Collective Memory and Cultural History: Problems of Method." *American Historical Review* 5 (1997): 1386–1403.

Connerton, Paul. *How Societies Remember.* New York: Cambridge University Press, 1989.

Cosgrove, Denis. *Social Formation and Symbolic Landscape.* Madison: University of Wisconsin Press, 1998.

Daniels, Stephen. "Arguments for a Humanistic Geography." In *The Future of Geography,* ed. R. J. Johnson, 141–158. London: Methuen, 1995.

Debrunner, Hans W. *A Church between Colonial Powers: A Study of the Church in Togo.* London: Lutterworth Press, 1965.

Dotse, J. M. *Shallot Farming in Anloga, Ghana.* Special Monograph by Curriculum and Teaching Department. Cape Coast, Ghana: University of Cape Coast, 1980.

Drewal, Henry John. "Performing the Other: Mami Wata Worship in Africa." *The Drama Review* 32, no. 2 (1988): 160–185.

Dumett, Raymond. "The Campaign against Malaria and the Expansion of Scientific Medical and Sanitary Services in British West Africa, 1898–1910." *African Historical Studies* 1, no. 2 (1968): 153–197.

"Einschräkung der Diakonissenarbeit in Keta." *Monatsblatt der Norddeutschen Missionsgesellschaft* 3 (1904): 22–24.

Ellis, A. B. *The Ewe-Speaking Peoples of the Slave Coast of West Africa.* 1890. Reprint, Chicago: Benin Press, 1965.

———. *West African Sketches.* London: Samuel Tinsley and Co., 1881.

Entrikin, Nicholas J. *The Betweenness of Place: Towards a Geography of Modernity.* Baltimore: Johns Hopkins University Press, 1991.

Ewegbalexexle apka enelia. Bremen: Norddeutsche Missiongesellschaft, 1936.

Fabian, Johannes. *Remembering the Past: Painting and Popular History in Zaire.* Berkeley: University of California Press, 1996.

Fianu, Daniel D. *The Hoawo and the Gligbaza Festival of the Asogli State of Eweland: A Historical Sketch.* Legon: Self-published, 1986.

Fiawoo, D. K. "Ancestral Worship among the Ewe-Speaking People of Southern Ghana: A Study in Religious Change." *Ghana Journal of Sociology* 5, no. 2 (1969): 18–22.

———. "Characteristic Features of Ewe Ancestor Worship." In *Ancestors,* ed. William H. Newell, 263–281. The Hague: Mouton, 1976.

———. *The Fifth Landing Stage.* 1943; Reprint, Accra: Sedco, 1983.

Flothmeier, Missionar. "Bilder aus unserer Arbeit." *Monatsblatt der Norddeutschen Missionsgesellschaft* 9 (1903): 86–87.

Forster, Missionary. "Die Tause der Erstlinge von Anloga." *Monatsblatt der Norddeutschen Missionsgesellschaft* 70 (1909): 84–85.

Foster, Philip. *Education and Social Change in Ghana.* Chicago: University of Chicago Press, 1965.

Fosu, Gabriel. "Disease Classification in Rural Ghana: Framework and Implications for Health Behaviour." *Social Science and Medicine* 15B (1981): 471–482.

Gaba, Christian R. *Scriptures of an African People: Ritual Utterances of the Anlo.* New York: Nok, 1973.

Gayibor, N. L. "Le Remodelage des Traditions Historiques: La Légend d'Agokoli, Roi de Notsé." In *Sources orales de l'histoire de l'Afrique,* ed. Claude-Hélène Perrot, 209–214. Paris: CNRS, 1989.

———. *Recueil des Sources Orales du Pays Aja-Ewe.* Lome, Togo: Department d'Histoire, University du Benin, 1977.

Geschiere, Peter. *The Modernity of Witchcraft.* Charlottesville: University of Virginia Press, 1997.

Gifford, Paul. "Ghana's Charismatic Churches." *Journal of Religion in Africa* XXIV, no. 3 (1994): 241–265.

Gilbert, Michelle V. "Ewe Funerary Sculpture." *African Arts* XIV, no. 4 (1981): 45–46, 88.

———. "Mystical Protection among the Anlo Ewe." *African Arts* XV, no. 4 (1982): 60–66, 90.

Gilles, Eva. "Causal Criteria in African Classifications of Disease." In *Social Anthropology and Medicine,* ed. J. B. Loudon, 358–393. London: Academic Press, 1976.

Goankar, Dilip Parameshwar. "On Alternative Modernities." *Public Culture* II, no. 1 (1991): 1–18.

Gocking, Roger. "A Chieftancy Dispute and Ritual Murder in Elmina Ghana, 1945–6." *Journal of African History* 41, no. 2 (2000): 197–219.

Gold Coast Annual Medical Report. Accra: Government Printing Press, 1907.

Gold Coast Handbook. London: West Africa Publicity, 1937.

Goody, Jack. "Anomie in Ashanti." *Africa* XXVII, no. 4 (1957): 356–363.

Gottlieb, Alma. *Under the Kapok Tree: Identity and Difference in Beng Thought.* Chicago: University of Chicago Press, 1992.

Greene, Sandra E. "Cultural Zones in the Era of the Atlantic Slave Trade: Exploring the Yoruba Connection with the Anlo-Ewe." In *Identity in the Shadow of Slavery,* ed. Paul Lovejoy, 86–101. New York: Continuum, 2000.

———. "Developing the Arts for Development." *Africa Notes* (Feb. 1998): 1–5.

———. *Gender, Ethnicity, and Social Change on the Upper Slave Coast.* Portsmouth, N.H.: Heinemann, 1996.

———. "The Past and Present of an Anlo-Ewe Oral Tradition." *History in Africa* 12 (1985): 73–87.

———. "Sacred Terrain: Religion, Politics and Place in the History of Anloga (Ghana)." *International Journal of African Historical Studies* 30, no. 1 (1997): 1–22.

———. "Social Change in 18th Century Anlo: The Role of Technology, Markets and Military Conflict." *Africa: The Journal of the International African Institute* 58, no. 1 (1988): 70–86.

Grove, J. M. "Some Aspects of the Economy of the Volta Delta (Ghana)." *Bulletin de L'Institut Fondamental d'Afrique Noire* XXVIII, no. 1–2 (1996): 381–432.

Gyekye, Kwame. *Tradition and Modernity: Philosophical Reflections on the African Experience.* New York: Oxford University Press, 1997.

Hackett, Rosalind I. J. "Charismatic/Pentecostal Appropriations of Media Technologies in Nigeria and Ghana." *Journal of Religion in Africa* XXXVII, no. 3 (1998): 258–277.

Halbwachs, Maurice. *The Collective Memory.* New York: Harper and Row, 1980.

Haley, Bruce. *The Healthy Body and Victorian Culture.* Cambridge, Mass.: Harvard University Press, 1978.

Harries, Patrick. "Under Alpine Eyes: Constructing Landscape and Society in Late Pre-colonial South-East Africa." *Paideuma* 43 (1997): 171–191.

Härtter, G. "Der Fischfang im Evheland." *Zeitschrift für Ethnologie* 38, no. 1–2 (1906): 51–63.

———. "Ein Schultag in Keta." *Monatsblatt der Norddeutschen Missionsgesellschaft* 1 (1890): 3–4.

———. "Sitten und Gebräuche der Angloer (Ober-Guinea)." *Zeitschrift für Ethnologie* 38 (1906): 40–51.

———. "Spiele der Evheer." *Quartalblatt der Norddeutschen Missionsgesellschaft* 38/1 (1897): 1–8.

Hatty, Suzanne E., and James Hatty. *The Disordered Body: Epidemic Disease and Cultural Transformation.* Albany: State University of New York Press, 1999.

Hayden, Dolores. *The Power of Place: Urban Landscapes as Public History.* Cambridge: MIT Press, 1995.

"Heidnisches Leben." *Quartalblatt der Norddeutschen Missionsgesellschaft* 68 (1873): 320–325.

Herbert, Eugenia. *Iron, Gender, and Power: Rituals of Transformation in African Societies.* Bloomington: Indiana University Press, 1993.

Hess, Janet. "Exhibiting Ghana: Display, Documentary and 'National' Art in the Nkrumah Era." *African Studies Review* 44, no. 1 (2001): 59–97.

Hill, Polly. *Studies in Rural Capitalism in West Africa.* Cambridge: Cambridge University Press, 1986.

———. *Talking with Ewe Seine Fisherman and Shallot Farmers.* Cambridge: African Studies Center, 1986.

Hobsbawm, E. J., and T. O. Ranger. *The Invention of Tradition.* Cambridge: Cambridge University Press, 1983.

Hogbeza, 1978. Accra: Arakan Press, 1978.

Hornberger, Christian. "Etwas aus der Geschichte der Anloer." *Quartalblatt der Norddeutschen Missionsgesellschaft* 82 (1877): 436–466.

———. "Wie es in Keta aussieht." *Monatsblatt der Norddeutschen Missionsgesellschaft* 25/295 (1875): 1380–1381.

Houlbrooke, Ralph. "Death, Church and Family in England between the Late Fifteenth and the Early Eighteenth Centuries." In *Death, Ritual and Bereavement,* ed. Ralph Houlbrooke, 25–42. New York: Routledge, 1989.

Isert, Paul Erdman. *Voyages en Guinée et dans les îsles Caraïbes en Amerique. Tirés de sa correspondence aves ses amis. Traduits de l'allemand.* Paris: Maradan, 1973.

Jackson, Michael, and Ivan Karp. *Personhood and Agency: The Experience of Self and Others in African Cultures.* Washington, D.C.: Smithsonian Institution Press, 1990.

Jackson, Peter, and Jan Penrose, ed. *Constructions of Race, Place, and Nation.* Minneapolis: University of Minnesota Press, 1993.

Jahoda, Gustav. "Social Aspirations, Magic and Witchcraft in Ghana: A Social Psychological Interpretation." In *The New Elites of Tropical Africa: Studies Presented and Discussed at the Sixth International African Seminar at the University of Ibadan, Nigeria, July 1964,* ed. P. C. Lloyd, 199–213. London: Oxford University Press, 1966.

Jenkins, Ray. "Confrontations with A. B. Ellis, A Participant in the Scramble for Gold Coast Africana, 1874–1894." *Paiduema* 33 (1987): 313–335.

———. "The Earliest Generation of Missionary Photographers in West Africa and the Portrayal of Indigenous People and Culture." *History in Africa* 20 (1993): 89–118.

Jewsiewicki, Bogumil. "Collective Memory and the Stakes of Power: A Reading of Popular Zairean Historical Discourses." *History in Africa* 13 (1986): 195–223.

Jewsiewicki, Bogumil, and V. Y. Mudimbe. "Africans' Memories and Contemporary History of Africa." *History and Theory* 32, no. 4 (1993): 1–11.

Jewsiewicki, Bogumil, and David Newbury, eds. *African Historiographies: What History for Which Africa?* Beverly Hills, Calif.: Sage, 1986.

Johnson, John William. *The Epic of Son-Jara: A West African Tradition.* Bloomington: Indiana University Press, 1986.

Jones, Adam. "Reindorf the Historian." In *Recovery of the West African Past: African Pastors and African History in the Nineteenth Century—C. C. Reindorf and Samuel Johnson,* ed. Paul Jenkins. Basel: Basler Afrika Bibliographien, 1998.

Jorion, P. "Going Out or Staying Home: Migration Strategies among the Xwla and Anlo-Ewe Fishermen." *MAST* 1, no. 2 (1988): 129–155.

Kea, Ray A. "Akwamu-Anlo Relations, c. 1750–1813." *Transactions of the Historical Society of Ghana* X (1969): 29–63.

Keane, Webb. "Materialism, Missionaries and Modern Subjects in Colonial Indonesia." In *Conversion to Modernities: The Globalization of Christianity,* ed. Peter van der Veer, 137–170. New York: Routledge, 1996.

Knuesli, A. "Afrikanisches Frauenleben: Lichtstrahlen vom Evangelium." *Monatsblatt der Norddeutschen Missionsgesellschaft* 68 (1907): 2–3, 10–11, 21–22.

Koslofsky, Craig M. *The Reformation of the Dead: Death and Ritual in Early Modern Germany, 1450–1700.* New York: St. Martin's Press, 1999.

Kramer, Fritz. *The Red Fez: Art and Spirit Possession in Africa.* London: Verso, 1993.

Kufogbe, S. K. "The Natural Resources of the Southern Ewes." In *A Handbook of Eweland.* Vol. 1, *The Ewes of Southeastern Ghana,* ed. Francis Agbodeka, 297. Accra: Woeli Press, 1997.

Kumekpor, Maxine. "Some Sociological Aspects of Beads with Special Reference to Selected Beads Found in Eweland." *Ghana Journal of Sociology* 6, no. 2/7, 1 (1971): 100–108.

Kuper, Hilda. "The Language of Sites in the Politics of Space." *American Anthropologist* 74 (1972): 411–425.

Larson, Pier. *History and Memory in the Age of Enslavement: Becoming Marina in Highland Madagascar, 1770–1822.* Portsmouth, N.H.: Heinemann, 2000.

Law, Robin. "Between the Sea and the Lagoon: The Interaction of Maritime and Inland Navigation on the Precolonial Slave Coast." *Cahiers d'Études Africaines* II4, XXIX-2 (1989): 209–237.

———. *The Slave Coast of West Africa, 1550–1570.* Oxford: Oxford University Press, 1991.

Lindemann, Mary. *Health and Healing in Eighteenth Century Germany.* Baltimore: Johns Hopkins University Press, 1996.

Lovell, Nadia. "Introduction." In *Locality and Belonging,* ed. Nadia Lovell, 1–24. London: Routledge, 1998.

Macchia, Frank D. *Spiritual and Social Liberation: The Message of the Blumhards in the Light of Wuerttemberg Pietism.* Metuchen, N.J.: Scarecrow Press, 1993.

MacGaffey, Wyatt. *Religion and Society in Central Africa: The BaKongo of Lower Zaire.* Chicago: University of Chicago Press, 1989.

Mahoney, Dennis F. "Human History as Natural History in *Die Lehrlinge zu Sais* and *Heinrich von Ofterdingen.*" In *Subversive Sublimities: Undercurrents of the German Enlightenment,* ed. Eitel Timm, 1–11. Columbia, S.C.: Camden House, 1992.

Malkki, Liisa. *Purity and Exile: Violence, Memory, and National Cosmology among the Hutu Refugees of Tanzania.* Chicago: University of Chicago Press, 1995.

Mamattah, Charles M. K. *The Ewes of West Africa.* Keta, Ghana: Advent Press, 1979.

Maxwell, John, ed. *The Gold Coast Handbook.* London: Westminster, 1928.

McCaskie, T. C. "Anti-Witchcraft Cults in Asante: An Essay in the Social History of an African People." *History in Africa* 8 (1981): 125–154.

———. *State and Society in Pre-Colonial Asante.* Cambridge: Cambridge University Press, 1995.

McClintock, Anne. *Imperial Leather: Race, Gender, and Sexuality in the Colonial Context.* New York: Routledge, 1995.

McDonald, George. *The Gold Coast Past and Present.* London: Longmans, Green and Co., 1898.

McLeod, Malcolm. "On the Spread of Anti-Witchcraft Cults in Modern Asante." In *Changing Social Structure in Ghana: Essays in the Comparative Sociology of a New State and an Old Tradition,* ed. Jack Goody, 107–117. London: International African Institute, 1975.

McWilliam, H. O. A. *The Development of Education in Ghana.* London: Longmans, 1959.

Medical and Sanitary Reports on the Gold Coast Colony and *Appendices.* Accra: Government Press, 1911, 1913, 1914.

Meyer, Birgit. "Christian Mind and Worldly Matters." *Journal of Material Culture* 2, no. 3 (1997): 311–337.

———. "Modernity and Enchantment: The Image of the Devil in Popular African Christianity." In *Conversion to Modernities: The Globalization of Christianity,* ed. Peter van der Veer, 199–230. New York: Routledge, 1996.

———. *Translating the Devil: Religion and Modernity among the Ewe of Ghana.* Edinburgh: University of Edinburgh Press, 1999.

Miller, Joseph, ed. *The African Past Speaks.* Folkstone, Kent: Dawson, 1980.

Minkley, Gary, and Rassoul Ciraj. "Orality, Memory and Social History in South Africa." In *Negotiating the Past: The Making of Memory in South Africa,* ed. Sarah Nuttail and Carli Coetzee. Cape Town: Oxford University Press, 1998.

Mobley, Harris W. *The Ghanaian's Image of the Missionary: An Analysis of the Published Critiques of Christian Missionaries by Ghanaians, 1897–1965.* Leiden: E. J. Brill, 1970.

Moore, Henrietta L. *Space, Text, and Gender: An Anthropological Study of the Marakwet of Kenya.* London: Guilford Press, 1996.

Morgan, Jim. "The Burial Question in Leeds in the Eighteenth and Nineteenth Centuries." In *Death, Ritual and Bereavement,* ed. Ralph Houlbrooke, 95–104. New York: Routledge, 1989.

Nandy, Ashis, and Shiv Visvanathan. "Modern Medicine and Its Non-Modern Critics: A Study in Discourse." In *Dominating Knowledge: Development, Culture, and Resistance,* ed. Frédérique Apffel Marglin and Stephen A. Marglin, 145–184. Oxford: Clarendon, 1990.

"Neger-Doctoren." *Monatsblatt der Norddeutschen Missionsgesellschaft* 24, no. 283 (1874): 131–1314.

"Not und Hülfe im Diakonissenhause in Keta." *Monatsblatt der Norddeutschen Missionsgesellschaft* 3 (1907): 69–72.

Nugent, Paul. "Ewe Nationalism." *Journal of African History* 33, no. 3 (1992): 495–496.

———. *Myths of Origin and the Origin of Myth: Local Politics and the Uses of History in Ghana's Volta Region.* Berlin: Das Arabische Buch, 1997.

Nukunya, G. K. "Afa Divination in Anlo: A Preliminary Report." *Research Review* (Legon) 5/2 (1969): 9–26.

——. "The Anlo-Ewe and Full-Time Maritime Fishing: Another View." *MAST* 2, no. 2 (1989).

——. *Kinship and Marriage among the Anlo Ewe.* New York: Humanities Press, 1969.

——. "Some Underlying Beliefs in Ancestor Worship and Mortuary Rites among the Ewe." In *La Notion de Personne en Afrique Noire,* ed. G. Dieterlen, 119–130. Paris: Editions du Centre national dela recherche scientifique, 1973.

Nukunya, G. K., P. A. Twumasi, and N. O. Addo, "Attitudes towards Health and Disease in Ghanaian Society." *Conch* 7, no. 1–2 (1975): 113–136.

"Offene Türin under widersacher in Anloga." *Monatsblatt der Norddeutschen Missionsgesellschaft* 68 (1907): 67.

Okoye, Ikemefuna Stanley. "History, Aesthetics and the Political in Igbo Spatial Heterotopias." *Paideuma* 43 (1997): 75–91.

Oman, D. J. *Report on the Direction of the Former Bremen Mission of the Government of the Gold Coast from June 1916 to March 1926.* Accra: Government Printer, 1927.

Ordnung für die Evangelischen Gemeinden der Basler Mission auf der Goldküste. Basel: Werner-Riehm, 1902.

Osswald, Carl. *Fifty Years' Mission Work at Keta.* Bremen: Norddeutsche Missionsgesellschaft, 1903.

Park, Chris C. *Sacred Worlds: An Introduction to Geography and Religion.* London: Routledge, 1994.

Parkin, David. *Sacred Void: Spatial Images of Work and Ritual among the Giriama of Kenya.* Cambridge: Cambridge University Press, 1991.

Pazzi, Roberto. *Introduction à l'histoire de l'aire culturelle aja tado-lome.* Series A: Études et Documents de Science Humaines. Lome: Université du Benin, Institut National des Science de L'Education, 1979.

p'Bitek, Okot. *African Religions in Western Scholarship.* Nairobi: Kenya Literature Bureau, 1971.

Piot, Charles. *Remotely Global: Village Modernity in West Africa.* Chicago: University of Chicago Press, 1999.

Plessing, Fredrick. "Briefe aus Keta." *Monatsblatt der Norddeutschen Missionsgesellschaft* 5/57 (1855): 244–248.

Poogie, John J. Jr., and Carl Gersuny. "Risk and Ritual: An Interpretation of Fishermen's Folklore in a New England Community." *Journal of American Folklore* 85, no. 335 (1972): 66–72.

Porter, Dorothy. *Health, Civilization, and the State: A History of Public Health from Ancient to Modern Times.* New York: Routledge, 1999.

Porter, Roy. *The Greatest Benefit to Mankind: A Medical History of Humanity.* New York: W. W. Norton and Co., 1998.

Prakash, Gyan. "Introduction." In *After Colonialism,* ed. Gyan Prakash, 3–17. Princeton: Princeton University Press, 1995.

Quarcoopome, Nii Otokunor. "Notse's Ancient Kingship: Some Archaeological and Art-Historical Considerations." *African Archaeological Review* 11 (1993): 109–128.

——. "Thresholds and Thrones: Morphology and Symbolism of Dangme Public Altars." *Journal of Religion in Africa* XXIV, no. 4 (1994): 339–357.

Ranger, Terence. "The Invention of Tradition in Africa." In *The Invention of Tradition,* ed. Eric Hobsbawm and Terence Ranger. Cambridge: Cambridge University Press, 1983.

———. *Voices from the Rocks: History in the Matopos Hills of Zimbabwe.* Oxford: James Currey, 1999.

Ray, Benjamin. *Myth, Ritual, and Kinship in Buganda.* New York: Oxford University Press, 1991.

Report of the Educationist's Committee Appointed by His Excellency the Governor on 5th March 1920 to Advise the Government on Educational Matters. Accra: Gold Coast Printing Press, 1920.

Robertson, G. A. *Notes on Africa.* London: Sherwood, Neely and Jones, 1819.

Roehr, Sabine. *A Primer on German Enlightenment.* Columbia: University of Missouri Press, 1995.

Rosenthal, Judy. *Possession, Ecstasy, and Law in Ewe Voodoo.* Charlottesville: University Press of Virginia, 1998.

Ryden, Kent C. *Mapping the Invisible Landscape: Folklore, Writing, and the Sense of Place.* Iowa City: University of Iowa Press, 1993.

Salkowski, E. "Anloga: Eine Hochburg des Heidentums." *Bremer Missionschriften* 20 (1907): 1–28.

———. "Eine offene Tür in Anlo-Ga." *Monatsblatt der Norddeutschen Missionsgesellschaft* 4 (1906): 30–32.

Schiek, Missionar. "Keta." *Monatsblatt der Norddeutschen Missionsgesellschaft* 22/263 (1872): 1193–1194.

Schlegel, Bernhard J. "Beitrag zur Geschichte, Welt-und Religionsanschauung des Westafrikaners, namentlich des Eweers." *Monatsblatt der Norddeutschen Missionsgesellschaft* 7, no. 93 (1858): 397–400, 406–408.

Schlunk, Martin. *Die Norddeutsche Mission in Togo: Meine Reise durchs Eweland.* Bremen: Verlag der NDMG, 1910.

Schoffeleers, J. Matthew. *River of Blood: The Genesis of a Martyr Cult in Southern Malawi, c. A.D. 1600.* Madison: University of Wisconsin Press, 1992.

Seidel, H. "Krankheit, Tod und Begräbnis bei den Togonegern." *Globus* 10 (1897): 40–45.

———. "System der Fetischverbote in Togo." *Globus* LXXIII, no. 18 (1898): 340–344.

———. "Der Yewe-Dienst im Togolande." *Zeitschrift für Afrikanische und Oceanische Sprachen* 3 (1897): 157–185.

Smith, W. David. *Stretching Their Bodies: The History of Physical Education.* London: David and Charles, 1974.

Sopher, David E. "Geography and Religions." *Progress in Human Geography* 5, no. 4 (1981): 510–524.

Spain, Daphne. *Gendered Spaces.* Chapel Hill: University of North Carolina Press, 1992.

Spiess, C. "Aus dem Leben eines Stadtgötzen." *Quartalblatt der Norddeutschen Missionsgesellschaft* 2/6–8 (1930): 14–15.

———. "Austribung eines böse Geistes." *Monatsblatt der Norddeutschen Missionsgesellschaft* 88 (1927): 30–31.

———. "Brautsitten under den Evhe-Negern in Togo." *Anthropophyteia* (Leipzig) 8 (1911): 173–180.

———. Ein Erinnerungsblatt an die Tage es Sklavenhandels in Westafrika." *Globus* (Braunschweig) 92 (1907): 205–208.

———. "Der Eintritt der Menstruation und die damit verbundenen Zeremonien bei den Evhenegern in Süd-Togo." *Anthropophyteia* (Leipzig) 8 (1911): 180–184.

———. "Fünfzig Jahre Missionsarbeit in Anyako." *Monatsblatt der Norddeutschen Missionsgesellschaft* (January 1908): 3–6.

———. "Heidenische Gebräuche der Evhe Neger." *Archiv für Religionswissenschaft* 15 (1912): 162–170.

———. "Der Legba-Kult in Seinen Verschiedenen formen an der Westafrikanischen Küste." *Bassler-Archiv* (Berlin) 6/4–6 (1922): 143–154.

———. "Sturz eines heidnischen Gottes." *Monatsblatt der Norddeutschen Missionsgesellschaft* 88 (1927): 109–110.

———. "Verborgener Fetischdienst under den Eveern." *Globus* 98 (1910): 10–13.

———. "We, Anglo and Atoko." *Monatsblatt der Norddeutschen Missionsgesellschaft* 10 (1898): 34, 35–36.

Spiess, Sophie. "Heidnische und Christliche Totenfeiern und Begräbnisse." *Quartalblatt der Norddeutschen Missionsgesellschaft* 2 (1931): 7–8.

Spieth, Jakob. *Die Ewe Stämme.* Berlin: Dietrich Reimer, 1906.

———. "Ein Gökenhain." *Monatsblatt der Norddeutschen Missionsgesellschaft* 5 (1893): 45–46.

———. "Krankenbehandlung bei den Eweern in Togo." In *Flugschriften des Bremer Vereins für ärtliche Mission,* 1–16. Bremen: Bremen Mission, 1909.

———. *Die Religion der Ewe

er.* Gottingen: Vandenhoeck and Ruprecht, 1911.

———. "Die Religiösen Vorstellungen der Eweer." *Monatsblatt der Norddeutschen Missionsgesellschaft* 3 (1906): 22–23.

———. "Von den Evhefrauen." *Quartalblatt der Norddeutschen Missionsgesellschaft* IV (1889): 1–8.

Stoler, Ann Laura. "Carnal Knowledge and Imperial Power: Gender, Race and Morality in Colonial Asia." In *Gender at the Crossroads of Knowledge,* ed. Michaela di Leonardo, 51–101. Berkeley: University of California Press, 1991.

———. "Sexual Affronts and Racial Frontiers: European Identities and the Cultural Politics of Exclusion in Colonial South East Asia." In *Tensions of Empire: Colonial Cultures in a Bourgeois World,* ed. Frederick Cooper and Ann Laura Stoler, 198–237. Berkeley: University of California Press, 1997.

Strachan, Henry. *Lessons in Elementary Hygiene for the Use of Pupils in Tropical Schools.* London: Constable and Company, 1913.

Surgy, Albert de. *La Pêche Traditionnelle sur le Littoral Evhe et Mina—De l'embouchure de la Volta au Dahomey.* Paris: Groupe de Chercheurs Africanistes, 1966.

———. *La Géomancie et le culte d'Afa chez les Evhé du littoral.* Paris: Publications Orientalistes de France, 1981.

Sutton, I. B. "The Volta River Salt Trade: The Survival of an Indigenous Industry." *Journal of African History* 22 (1981): 43–61.

Terdiman, Richard. *Present Past: Modernity and the Memory Crisis.* Ithaca: Cornell University Press, 1993.

Thomas, Charles W. *Adventures and Observations on the West Coast of Africa and Its Islands.* 1860; Reprint, New York: Negro Universities Press, 1969.

Thomas, Keith. *Religion and the Decline of Magic.* New York: Scribners, 1971.

Thornton, Robert J. *Space, Time, and Culture among the Irawq of Tanzania.* New York: Academic Press, 1980.

Toepfer, Anna. "Ein Frauenbrief aus Keta." *Monatsblatt der Norddeutschen Missionsgesellschaft* 2/10 (1885): 21–26.

Trotter, David. "Colonial Subjects." *Critical Quarterly* 32, no. 3 (1990): 3–37.

Tuan, Yi -Fu. "Space and Place: A Humanistic Perspective." *Progress in Geography: International Reviews and Current Research* 6 (1974): 211–252.

——. *Space and Place: The Perspective of Experience.* Minneapolis: University of Minnesota Press, 1997.

"Die Unruhen in Anglo-Gebeit." *Monatsblatt der Norddeutschen Missionsgesellschaft* 3 and 4, no. 10 (1885): 36–58.

Vansina, Jan. *Oral Tradition.* Harmondsworth, England: Penguin Books, 1965.

Wagner, Michele. "Environment, Community and History: 'Nature in the Mind' in Nineteenth and Early Twentieth Century Buha Tanzania." In *Custodians of the Land: Ecology and Culture in the History of Tanzania,* ed. Gregory Maddox, James L. Buglin, and Isaria N. Kimambo, 175–199. London: James Currey, 1996.

Ward, Barbara E. "Some Observations on Religious Cults in Ashanti." *Africa* XXVI, no. 1 (1956): 47–61.

Werbner, R. P., ed. *Regional Cults.* London: Academic Press, 1977

——. *Ritual Passage, Sacred Journey: The Process and Organization of Religious Movement.* Washington, D.C.: Smithsonian Institution Press, 1989.

Westermann, Dietrich. *Die Glidyi-Ewe in Togo.* Berlin: Mitteilungen des Seminars für Orientalische Sprachen an der Universität Berlin, 1935.

——. *The Study of the Ewe Language.* London: Oxford University Press, 1930.

Widenthal, Lora. "Race, Gender and Citizenship in the German Colonial Empire." In *Tensions of Empire: Colonial Cultures in a Bourgeois World,* ed. Frederick Cooper and Ann Laura Stoler, 263–283. Berkeley: University of California Press, 1999.

"Wie man zu Anyako die Pocken vertreibt." *Quartalblatt der Norddeutschen Missionsgesellschaft* 68 (1873): 321–324.

Williams, Perry. "The Laws of Health: Women, Medicine and Sanitary Reform, 1850–1890." In *Science and Sensibility: Gender and Scientific Enquiry, 1780–1945,* ed. Marina Benjamin, 60–88. Oxford: Blackwell, 1991.

Witte, P. A. "Der Zwillingskult bei den Ewe-Negern in Westafrika." *Anthropos* XXIV, no. 5-6 (1929): 943–951.

Wyllie, R. W. "Ignorance and Etiological Anarchy." *Anthropos* 89, no. 1 (1994): 191–193.

——. "Introspective Witchcraft among the Effutu of Southern Ghana." *Man* 8, no. 1 (1973): 74–79.

——. "Kponoe and the Tado Stool: A Problem in the Interpretation of the Anlo Migration Tradition (Ghana/Togo)." *Anthropos* 72, no. 1/2 (1977): 119–128.

——. "Migrant Anlo Fishing Companies and Socio-political Change: A Comparative Study." *Africa* XXXIX, no. 4 (1969): 396–410.

Zöller, Hugo. *Das Togoland und die Scklavenküste.* Berlin: W. Spemann, 1885.

Zunz, Olivier. "Introduction." In *Reliving the Past: The Worlds of Social History,* ed. Olivier Zunz, 3–10. Chapel Hill: University of North Carolina Press, 1985.

DISSERTATIONS, THESES, LONG ESSAYS, AND UNPUBLISHED PAPERS

Adanua, Anthony Kwame. "Adevu: A Study of Ve Hunter's Music." Music Diploma Thesis, Institute of African Studies, University of Ghana, 1990.

Adjorlolo, Theophelus W. "The History of Education in Anlo with Special Reference to Keta, from 1850–1960." B.A. Long Essay, History Department, University of Ghana, Legon, 1977.

Agbeko, Dan Atsu. "Elements of Art in the Worship of the Afa-Cult among the People of Dzodze." Long Essay, Department of Art Education, Specialist Training College, Winneba, n.d.

Agbenyegah, Logo Patrick. "Perceptions of Childhood Disease in Mafi, Volo, Battor and Dorffor Traditional Arts in the Volta Region." B.A. Long Essay, Department of Sociology, University of Ghana, Legon, 1993.

Aguigah, Dola A. "Le Site de Notse: Contribution à L'Archeologie du Togo." Ph.D. thesis, Doctorat de Troisième Cycle, Université de Paris, 1986.

Ahiable, Julius Kwame. "Physical Education in Anlo Schools from 1933 to the Present Time." Long Essay, Specialist Training College, Winneba, Ghana, 1969.

Akoussah, Peter Kwami Akli. "Afa Divination as a Means of Social Control." B.A. Long Essay, Department of Sociology, University of Ghana, Legon, 1978.

Amable, Sophia. "The 1953 Riot in Anloga and Its Aftermath." B.A. Long Essay, History Department, University of Ghana, Legon, 1977.

Amegashie, Justice Mokpokpo Yao. "The Concept of Renewal: A Study in Anlo Thought." B.A. Honors Thesis, Department for the Study of Religions, University of Legon, Ghana.

Anyidoho, Kofi. "Death and Burial of the Dead: A Study of Ewe Funeral Folklore." Master's thesis, Indiana University, 1983.

———. "Oral Poetics and Traditions of Verbal Art in Africa." Ph.D. diss., University of Texas at Austin, 1983.

Atieku, Ebenezer. "Colour in Anlo Traditional Religion." Long Essay, Department of Art, Specialist Training College, Winneba, 1978.

Ayayee, Charles Nani. "Twins and Their Ceremonies among the Anlos." B.A. Long Essay, Department for the Study of Religions, University of Ghana, Legon, 1975.

Bensah, Christian R. K. "Anlo Belief in Life after Death." B.A. Long Essay, Department for the Study of Religions, University of Ghana, 1979.

"Church of Pentecost." Unpublished manuscript. Institute of African Studies, University of Ghana, Legon.

Dogbe, L. T. K. "The Significance of Body Marks in Anlo." Art Diploma, Specialist Training College, Winneba, 1971.

Dotse, C. K. "The Development of Death Sculpture in South Anlo Traditional Area." Long Essay, School of Art, Home Science and Physical Education, Winneba Specialist Training College, 1976.

Dotse, J. M. "Agricultural Geography of the Keta District." Master's thesis, University of Ghana, Legon, 1969.

———. "The Geography of Transportation in the Anlo District." B.A. Honors Thesis, University of Ghana, Legon, 1966.

Dovlo, Elom. "Sexual Morality among the Anlo Ewe." B.A. Long Essay, Department for the Study of Religions, University of Ghana, Legon, 1976.

Egblewogbe, Eustace Yaw. "Ewe Personal Names: A Sociolingustic Study." Ph.D. Thesis, University of Ghana, 1977.

Fiawoo, Dzigbodi Kodzo. "The Influence of Contemporary Social Change on the Magico-Religious Concepts and Organization of the Southern Ewe-speaking Peoples of Ghana." Ph.D. diss., Edinburgh University, 1959.

Fiawoo, D. K., D. N. Nortey, E. H Mends, J. M. Assimeng, and P. A. Twumasi. "Funeral Customs in Ghana: A Preliminary Report." Unpublished Paper, Department of Sociology, University of Ghana, Legon, 1978.

Gaba, Kue Abota. "The History of Anecho, Ancient and Modern." Deposited at Balme Library, University of Ghana, Legon, 1965.

Gabegbeku, Vincent K. "The Socio-cultural Significance of Traditional Festivals: The Case of Hogbetsotso of the Anlo-Ewe." B.A. Honors Thesis, Department of Sociology, University of Cape Coast, 1993.

Geurts, Kathryn Linn. "Sensory Perception and Embodiment in Anlo-Ewe Cultural Logic and Symbolic Life." Ph.D. diss., University of Pennsylvania, 1998.

Greene, Sandra E. "The Anlo Ewe: Their Economy, Society and External Relations in the Eighteenth Century." Ph.D. diss., Northwestern University, 1981.

Kea, R. A. "The Salt Industries of the Gold Coast, 1650–1800." Institute of African Studies, University of Ghana, Legon, 1966.

Kumado, Cletus Experience Kofi. "Customary Constitutional Rules and Procedures for Enstoolment and Destoolment of a Chief among the Anlo-Ewe." L.L.M. Degree Thesis, University of Ghana, 1974.

Lotsu, Emily Angela Essie. "Women in Fishing: A Study of the Significance of Women's Roles in the Fishing Industry at Anlo-Afiadenyigba." B.A. Long Essay, Department of Sociology, University of Ghana, Legon, 1994.

Meyer, Birgit. "Christianity and the Arise of the Ewe Nation: On the Encounter between German Pietist Missionaries and Ewe Mission Workers." Paper presented at the International Conference on "Religion and Nationalism in Europe and Asia" at the Research Center on Religion and Society, University of Amsterdam, 1995.

———. "Translating the Devil: An African Appropriation of Pietist Protestantism— The Cast of the Peki Ewe in Southeastern Ghana, 1847-1992." Ph.D. diss., University of Amsterdam, 1995.

Mitchell, Vernay. "Choice and Resistance in Ethnic Relations among the Ewe in a Developing Togolese Town." Ph.D. diss., Columbia University, 1998.

Quarcoopome, Nii Otokunor. "Rituals and Regalia of Power: Art and Politics among the Dangme and Ewe, 1800 to present." Ph.D. diss., University of California, Los Angeles, 1993.

Selormey, Emily. "The Importance of Beads with Particular Reference to the Anlo Traditional Area." Long Essay, Specialist Training College, Winneba, 1978.

Senaya, Roseville Ediefiam. "Ancestral Worship in Anloland: An Artistic Expression." B.A. thesis, School of Art and Design, Specialist Training College, Winneba, 1983.

Sorkpor, G. A. "Geraldo De Lima and the Awunas, 1862–1904." Master's thesis, Institute of African Studies, University of Ghana, 1966.

Souza, Dzifaa Kobla de. "The Religious Significance of Rites of Passage among the Anlo-Ewe." B.A. Long Essay, Department for the Study of Religions, University of Ghana, Legon, 1979.

Tagbor, F. R. K. "Marriage, Birth and Death Ceremonies in South Anlo." Long Essay, Specialist Training College, Winnega, n.d.

Torgby, Richard Tetteh. "The Origin and Organization of the Yewe Cult." B.A. Honors Thesis, Department for the Study of Religions, University of Ghana, Legon, 1977.

Wendl, Tobias. "Preliminary Results of My Mama Wata Field Work among the Ewes of Togo and Ghana, 1985/86." In author's possession.

ARCHIVAL AND ORAL SOURCES

National Archives of Ghana, Accra

ADM 1/2/5
ADM 1/2/12
ADM 1/2/42
ADM1/2/361
ADM 11/1/450
ADM 11/1/228: Quittah Lagoon
ADM 11/1/1113
ADM 11/1/1457: Report on the Education Department
ADM 11/1/1661: Administrative Papers of the Secretary of Native Affairs
ADM 11/1/1679: Native Customs and Fetish
ADM 39/1/1, 120, 161
ADM 39/1/173: Keta Lagoon
ADM 39/1/206: Keta Sanitary Committee
ADM 39/1/602: Togbi Sri II, Awoame Fia of Anlo, 40th Anniversary Celebration of . . .
ADM 41/1/5, 8–9
ADM 41/1/15–19, 35
ADM 41/4/20, 28, 30, 35: Civil and Criminal Record Book, Keta
ADM 41/5/2: Inspection Book
ADM 121/1/1475: Report on the Education Department (1852–1897)

National Archives of Ghana, Ho

Item Number 21—Fetish Customs 30/1909–15/6/28

Anlo Traditional Council Office, Anloga, Ghana

Anlo Council Minute Book (29 June 1934–5–7 November 1946)
Traditional Council Minute Book, March 1947–April 1952

District Court Grade II, Anloga, Ghana

Judicial Council Court Record, 1918

Staatsarchiv, Bremen, Germany

Vom Hexenglauben der Eweer. Unpublished manuscript. C. 1932. (Norddeutsche Missions-Gesellschaft: 7, 1025. Keta: 14/1).

Public Records Office, Kew, Great Britain

T70/33: Treasury Papers, African Companies.

ORAL INTERVIEWS

No. 14: Interview with Togbui Trygod Yao Zodanu, 11 August 1978, Anloga.
No. 20: Interview with Togbui Alex Afatsao Awadzi, 30 August 1978, Anloga.
No. 22: Interview with Togbui Trygod Yao Zodanu, 1 September 1978, Anloga.
No. 29: Interview with Miss Florence Adama, 24 September 1978, Agbosome.
No. 37: Interview with Boko Seke Axovi, 4 October 1978, Anloga.
No. 45: Interview with Togbui Dzobi Adzinku, 8 November 1978, Anloga.
No. 53: Interview with Togbui Afatsao Awadzi, 16 December 1987, Anloga.
No. 54: Interview with Togbui Tse Gbeku, 16 December 1987, Anloga.
No. 56: Interview with William Tiodo Anum Adzololo, 22 December 1987, Anloga.
No. 57: Interview with Robert G. Kofi Afetogbo, 22 December 1988, Anloga.
No. 62: Interview with K. A. Mensah, 5 January 1988, Anloga.
No. 64: Interview with J. N. K Dogbatse, 5 January 1988, Anloga.
No. 67: Interview Togbui Aklorbortu Efia Nunyanu, 6 January 1988, Anloga.
No. 69: Interview with Togbui Dzobi Adzinku, 7 January 1988, Anloga.
No. 72: Interview with Christian Nani Tamaklo, 13 January 1988, Keta.
No. 74: Interview with A. W. Kuetuade-Tamaklo, 19 January 1988, Tegbi.
No. 76: Interview with Togbui Aklorbortu Efia Nunyanu, 6 January 1988, Anloga.
No. 81: Interview with Togbui Joachim Acolatse IV, 26 January 1988, Keta.
No. 91: Interview with Togbui Joachim Acolatse IV, 5 February 1988, Tema.
No. 97: Interview with J. G. Kodzo Vordoagu, 24 February 1988, Tegbi.
No. 100: Interview with Togbui Awusu, II, 29 March 1988, Atoko.
No. 113: Interview with Togbui Aklorbortu Efia Nunyanu, 10 February 1996, Anloga.
No. 116: Interview with Togbui Tretu, 13 February 1996, Anloga.
No. 117: Interview with Kwasi Tome, 14 February 1996, Anloga.
No. 118: Interview with Aklorbortu Efia Nunyanu, 14 February 1996, Anloga.
No. 121: Interview with Togbui Awusu II, 18 February 1996, Atokor.
No. 134: Interview with Elvis Adika, 28 March 1996, Anloga.
No. 138: Interview with Togbui Kojo Lavoe, 3 March 1996, Srogbe.
No. 141: Interview with Mama Daolo, 13 March 1996, Whuti.
No. 144: Interview with Mama Daolo, 15 March 1996, Whuti.
No. 148: Interview with Mama Semefa, 17 March 1996, Anloga.

No. 151: Interview with Mama Nanevi, 19 March 1996, Anloga.
No. 152: Interview with Togbui Awuku Dzrekey, 19 March 1996, Whuti.
No. 153: Interview with Togbui Tekpor Sedzorme, 20 March 1996, Anloga.
No. 154: Interview with Togbui Tekpor Sedzorme, 21 March 1996, Anloga.
No. 157: Interview with Sedzorme, 23 March 1996, Anloga.
No. 158: Interview with Mama Ami Nutsugah, 24 March 1996, Whuti.
No. 162: Interview with Togbui Awuku Dzrekey, 25 Mach 1996, Whuti.
No. 165: Interview with Tekpor Sedzorme, 27 March 1996, Anloga.
No. 168: Interview with Togbui Sorkpor, 19 April 1996, Anloga.
No. 169A: Interview with Togbui Sorkpor, 19 April 1996, Anloga.
No. 170: Interview with Togbui Tekpor Sedzorme, 14 April 1996, Anloga.
No. 171: Interview with Togbui Awuku Dzrekey, 18 April 1996, Whuti.
No. 172: Interview with Mama Dzagba, 19 April 1996, Anloga.
No. 173: Interview with Tekpor Sedzorme, 15 April 1996, Anloga.
No. 175: Interview with Togbui Klomegah, 20 April 1996, Anloga.
No. 176: Interview with Tekpor Sedzorme, 20 April 1996, Anloga.
No. 177: Interview with Togbui Akpate I, 22 April 1996, Srogbe.
No. 180: Interview with Togbui Akpate I, 23 April 1996, Srogbe.
No. 181: Interview with Hianvedzu Nyamadi, 23 April 1996, Anloga.
No. 185: Interview with Aklorbortu Efia Nunyanu and Zanyiedo Kwawukume, 27 April 1996, Anloga.
No. 188: Interview with Mama Xaedo Worgbale, 29 April 1996, Anloga.
No. 189: Interview with Togbui Tudzi, 20 April 1996, Anloga.
No. 190: Interview with Aklorbortu Efia Nunyanu and Zadzie, 30 April 1996, Anloga.
No. 191: Interview with Togbui Aklorbortu Efia Nunyanu and Zadzie, 2 May 1996, Anloga.
No. 192: Interview with Togbui Tudzi, 3 May 1996, Anloga.
No. 193: Interview with V. Y. Dotsey, 4 May 1996, Anloga.
No. 194: Interview with Sister Mary, 6 May 1996, Anloga.
No. 195: Interview with D. D. Deku, 6 May 1996, Anloga.
No. 196: Interview with Pastor P. K. Larbi and elders, 7 May 1996, Anloga.
No. 198: Interview with Mama Korfobu Diaba, 11 March 1996, Srogbe.
No. 199: Interview with Togbui Ayike, 12 May 1996, Srogbe.
No. 202: Interview with Togbui Tudzi, 15 May 1996, Anloga.
No: 203: Interview with Aklorbortu Efia and Zanyiedor Kwawukume, 16 May 1996, Anloga.
No. 204: Interview with Togbui Sewornu, 5 June 1996, Anloga.
No. 205: Interview with Kofi Sorkpor, 8 June 1996, Anloga.
No. 209: Interview with Togbui Dedzo Megbemegbi, 13 June 1996, Anloga.
No. 212: Interview with Kwasi Tome, 18 June 1996, Anloga.
No. 218: Interview with Togbui Nyable and others elders of Tsiame, 13 July 1996, Tsiame.
No. 215: Interview with Mama Daolo, 21 June 1996, Whuti.
No. 230: Interview with Mama Nugblanuitor, 20 July 1996, Srogbe.
No. 234B: Interview with Togbui Tudzi, September 1996, Anloga.
No. 234D: Interview with Akorbortu Efia, 15 September 1996, Anloga.
No. 239: Interview with Togbui Kwasi Tome, 9 September 1996, Anloga.
No. 240B: Interview with Tobui Kofi Ahosu et al., 1 September 1996, Notsie, Togo.
No. 243: Interview with Colonel Courage Togobo, October 1996, Accra.

Index

Page numbers for illustrations are italicized.

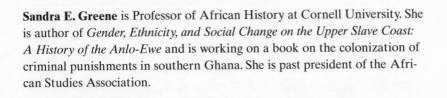

Sandra E. Greene is Professor of African History at Cornell University. She is author of *Gender, Ethnicity, and Social Change on the Upper Slave Coast: A History of the Anlo-Ewe* and is working on a book on the colonization of criminal punishments in southern Ghana. She is past president of the African Studies Association.